MW01143911

A MEMOIR OF TOXIC WORK,
MINDFULNESS, AND INNER PEACE

Breakthrough

SUNITA DEVI ALVES

Copyright © 2022 by Sunita Alves

All rights reserved. No part of this publication may be reproduced in any form, or by any means, electronic or mechanical, including photocopying, recording, or any information browsing, storage, or retrieval system, without permission in writing from the author. It is illegal to copy this book, post it to a website, or distribute it by any other means without permission.

Published in Canada. Visit the author's website at www.SunitaAlves.com.

Stylistic Edit: Lee Parpart, Iguana Books

Copy Edit: Jennifer Trent

Cover and Interior Design: Laura Boyle Design

Illustrator: Jessica Alves

Author and Illustrator Photographs: Memories By Alexa Photography

978-1-7782616-4-0	EPUB
978-1-7782616-3-3	PDF
978-1-7782616-2-6	Paperback
978-1-7782616-1-9	Hardcover book

This work depicts actual events in the author's life as truthfully as recollection permits. While all persons within are actual individuals, and work experiences are real, names and identifying characteristics have been changed to respect the privacy of individuals and corporations, except where permission has been granted by immediate family members.

The content of this book is for informational purposes only and is not intended to diagnose, treat, cure, or prevent any condition or disease or to give legal advice. This book is not a substitute for consultation with a licensed medical, healthcare, or legal practitioner. Sunita Alves has no responsibility for the persistence or accuracy of URLs for external or third-party Internet websites referred to in this publication and does not guarantee that any content on such websites is, or will remain, accurate or appropriate.

The suicide of a colleague is mentioned in this book. If you or anyone you know is at risk of suicide or self-harm, please immediately call a local support number such as:

Canada: 1-833-456-4566 | https://www.crisisservicescanada.ca/en/
USA: 1-800-273-8255 or 9-8-8 | https://suicidepreventionlifeline.org/

"Jailbreak" from *Distilled: Poems on Eldering* by Maya Spector, forthcoming in 2022 by Maya Spector. Copyright 2022 by Maya Spector. Excerpt reprinted by permission of Maya Spector. Direct Link: https://barryandmayaspector.com/mayas-writing

"Finding Peace" from *A gift of peace* by Vicki L. Flaherty. Copyright 2017 by Vicki Flaherty and Mostly My Heart Sings. Excerpt reprinted by permission of Vicki L. Flaherty. Direct Link: https://mostlymyheartsings.wordpress.com/2012/11/05/a-gift-of-peace/

CONTENTS

Introduction   1

Prologue — My Attempt to be Superwoman
Falls Apart in Front of Me   3

PART 1: SEEDS OF FEAR AND STRENGTH

Chapter 1 — Setting the Bar   7
Chapter 2 — Expectations with Limitations   12
Chapter 3 — Never Not Be Afraid   18
Chapter 4 — An Engineer Building Self-Worth   24
Chapter 5 — Simply the Best   29

PART 2: TOXIC WORK

Chapter 6 — Physiological Burnout   38
Chapter 7 — The Spirit of a JTekker: Heart & Soul   44
Chapter 8 — Spiritual Burnout   50
Chapter 9 — The Organization is Sick   58
Chapter 10 — Integrity vs. Work   67

PART 3: JAILBREAK

Chapter 11 — A New Relationship with Work   74
Chapter 12 — The Woo Comes Calling   82
Chapter 13 — Life Class Begins   91
Chapter 14 — Flipping the Script   98
Chapter 15 — Wholehearted at Work   105

PART 4: HEARTBREAK

Chapter 16 — Dark Shadows   118
Chapter 17 — Some Highs and a Big Low   128

Chapter 18 — Yard Sale   137
Chapter 19 — Broken   142
Chapter 20 — Surrender   149

PART 5: BREAKTHROUGH

Chapter 21 — Quiet   162
Chapter 22 — A Soft Landing   167
Chapter 23 — The Dharma Finds Me   175
Chapter 24 — Noble Silence Speaks   182
Chapter 25 — A New Worldview   191
Chapter 26 — Awake in the World   199

PART 6: BREAKING OPEN

Chapter 27 — Coming Home   207
Chapter 28 — Cleared for Work   213
Chapter 29 — Finding the Dharma in the Real World   220
Chapter 30 — Dharma Doors   226
Chapter 31 — The Heart as CEO   234
Chapter 32 — The Real Work   239
Chapter 33 — Healing a Toxic Work World   245

Epilogue — Begin Again   251
A Note on Honouring Buddhism   256
Acknowledgements   258
Appendix A — Mental Health at Work Log   260
Appendix B — Compassion, Joy and Kindness Toolbox   266
Appendix C — Glossary   269

For Tom, Jessica, and Sophia.
You have seen me at my best and worst and love me anyway.

"Although the world is full of suffering, it is also full of the overcoming of it."

— Helen Keller

Introduction

When I asked my niece what university programs she was considering, I didn't expect a discussion about work values from someone who had just turned seventeen.

"I'm thinking about software engineering, but I'm not going to work like your generation did," she told me.

She is South Asian like me, living near Toronto, Canada. Her parents and I work in the tech industry and are squarely Gen X. Our parents, immigrants with an extremely demanding work ethic, shaped us into high achievers who value financial security. We modeled our self-sacrificing Guyanese Canadian parents but got white-collar jobs instead of being shift workers. This should have resulted in a more satisfying life, yet somehow I think we're more stressed and have less time than the generation before. Now our kids see our approach to life and believe there is a better way, just as every generation does.

My niece went on to say that money is not as important to members of Gen Z because they value quality of life more than financial gain. I smiled, glad to hear her sounding so confident in her intention to be happy. Yet I worry for her because I've been in tech and learned first-hand how hard it is to prioritize life-work balance while also succeeding in the field. I'm all too familiar with the ethical stress of certain practices within the tech world, especially as a woman within a power-and profit-driven industry. I prospered in my career, but there was a price to be paid, and it was all on the side of mental health.

It took me decades and a great deal of luck — or what I now think of as a high degree of synchronicity — to connect to my inner truth and find a balanced relationship to life and work. I never intended to expose my deepest inner thoughts about this journey in a memoir, but as I navigated tough decisions about going to HR or taking a medical leave, I looked for and didn't find any stories that had a voice like mine. As Toni-Morrison once wrote, "If there's a book you want to read, but it hasn't been written yet, then you must write it." This memoir is for anyone who is struggling with work-life balance, especially but not exclusively in the field of high tech. More specifically, it's also the story of a South Asian woman, a Canadian settler, an employee, a child, and a soul becoming whole.

My Attempt to be Superwoman Falls Apart in Front of Me

Doctors' waiting rooms seem so cold without the presence of the doctor. The one I'm in is painted light blue, but under the fluorescent lights it looks colourless. There is just enough room for two chairs at the end of the examination table. Someone has stuck a line of toy train decals on the wall, at just the right angle for a child to see if they're lying on the table. I've seen these train decals countless times over the past decade of routine checkups for the kids and me and impromptu visits for rashes, ear infections, and sprains. Today I'm here on my own, and the reason for my visit is anything but routine.

It's February 2018, and after twenty-three years of working in the tech industry as an engineer and project manager, I think I've lost my mind. I can't cope with even the simplest things, never mind how much I used to juggle between work and family. In the past, when things got tough, as the saying goes, I got going. As a take-charge person and a natural multitasker, I went into plan mode. The old me could figure out multiple solutions and think through various factors to settle on the best path forward for all involved. Whether it was the customer changing their mind at work (they always do) or my daughter having problems with the new way of teaching math (it was unnecessarily complicated), no problem was too great for me. Like the cheery blue train from *The Little Engine That Could*, a book Dad read to me as a child, my motto has always been, "I think I can, I think I can, I think I can." Except for weeks now, life has been getting grim, and the old me has begun to seem like a past self who no longer lives in my body. Problems that used to seem manageable now seem insurmountable. I have alien feelings of helplessness, and I can't motivate my way out of them.

The Sunita who routinely earned kudos at work for rising to any challenge has given up. The woman who anticipated her family's needs and efficiently ran the domestic front has disappeared. In her place is an interloper: a messy, distracted, shadow mom who knows she brings the family down with sad expressions and angry responses to innocent questions. Shadow Sunita knows that she used to care deeply about her work and her family, but she — I — can't seem to find those feelings anymore. I've been feeling around inside of me for who I used to be, and I keep coming up empty. My mind feels heavy and slow and sad. I'm tense and on guard. I can't remember the last time I felt truly relaxed or at ease. Each day I feel worse instead of better, and I can't seem to find the can-do attitude anymore to turn myself around. Like blackout blinds these feelings have darkened my world, and I am terrified of losing the light.

Dr. Joshi enters the room and closes the door behind her. Her calm and friendly demeanor immediately begins to radiate out, warming up the space. She's the kind of doctor — the kind of person — who makes you feel the full force of her attention. She sees you. She cares. She is focused only on you. Dr. Joshi is a brown woman like me. She's a few years younger and, like me, she's a working parent. I really feel I can identify with her. I believe that she wants me to be as healthy and as happy as I can be. No matter why I'm in her office, even if I'm just there to get a seasonal flu shot, she checks on my mental health. She asks how I'm doing and inquires about any stress in my work and home life. In the past, I've always been able to reassure her that I was fine, despite trying to be superwoman and juggle all the balls.

Now I feel like I'm a big mess on the floor of her office, and I don't even know where to begin. On the surface, everything looks fine. I have a great job as a project manager with great pay at one of the best-known tech companies. But something is not right. Work — that part of my life that used to energize me and that to a large extent defined me — has begun to seem toxic. I need someone objective to tell me if work isn't safe for me anymore. Dr. Joshi is a GP, not a therapist or psychiatrist, but I trust her to hear me out and tell me if I have a legitimate problem or if I am overreacting. She scans my folder briefly and then makes eye contact and smiles.

"Tell me, Sunita, what's going on?"

PART 1

Seeds of Fear and Strength

"And I began to recognize a source of power within myself that comes from the knowledge that while it is most desirable not to be afraid, learning to put fear into a perspective gave me great strength."

— Audre Lorde, "The Transformation of Silence into Language and Action"

CHAPTER 1

Setting the Bar

I'm not sure I would even know the name of the country I was born in if I didn't hear it from my parents. I am an Indo-Caribbean-Canadian woman, descendant of indentured servants who travelled in the late 1800s from India to British Guiana to work under inhumane conditions that African slaves had been freed from in 1834. From an economic point of view, plantation owners wanted to maximize profits which meant using Indian workers versus the higher-cost local workforce of recently emancipated slaves. My ancestors (both male and female) worked in these sugar plantations under the brutal tropical heat to make a better life for their children. Once freed of their work term for the British Crown, my family prospered by working for themselves.

Several decades later, Mom's parents owned a convenience store, the house above the shop, and land. Dad's parents were very wealthy, expanding the fertile land they earned through indentured labour into a coconut plantation and a village with several family homes. Guyana gained independence from Britain in 1970 and is the only English-speaking country in South America, but the English is full of Hindu words for family and food. The patois emerged as African, Amerindian, Portuguese, Spanish, Chinese, Dutch, British, and French cultures came together in the Caribbean. For example, "How many children do you have?" is said as "How much pickney yuh get?" Pickney is patois for child, and my family says it like "pick-uh-nay." My family calls this broken English.

While the Hindu language didn't survive to my generation of the Indian diaspora in Guyana, how we address our relatives is still a tradition I share with the culture in India. I call my maternal grandmother Nani and maternal grandfather Nana. If I had grown up with my paternal grandparents, I would have called them Ajee and Aja. I remember my Canadian school friends being confused that I called my grandfather Nana, the same name that many of them called their grandmothers.

I grew up in Guyana with this mix of Hindu words and lively patois, the salty ocean breeze, the silty tides leaving the beach strewn with pebbles, and palm trees waving under the equatorial sun. However, I don't remember very much. My memories are like mosquitoes that appear and disappear as you try to track them. Sometimes when I walk by a school bus, the smell of diesel brings me back to childhood. I can sense the cool feel of the hand-held slates and silky feel of the slim chalk pencil we used in school. I remember a dark green plant and breaking the thick leaves to see a milky white substance oozing out. At school, the teacher threw candies in the air, and the kids would scramble to grab them. I recall the crispness of tissue paper as we made kites at Easter time. Another flimsy memory is of holding my hand out to get hit with the ruler. I don't know what I did to anger the teacher, but I remember the shame and embarrassment at being singled out for being bad. Other than this, I don't remember any homes, toys, or friends. I don't even remember my younger brothers. I should have these memories because I immigrated to Canada when I was seven years old, but all my clear memories are from Grade 3 and up.

Did I just leave these memories behind with the abrupt move to a new country? After all, in one day I lost my home and found myself in an alien place that was bitterly cold, with the claustrophobic feel of a toque, mittens, and coat on my body, and the bite of snow on my face. My parents left the country secretly because they didn't like how the communist-leaning government was evolving and felt our freedoms and rights were in jeopardy. They had just a few hundred dollars and three kids in tow, and stayed with friends until they could afford a home. It would have been an abrupt and confusing change for us. I would have woken up in my tropical country and gone to bed in a foreign place without understanding why.

Maybe the stress of such a move and starting a new school wiped out my memories. Maybe I buried away my past because I could sense how important it was for my parents to make it in Canada and move forward. Perhaps I felt I had to be a good girl and not complain, so I didn't burden them further. Maybe I was told that as the oldest child, I needed to be a big girl now.

Work became everything to our family as my parents strove to stop living with friends and relatives and afford their own home. And what they worked so hard for was always clear: to enable the highest possible education for us. The bar was set high — at minimum a master's degree, ideally a medical or law degree. My parents wanted me to shoot for the stars. They were working hard and striving for the best life they could make. And they wanted me to do more than they accomplished by giving me the opportunity for the best education. Although cash poor, they put money into a savings program for university long before RESPs existed. My parents did without fancy clothes and luxuries, but they bought a piano and paid for lessons to help me excel in the university application process. I knew from early on that they were pinning their hopes on me to be the one to go to medical school, and I had to take my academic success, and thus future career success, very seriously. We had cheap used cars, but an expensive, brand-new Encyclopedia Britannica set. I worked hard in school and piano practice because I loved learning, and I wanted to make them proud.

***

My grandmother was my early role model when it came to work. Although she didn't know how to read or write well, she ran a business, picked up the slack from a husband who liked to sit around drinking rum with his buddies, and was determined that her children would be educated.

"I never wanted your mom to marry so young," my grandmother will tell me. It's a story I've heard her tell a few times. "It was arranged for her to go to Canada and study medicine, but then your dad came." At this point, Nani will look just a little wistful at what could have been.

Mom was only seventeen when her marriage was arranged, eighteen when she married, and nineteen when she had me. I never say to Nani that I wouldn't exist if Mom had come to a Canadian university. That wasn't the point anyway. I understood from this story that as women, we had expectations and duties to fulfill. And although I would not be in an arranged marriage, I would be expected to have the education that Mom and Nani never had. Mom has never voiced regrets to me about wishing she had had a different life. She is a dedicated and loving mother and embraced her role fully. Still, I knew from when I was quite young — as early as elementary school — that both my parents wanted more for me.

My grandmother was sixteen years old when she married a man, really a boy, selected by her family. She was seventeen when she gave birth to my mother. I was her first grandchild when she was only thirty-six years old. Nani never finished high school because homemaking was the priority for girls at that time. As a result, my grandmother has only a rudimentary level of reading and arithmetic. Mom did finish high school and tells me her favourite subject was biology, and she believes she could have been a good doctor. But she loves her children and wouldn't want it any other way. When my brother came along, I was a handful at two years old, wanting to be held all the time and needing to be told stories as a distraction so I would eat. My parents shipped me off to stay with my grandparents to give my young mother a break. It's common in my extended family to have grandparents be significant caregivers. I often stayed with my grandparents in my first five years of life, even going to preschool while living under their roof. I can imagine they doted on me and made my spoiled ways even worse. I don't remember much from those years, but the importance of work seeped into my bones from my family and culture.

But I saw that while sons and daughters had to meet their parents' expectations, there were different societal rules for the power, freedoms, and choices applied to girls versus boys. I was treated as if I was fragile and required more protection than my younger brothers. I constantly heard the phrase "Walk, don't run!" and I had to slow down and be less rowdy. Whereas my brothers could storm through the house and run wild, I had to temper myself. My parents did give me many freedoms in elementary school to go out and play with both male and female friends. However, once high school came, I noticed they were reluctant to let me go out if boys were included. My oldest brother, an entire two years younger, didn't get the scrutiny I endured. I had a high bar of expectations to meet, yet I also had limitations instilled into me because I was a girl.

CHAPTER 2

Expectations with Limitations

"But all my friends are going!" I cried. "It's not going to be unsafe just because we're at a hotel. Teachers are even going!"

I was talking about Academic Decathlon, a high school club. This was the Olympics of the mind, and my parents had decided that I would not be allowed to attend a gathering of participants at a local hotel. Each year, Decathlon organizers picked a different decade as the basis for wide-ranging study. As a school team, we competed in academic subjects like math and public speaking, literature, music, and art. I learned how to recognize the voices of Billie Holiday, Louis Armstrong, and Ella Fitzgerald so I could identify them when a snippet of a song was played. The final competition was coming up, and the other school teams were in town, staying at a local hotel. It was a very studious and nerdy thing to do with your after-school time, and I loved being part of this team. Many of my friends were going to the hotel to hang out. It was innocent fun. But Dad saw red flags with teenage boys and hotels, and said I couldn't go. I was so upset that I was studying above and beyond the school curriculum, which my parents wanted, but I couldn't enjoy this evening out because I was a girl and thus, somehow, at a disadvantage. I was fifteen years old, and my Canadian friends had so many more freedoms. Although we lived in Canada, we had not left behind the notion from Guyana, and even from India, that women were property to be kept safe. Women were vulnerable to the people who held psychological power over them and to those who could overpower them physically. Dad held onto these notions as firmly as if he was still living in Guyana. Mom was different; when she saw me crying, she bent the rules. After talking to a teacher who was supervising the hotel social, she drove me there secretly. Dad was working the night shift, and he never knew.

Childhood is a time where you start to understand who matters more and who matters less. I already knew gender made a difference, but I also came to learn there was more status for anyone in my family who was a medical doctor and anyone who was educated — so professors and engineers counted too, but just not as much. I also learned that the older aunts and uncles were more respected, and the younger ones could be made fun of. I heard whispers of gossip at family gatherings that some of the women were mean to their mothers-in-law living with them. I learned that people in my family with light skin were beautiful, and people with dark skin were somehow lesser. A dark-skinned woman was worse than a dark-skinned man because it lessened her beauty. I am still told to this day not to be in the sun too much because it could "black" my skin. White people were viewed to be higher in status, almost in a master-servant sense left over from the British colonial days. I grew up hearing racial slurs against Black people and Asian people. There was a well-defined and unwritten hierarchy of who was more important in the world.

Maybe to help fill in the holes of my memory, I created a family tree to catalog my relatives and understand the relationships. I was confused as to why Mom's aunt was addressed as "mausee" and Dad's aunt as "di-dia." They both meant aunt, but it depended on if they were paternal or maternal, and on birth order too. With ten siblings on Dad's side, I had over thirty first cousins. As I started mapping out my family, I uncovered more than just my genealogy. I learned that my grandmothers lived hard lives with traumatic losses.

Nani wanted lots of children, but she only had two — Mom and my uncle. She told me once, maybe when I was looking at my highly imbalanced family tree, that she couldn't have more children and that it was a disappointment to her not to have a big family. Her husband, my Nana, was a figurehead of our family, and everyone loved him. He was a warm and charming man. He was a loving grandfather in my memories of him in Canada. I seem to have this story in my mind that Nani lost a child and that it caused her to be incapable of having more children. I don't ever remember hearing this story. I never wanted to ask about it because another part of the story was something even a child knows should never be spoken of. The other part of the story is that she lost the child because of domestic abuse, but I don't know how I would know such an awful thing. It seemed like everyone knew Nana had a terrible temper, though that was never my experience. I do remember feeling that the maternal side of my family tree seemed tragic. Perhaps I had a vivid imagination and a flair for the dramatic, like my childhood heroine, Anne of Green Gables.

I can imagine Nani at sixteen years old, fair-skinned with light brown eyes, likely from some British blood in our ancestry. Her legal name is Juignee, a Punjabi or Urdu word that could mean many things, though firefly is my favourite that came up on a web search. She would have been petite and gentle and wanting to please. That girl still shines through in her eighties when she smiles or pulls her great-grandchildren in for a hug. She is the light in our family because she gives grandmother love — the kind that loves you just for being you and that blankets you in warmth and goodness.

Nani would have been totally powerless in her marriage because once a girl leaves her parents' house, she is at the mercy of her husband and his family. Often the lowest in rank, she would have been an easy target and expected to serve those with higher standing. She'll tell you that her life was hard, but she endured it to raise her two children and send them to school. Her dream was for them to have an education, because she never learned to write and read properly. She saw that dream come true for my uncle, who became a successful and well-respected engineer in the US. Nani arranged for Mom to come to Canada to study medicine. However, when Dad blew into town, a freshly minted engineer from England ready for a wife, Nani had to change her plans. Nani tells me her mother-in-law forced Mom's arranged marriage, and she had no choice but to cancel Mom's education and push her into marriage at the age of eighteen. When Mom learned I was writing about her marriage, she gave me a totally different account. Mom said Nani was happy to have her married to a catch like Dad. It makes me wonder if Nani had vowed to have more for her daughter, but the cultural mentality to have a woman married as soon as possible won out. Maybe telling me the story the way her heart had wanted it to be is an easier memory for Nani to have.

Dad's mother, my Ajee, was also in an arranged marriage, and her life also had loss. I never got to meet her. Her name was Kowsilla, drawn from the Ramayana, an important Hindu text. It is a version of the name Kaushalya, who was Lord Rama's mother and part of the Kosala tribe. The naming of children follows a traditional pattern in India, and this practice continued in Guyana. The process is referred to as "open book" and is more about the astronomical calendar than religion. Mom tells me that after having a baby you visit a pandit who is a Hindu holy man or priest. Unlike Christian priests, pandits can be self-proclaimed. The pandit, always a man, opens his book, cross-checks the time of birth, and tells the parents the baby's name, or at least the first few letters, to have the most blessed life. This book is called the Patra and is issued annually like a farmer's almanac.

All of Kowsilla's children and Juignee's children were named by open book process. The names were foreign to me on the family tree because they were the legal names I had never heard anyone use. Aunty Etto's real name was Soorsatie, and Uncle Bob's real name was Lachman. I found it very odd that their real names were so different sounding. Almost everyone had a nickname that was shorter or more anglicized. Mom's book name, Mohinie, was dropped, and people called her Patsy or Pats. I also learned that Dad rejected my book name, which was Manhila, and named me Sunita instead. He liked the name from his favourite 1967 Bollywood movie, *Farz*. I was told that I was mesmerized when I heard my name in one of the songs on the soundtrack, *Baar Baar Din Ye Aaye/Happy Birthday To You*, which was always played for my childhood birthdays.

Dad doesn't have a lot of tolerance for ideas he thinks are useless, and he broke with tradition to name us. As I squeezed Kowsilla's children and their offspring onto the legal-size paper for the family tree I was creating, I learned that Dad had a lot of strong feelings about how his mother was treated.

Dad was only nine when his mother died in childbirth along with her thirteenth child. She must have been pregnant every year of her married life. He has told us about his love for his mother and his sadness at how she was horribly mistreated. In his family, the head of the family was his grandmother, who everyone called Mai. Mai took away Kowsilla's first two children to raise as her own; her power over her daughter-in-law and son was that great. Dad is so bitter about this because of how much it hurt his mother and hurt him to see these first-born sons raised with more power and status, more food, and more clothes than the rest of the siblings. Mai's motive was to groom these eldest boys to go to England and become doctors, and she wanted to be in control of their upbringing. Dad is angry that his mother's rights to raise her own children were taken away. He remembers her anguish at watching them be raised literally next door, never calling her Mother. I cannot imagine the powerlessness and loss my Ajee felt at having her babies taken, but I can feel the pain that my father still carries.

My culture had drilled into me that women were not as valuable as men — they didn't have the choices or freedoms men had. They were seen as property by many of the male role models in my family who I loved and looked up to. Even as I was raised in the progressive Western culture of the Greater Toronto Area, these family dynamics still weakened my self-worth and sense of safety. However, I came to know that women in my family were strong. They persevered through lives where their husband or mother-in-law had power over them. Although they were not treated with love, their power was in the love they gave forward. They had *power within,* even while they were under the power of others and limited by their status as women.

I was fascinated by women like Helen Keller, Florence Nightingale, and Marie Curie, role models who told me that I didn't have to have limitations. I latched on to the belief that my intellect gave me equality and independence. I strove for everything the world had to offer and gender was not a limitation. This was the message I received in my new home in Canada. But my upbringing always seemed to bump up against those tenets, and I struggled with a paradox. How could I embrace my own power when I was socialized to believe that women were less capable than men?

All through school and then later, as I headed into my adult work life, my mind was a jumble of conflicting fears and beliefs. In some ways I was lucky: I didn't fear being smarter than the boys, or worry when they taunted me for being taller than most of the other students in middle school. And I didn't feel pressured to look a certain way or to conform to Western, Barbie-inspired standards of beauty. I was okay being nerdy. Unlike some girls in high school, I didn't care about being popular, or worry about whether my clothes were trendy, and I barely bothered with makeup. I was really good at math and didn't care who knew it. But I *did* suffer from a chronic need to please, and I feared being reprimanded or falling short of anyone's expectations. The idea of doing a mediocre job on any task was intolerable to me. I would put enormous effort into my academic work to gain approval and avoid criticism or failure. As a young woman, I also became hyper-aware of threats to my physical safety. This fear was like a contagion that Mom instilled into me. I became afraid of walking alone, especially if the streets were deserted or it was late at night. If a man appeared, I would go on high alert and be fearful if he followed me or paid too much attention.

Although I wasn't as oppressed as my grandmothers, these mixed messages about women were confusing. I was supposed to be just as intelligent as a man but at the same time understand that I had limitations as a woman. Even beyond culture and gender, my parents overprotected me because of how many times I struck terror into their hearts.

CHAPTER 3

Never Not Be Afraid

"You're a girl child," I would hear growing up.

That statement was never fully unpacked, but it could mean different things. It could mean I didn't do the outside yard work with Dad because that's not what girls did. It could mean I was expected to help Mom around the house because that was women's work. For many South Asian women, being a girl means they have to learn to cook Indian food, like roti and curry, and keep house. Mom tried with me, but I was good at making arguments that I needed to study, read, or practice piano. I knew I could play the homework card and get out of doing things I didn't like. So I didn't do much more in the way of domestic chores than my brothers had to do.

It wasn't just that they wanted me to focus on education. Being called a "girl child" was about treating me as if I was made of glass. There was this pervasive sense that I had to be careful and play it safe because I was always in danger of dying abruptly. Their worry was a heavy anchor on childhood freedom and fun. But that worry was likely justified because of how many times they almost lost me in childhood.

The first part of my life is a black hole, memory-wise, but I was told the stories of calamities and near death over and over again. Without my own memories the tales I heard in childhood seemed like a fairy tale. Dad would say I ran so much I could barely stop to change directions. They were always trying to keep their eye on me, but somehow I literally fell into trouble.

I'm told that when I was about four years old, I jumped and ran so hard while playing that I hurt my stomach and couldn't stop having diarrhea. Mom was distressed after the doctor said nothing was wrong with me and took me to her Aunty as a last measure. In the 1970s some Guyanese people still trusted healers because for decades that was the only reliable source of medical care. I'm told the Aunty quickly realized she had to do "nara" on my stomach to fix the issue. Nara is a term used by Indian labourers in the Caribbean. As a noun, nara means an issue with the intestines after having a severe strain to the area or a bad fall. As a verb, nara means to pull or rub the stomach to get things back into place. After Aunty did some strong massaging to my stomach, the story goes that I went from horrible pain to playing outside like I'd never been writhing in pain. It always felt that this was a magical event filled with mystery, like going to a sorcerer. I never quite understood how scared Mom must have been until I became a mother myself. To me, it was just a fantastical story.

My parents tried to keep their eye on me and keep me safe, but I evaded their watch a couple of years later. Dad worked in sugar refineries with large estate homes provided for the families of top workers. When they told me stories of having a private clubhouse and Mom lunching with the other wives while the men went to work it seemed like we lived in a splendid country club. We resided in several sugar estates with names that sounded like far-away kingdoms, such as Rose Hall, Skeldon, Leonora, and Uitvlugt (pronounced in patois as "Highfluck"). The refineries were all near the ocean for manufacturing and shipping ease, and from photographs the homes looked like pops of bright colour amidst palm trees, hibiscus, and bougainvillea.

At Uitvlugt, I would have been around six years old but went to school in the neighbouring estate of Leonora, a couple of miles down the west coast. The head manager of the Uitvlugt refinery had a driver and the latest model of Land Rover at his disposal. Since they were both idle during the workday, they drove the estate kids to school and back. One day the Land Rover came back to the expectant parents waiting for their kids, but I wasn't on it. As the story goes, my parents frantically searched for me and found me, wandering on the road. Somehow I found the right road and direction towards my house. I have no idea why I didn't get into the Land Rover or how the driver and my teacher fumbled the handoff. I just knew it scared my parents terribly to have me missing during those few hours.

Dad got a promotion from assistant factory manager to factory manager, and we moved to Leonora sugar estate where my school was. Because of the more senior position, we got a bigger home, and this one had a heavy wooden wall bookcase made of a dense native rosewood called wamara. Presumably, a bigger home meant I had more room to run. I would grab the bookcase to swing myself into the next room, and eventually the hardware that kept it on the wall came loose. My momentum as I ran past it was enough to pull it off the wall, and it came crashing down on me. The heavy structure would have crushed me had it not been for a freezer that slowed its fall — I came away with just a broken arm because I had time to roll out.

The last of my childhood catastrophes was drowning at six years old. Leonora estate had a clubhouse where I'm told I was a frequent visitor for ice cream and peanuts. My parents were on the patio watching me swim in the shallow above-ground pool. I ran to jump into the concrete pool but tripped on the side, hitting my head on the bottom and passing out underwater. Neither Mom nor Dad saw this, but luckily someone else noticed this act of clumsiness and got their attention. Dad, who knew CPR from his studies in England, went into action and revived me. I do have a vague memory of falling backward out of a tunnel and away from a bright light as I returned to consciousness.

This elusive memory is one of the few I have of these incidents. I only know of them because I've been told how careful I had to be and how worried Mom, Dad, and Nani were whenever I ran around in horseplay with my brothers or cousins. It must have seemed to them every time they took their eyes off me, I got into something that ended up with a trip to the hospital. To be fair, I was a tall, gangly girl who grew too fast for her motor skills to catch up, and as a result I was very clumsy.

It was while my parents were living at Leonora estate that they snuck out of the country. They told everyone except a few close friends and family that they were going on a vacation, but really, they were immigrating to Canada.

Leaving Guyana did not leave my childhood safety drama behind. My parents soon found out from a Canadian doctor that I had a hole in my heart. I had open-heart surgery at SickKids hospital in Toronto when I was eleven. While the operation was successful, I don't think my parents ever recovered from the fear of having a child in the hospital like that. I had no fear of the surgery that I can recall. I do remember thinking what an adventure it was to be in downtown Toronto. I had a Hello Kitty autograph book, and I had my surgeon and nurses sign it like I was on a movie set. I remember waking up in the ICU in terrible pain where the saw had split open my breastbone. I still recall the utter relief as tiny ice chips were fed into my parched mouth.

I made a crazy-fast recovery, leaving the hospital in just over a week. Still, it took a few years of monitoring to ensure there were no problems. My parents didn't like it if I ran around and got out of breath. I had yearly stress tests on my heart until I got the all-clear when I was in my freshman year at high school. Even then, my parents continued to worry about me. In all the years since, they have never stopped. I think my family motto should be the one from the animated movie, *The Croods*: "Never Not Be Afraid." To this day, Mom will be in a panic if she hasn't been able to reach me.

While I can smile now at Mom's worrying, as a teenager I felt suffocated and overly surveilled compared to my Canadian friends' freedoms. This fueled my desire for independence. I wanted to live a life free of fear. The surest way to do that was to get a job. A job, to me, meant freedom, choice, and agency. I was a high achiever in school, motivated by the day I would leave home and not be controlled by anyone. Excelling in school met my need to be an achiever so as to meet my parents' expectations and my own need for independence.

***

I dreamed of a job where I could have the freedom to make fun, joyful choices. When my last year of high school arrived, I considered many careers. I thought about going into the army for fun, travel, and freedom. My parents were terrified when I mentioned this because I could be harmed, whether from warfare or the toxic military culture of power-abusing men. I spent a lot of time considering medicine or even the law (the next best thing) that I had been groomed for. But I shied away from them because they felt wrong.

I wonder now, with the distance of many years, if role models of feminine power being quiet and behind the scenes contributed to that teenager's decisions. At an instinctual level, I didn't trust situations where the power differential between people was too great. My grandmothers' marriages, and even my mother's, had such big power differentials, and I didn't want to replicate that in my career by having power over patients or clients. My family valued privilege so much, to the point of taking away my eldest uncles from their mother to groom them for elite professions. It turned me off any kind of career designed to win power and glory.

I didn't have this insight as an eighteen-year-old deciding what programs to apply to in university. I just knew the thought of having power over others made me deeply uncomfortable. I shrank from positions of authority. I didn't want others to look up to me and see me as having a higher status than them. To avoid being put into any kind of "power over" work, I chose to be an engineer. This career seemed to be more about working as a team of equals than occupying a position of prestige and status. I picked Engineering Physics because it didn't limit me and kept my options open to tack on a medical, law, or business degree if I changed my mind.

However, after four years of fun and hard work at university, I knew I was done with school. I wasn't interested in being anything but an engineer. My parents were disappointed I wasn't going for even a Master's degree. But Dad took it in stride and applied for jobs on my behalf. He didn't want an unemployed dependent at home. After all, any job is better than no job. He printed my resume and signed my name, and dropped it off at a large IT company headquartered in the mall where he banked. I had never heard of them, so when they called me for an interview, it was a bit of a shock. I had never envisioned working for a company that sold computer services. However, I was glad to have a job and one where I could live at home while I built up some savings.

I moved back home with knowledge about nuclear reactions, lasers, and semiconductors. But what I really learned during my degree was that I loved technology, problem-solving, and the satisfaction of accomplishing work as a team rather than as an individual. So even though I didn't seek out my first job, I was happy to hear I could use my engineering skills supporting a big automotive manufacturer where a lot of cutting-edge technology was being used, like robotics.

What I didn't realize was that although I had independent means, I would still be limited by my mental beliefs and those of my parents while I lived with them. My parents are extremely generous with money, time, and love. Their first new car in Canada was bought for me. I came home after finishing my second year to a shiny green Pontiac Grand Am with a giant pink bow on the roof. I'll never forget Dad handing me the keys. The neighbours still talk about this. From finding me a job to buying me a car, there is nothing my parents would not do for me. Having that kind of love and security is a blessing, and I know I'll always have safe harbour because of their love. Yet I still wanted more. I wanted respect and autonomy.

CHAPTER 4

An Engineer Building Self-Worth

I carried into my first job the need for approval, self-worth and validation. Although I had the success of a university degree, I was a mess on the inside. From childhood and culture, I had absorbed the idea that the world was different for me as a woman than it was for my brothers. It wasn't just about my childhood escapes from calamity. The fear permeating my upbringing had to do with the idea that women were weaker than men — as a woman, you could be assaulted, raped, and overpowered by a man. My family was more worried if I went out late at night than if my brothers did. In the workplace, and in social situations, I lived with a constant low-level fear of being too outspoken, too "bitchy," or too bossy. I worked hard to be seen as a reasonable woman and constantly monitored how I appeared to others.

Living in Canada gave me choices I would not have had in Guyana. I was able to get an education and choose who I would marry. But I still lived with Guyanese traditions and my own family's expectations surrounding what a woman could be. I was filled with the sense that somehow I was lesser and weaker than the men in my family and men in general. I often felt powerless. All of this meant that I was a mixed bag of fearlessness and fearfulness as I entered the workforce.

My first strong bid for freedom came, ironically, in the form of not wanting a curfew at the age of twenty-two. I wanted to take the world by storm, but my parents didn't like it if I stayed out late with the new friends I was making at work. My office was in the high-tech General Motors of Canada headquarters in Oshawa. The glassy building reflected the sky and nestled into a marsh on the shores of Lake Ontario, adjacent to Darlington Provincial Park. Shiny high-end cars such as Corvettes and Camaros were displayed at the front entrance. There was a cohort of new grad hires that spring. We were put into a training program to learn business etiquette like how to answer the phone, how long your skirt had to be (not higher than your fingertips when standing with arms at your side), and that a suit top and bottom must be the same colour and fabric (preferably navy blue). Our group wanted to party when class was over and was out until last call, even mid-week. Mom did not like me going out like this and sat up waiting, spoiling the sheer joy I had from this new freedom. She put the emotional load of her worry back onto me as guilt. I was free of my studies and had landed the degree and the job, but I didn't have my full independence.

Tom, a computer science grad, was also part of the business training/ partying group. He was a good listener to my complaints and had his own share of limitations in high school from his German immigrant parents. I should have probably known he liked me when he accompanied me to the Eaton Centre to buy business suits. He was a good shopping friend because he was honest if I tried something that didn't look good. He also encouraged me to invest in good pieces because I was worth it.

We hung out a lot, and he noticed that when someone paid me a compliment, I didn't acknowledge it. I would get a funny feeling and couldn't admit that I was worthy of their praise. I wanted to push it away and pretend it never happened. He said, "Sunita, you have to say thank you when someone gives you a compliment. I want to hear you say thank you." Initially, he would clear his throat or stare at me with insistent eyes or gesture with his head to prod me to say thank you. I didn't want to say the words, but I did with his encouragement. It pained me physically to adopt this new habit. For a long time, I felt pressure in my throat and chest whenever I said those simple words — thank you — in response to praise. I'm not sure I was this way in high school or university, where I was judged on marks, but in the world of work, I was uncertain if I would measure up. I was no longer in the academic world. At university, we worked like a team sport; we were all in the same lifeboat, and we helped each other succeed.

But work was competitive, and getting ahead wasn't based on a uniform grading method. In the business world, getting ahead depended on whether you could get airtime in meetings and if you came across as confident and assured. I struggled with that. This is where the fearfulness in me came up. I was introverted and wanted all the facts before I would add to the conversation or debate someone. Speaking on the fly felt scary, and I wasn't sure if I would sound dumb. Even when I spoke up, I felt my voice ended in a question mark, which irritated me. One would think that having graduated from a tough intellectual program like Engineering Physics I would have been confident to speak up and accept recognition for my abilities, but my insecurities made it difficult to believe in myself. When things went well and I received compliments, I struggled to feel the positive impact of those words. I wanted to quickly brush the praise aside and shrink away from attention. I also didn't want to trip up and do anything wrong. I have that early memory of a teacher in Guyana hitting me with a ruler as the class looked on, but I can't recall why. Although I remember the sting on my hand, the sting of the shame was worse. Tom was so different in his outlook. Maybe this is why I fell in love.

Tom is a first-generation Canadian — tall, blue-eyed, and confident. The differences between us are many. Our differences are more on the inside than the outside, even though he is white and I am brown. He believes you should go for something even if you don't meet all the criteria — that job descriptions are not as important as being a good fit for the leadership team. I believe I need to have all the requirements, or I won't even apply for a job. He believes nobody should push you around at work, and that you can and should stand up for yourself even if it pisses someone off. I believe that I should not rock the boat. He doesn't care much about catering to people's egos, whereas I often over-think others' feelings. I'll accommodate to make someone else more comfortable without thinking about whether it's worth it or how I might be inconvenienced. He believes in taking risks. I play it safe.

Tom started pushing me out of my comfort zone to help me improve my self-esteem. He was the first person to really say to me, "You are better than many people. You are more than qualified. Go for it, and don't let anyone hold you back — especially yourself." From the look in his eyes, I could tell that he was seeing me for my skills and abilities, with no regard for my gender, limited physical strength, or race. It was the beginning of finding my work identity and carving out a new relationship with my-self — one in which I believed I was the worthwhile and accomplished person he saw when he looked at me.

The other reason I liked Tom was that he saw my flaws and called me on them. I was not an easygoing person. I was high-strung and wanted to be in control. I've been told a few times — well, many times — that I have a need to be right. I could go overboard proving my point, and it wasn't nice at all for those on the other end. I always tried to be the best, always be right, never fail or screw up. But under all that armour hid the truth — I didn't think I was as good as anyone else. I know that I made people feel bad with how aggressively I argued things. Why did I have to be so righteous? So obnoxious?

Because it was life or death for me to not be wrong.

My self-worth, and maybe even my sense of self, was tied into having a valid place in the world. Deep inside, I was just not enough as I was. Being close friends with a work colleague is quite an opportunity because Tom had first-hand knowledge of the work version of Sunita. He opened my eyes to how I shortchanged myself and when I needed to play bigger — speak up, sell myself more, take credit where it's due. He also gently helped me be less argumentative and willing to acknowledge when I was wrong (this is still a work-in-progress).

It's wonderful to have someone believe in you and see you without lim-itations. But to actually change my ways, I had to change from the in-side out. I had to find a more confident voice within. Of all the things that were going on at an automotive manufacturing company, one of the least likely was a coaching program called Discovering You on the Quest Empowerment Seminars — Phases I & II. I believe this program was inspired by an executive from the American arm of the automotive company who went on a vision quest in the American southwest. I heard this seminar was life-changing, and it was open to me since our companies were partners. My manager at the time recommended it to me. He likely saw some of the self-confidence issues that Tom was seeing in me.

I signed up for the seminar, which ran November 17–20, 1995 at the Oshawa Travelodge, and paid for it myself using up personal days to attend. I was a bit nervous about going because it seemed to be more related to psychology than professional training. I was worried about whether it was legitimate or some wacky, brainwashing event. Tom encouraged me to try it. To calm my fears, he joked that he'd come extract me if it turned out to be a cult.

I could never have imagined this seminar would lead me to write on a page of hotel stationery, "I am a rejected, insecure, ridiculed person." Nor could I have imagined I would turn that dark belief around with the help of one of Tina Turner's most famous songs.

CHAPTER 5

Simply the Best

The seminar ended up being valid therapy that let me confront some of my inner beliefs. In retrospect, I probably should have been going to a therapist regularly in my twenties to unwind some of the conditioning and strategies I had adopted from childhood and absorbed from my South Asian culture. But I didn't know about therapy, and I didn't have a lot of spare money. Still, in the four days of group work and individual work, I learned something about myself — principally, that I had low self-worth. And the way I managed that was to be perfect and to be right. To never screw up or be imperfect or fail in anyone's eyes. The course didn't actually fix or heal this in me in such a short time, but it started the process. And the ability to take risks, to be okay with failure, and to see myself as an equal were important skills and beliefs for me to have if I wanted to really grow in my career as a competent engineer.

One of the things we did at the culmination of the course was to take a song we were assigned and sing the vocals to the rest of the group and make them believe it came from the centre of our being. The song I was given was "The Best" by Tina Turner. Of course, that was the last thing I believed, but I see the wisdom of this song pick for me. And there was a twist. I had to learn and sing the words in the first person. So instead of saying, "*You're* simply the best," I had to turn it around and sing, "*I'm* simply the best," and so on. This was so hard to practice because the words just felt like arrows piercing my heart. But maybe that's what they were supposed to do — shred the armour my heart had built around it and let in the magic of the world. Turning the song around to sing it to myself was armour piercing. It hurt to sing the new words, but when the moment came, I put on the tallest heels I had and a purple halter dress that flew up when I twirled. After all, I had to do justice to Tina. The instructor said she wanted to see my nostrils flare when I sang, just like Tina's did when her heart and soul were in it. I actually practiced nostril flaring in the mirror, and it was an excellent gauge to see if I was truly letting go.

When my time came to sing, I went up to the front of the room and felt everyone looking at me. I've heard that for some people, the fear of public speaking is akin to the fear of death. For me, public singing is worse than death, especially since I'm tone-deaf and can never figure out the beat. But everyone smiled and encouraged me, and I felt safe enough after all the bonding we had done. I sang that song to my group, and the words came from another place than my normal voice. I didn't stumble over the turn-arounds to the first person. I sang like I was pouring the language of love into myself. My nostrils flared of their own accord. This voice I had never heard before busted out and sang to me as if it was some loving being who cherished me. It was my inner Voice. I still play this song before I have to speak in public or go for a job interview. I do it to short-circuit my brain and stop it from trying to tell me that I'm not going to measure up. The song reminds me that when my inner Voice is speaking, I owe it to myself to speak lovingly, just as I would to someone I care about. And I still sing the words turned around to the first person.

Singing that song to myself was a breakthrough moment. I started to believe in myself and see that I had something of value to contribute. It wasn't that I was good enough in someone else's eyes. It was me who had to see this. It was my brain that had to stop saying I wasn't good enough. It was amazing timing that I could do this internal work at the start of my career. It was only a beginning — I still had far to go to unravel and heal what had caused me to be so scared of playing it too big or being too loud.

But the unconscious messages about women that had come to me from my culture had started to shake loose. I began to see the manipulation that was wrapped up in the idea that women should not be too forward, and that they should always be conscious of their position, blindly respecting those above them, not questioning authority, putting their own needs aside, and finding their purpose in meeting the needs of others. I say "began to see" because, twenty-five years after the seminar, I'm still working on understanding these limiting ideas about women and how they relate to my own sense of self. It's an onion that takes a lifetime to peel back, but I removed the first few layers, which were the biggest layers, at that seminar.

Between the seminar and Tom's influence, I started to see myself as a woman and not just a child obligated to make her parents happy without regard for her own needs. I knew my parents would only let me have my own life if I was married or moved out. I was on the move-out plan. I certainly did not want to get married when I felt like such a mess inside. But the seminar gave me a glimpse of myself as a powerful, confident woman who could stand up for her wants. When Tom mirrored this portrait back to me, that's when I knew I had found my life partner. I found the man and best friend who believed in me and in no way needed me to be anything other than a true and equal partner. In fact, he said he was so happy to have found a woman who didn't need a man to support her or who didn't just want to have babies and stop working. We both saw in the other something we wanted.

It was only because I had gone through the Quest empowerment seminar that I was able to decide to get married, and to marry someone like Tom who didn't buy into my cultural norms. I wanted someone who wasn't conditioned to think it was his right to have power over a woman. I didn't want to be expected to cater to his needs or be left out of important decisions. I wanted a relationship that was different from those that populated my family tree. I just didn't know how my parents would react to my decision to marry outside of our culture. The first time Tom came over he was driving a VW Golf with darkly tinted windows that made it impossible to see who or what was happening in the car. I suspected that Dad knew why a young man would want such a vehicle, but they welcomed him fully into our lives once they began to see in him what I saw: an honest, hard-working and loyal person who would stand by me. Tom loves my parents, and he was soon assimilated into the Guyanese culture. He drinks Johnnie Walker scotch with Coke. He also eats dahl and roti with his hands while I still use a spoon, like a child, so my fingers don't burn. Tom also learned that in my family, work means life. Prosperity in my Guyanese family meant always saying yes to work. Yes to overtime shifts. Yes to working on holidays and long weekends. Yes to more than one job — multiple jobs are a badge of honour.

Tom jokes about how many jobs I take on at work. I'll be full-time with a project and then take on another big task. He shakes his head about how stubborn I can be about pushing back when I'm given more work than I can comfortably handle. He references the "Hey Mon" skits from the '80s show *In Living Color*. "Hey Mon" is a skit about "the hardest working West Indian family, the Hedleys." The Hedleys are horrified if you only have one job, since they view that as the height of laziness. They would say, "Yuh get one job? Meh get six job!"

These skits nailed the work ethic of many West Indian families whose parents constantly instill the value of work into their children. My parents would work night shifts, even when sick. They would come home, get a bit of sleep, throw a party for a hundred people, renovate the house, overhaul the car engine, tend the garden, and keep the house full of delicious Indian food like roti, dahl, and curry. I grew up suffocated from being over-protected for fear I would die somehow and knowing deep in my bones that work meant prosperity, which really meant safety. Safety to have enough money to buy things, go on vacation, pay off the house, and save for a university education.

I am an approval seeker and people pleaser, which is one of the reasons I don't push back on work. As a female in Indian culture, I was brought up to make sure people were comfortable around me. The rules were clear: Don't be too noisy or act like a boy. Defer to authority. Be pleasant. Learn to cook. Make a home warm and inviting. I learned that being a good girl meant pleasing people. I never wanted to feel the sting of disapproval or disappointment. I avoided that feeling by being an overachiever and not pushing back. Of course, I was a horrible teenager to my parents — rude, moody, and insolent — because they loved me unconditionally and I could let off steam with them. But to anyone else, I was nice and pleasant and bottled it up if I was angry or upset with them. I have never been without financial security, but my need for approval — to be the person who stepped up and got the job done — was strong. I had one foot in an older identity, which held that my gender and race put me lower in the scheme of society than other groups, and another foot in the new identity of my gender and race not being something to hold me back.

***

Even during my wedding to Tom, I was reminded of this paradox. We had a traditional Hindu ceremony on a Friday in August 1996 in my parent's backyard, followed by a traditional Catholic wedding on Saturday. The first time I got married, I wore a red sari with elaborate designs in gold thread. I remember how heavy the material was and how beautiful I felt with the red veil pinned onto my hair. As I was walking to Tom and he was waiting for his first glimpse of me, an aunt said, "Walk slowly and keep your eyes on the ground. A bride doesn't look directly into a man's eyes." I kept my eyes downcast, which is why my first glimpse of Tom was his feet, while he could look openly at my whole self. In a Hindu marriage ceremony, only bare feet are allowed during the wedding rites. The next day, at our second wedding, I was again wearing a heavy dress and veil, but this one was made of white silk and tulle. As I walked down the aisle in the church, my gaze was level, and I smiled into Tom's eyes as he stood beside the altar. My two marriages were less than twenty-four hours apart and showed how I walked in two different worlds.

In my working life, I also had two different worlds. At work, I was treated as an equal even if I was the only person of colour or woman in the room — my ideas and voice were welcomed and people seemed happy if I stepped up to lead. But on the inside, I still felt like an imposter who had to be perfect and never fail. Sometimes the people I worked with were easier on me than I was on myself. I was driven by this need to always reach for the next thing. I didn't spend too much time being satisfied once I reached a goal. It was always about looking to the next opportunity to be an achiever. In my field, at that point in my career, that meant becoming a professional engineer, which for most people is a minimum two-year process. However, I earned my license as soon as possible with the support of my workplace mentor, a professional engineer at General Motors. My work centred on the programming of automatic guided vehicles that retrieved steel from a multi-story storage bay and delivered them to huge presses to be stamped into car parts like fenders and hoods. These squat driverless vehicles made me smile whenever one crossed my path on the factory floor. Some of the code I programmed allowed them to move around safely and productively. Still, I worried that I should be doing more with my degree in engineering physics. Programming wasn't that enjoyable for me, even in an exciting world like automotive manufacturing.

A few months after I received my professional license, the Professional Engineers Ontario magazine arrived. The magazine was included as part of my license fee for being a professional engineer, or "P.Eng." as we are referred to in Ontario, and this edition included a salary survey. I checked the survey and noted to Tom that my salary was about $15,000 lower than the median salary in my field. I felt I should be paid more because I certainly didn't do average work — my projects were challenging and often what a more senior person would take on. As I was getting angry about this, Tom said in his straightforward way, "Why don't you ask for a raise?" I remember feeling like that was an insane idea. "It's not annual evaluation time," I said. "They don't give raises mid-year." Really, what I was feeling was fear.

"So? You'll never know if you don't ask," he said, like this was obvious. But to me, it felt wrong to just ask for more money. Too forward. Too blunt. Too direct. But a part of me wanted fairness too. So I overcame my first reactions by believing I was worthy, just like I had written in a mission statement during the empowerment seminar. I wrote a lengthy data-supported email because that way felt a little safer than just walking into my manager's office and having a conversation, which I'm sure is what Tom would have done. I cited the salary survey and stated that I thought I should at least make the median salary for my job responsibilities. I cited the fact that our company publicly supported women in technology. My manager agreed right away without any pushback, but said he couldn't bring me up to my requested salary all at once because it was too big a jump. Instead, I would get my raise in two parts, a few months apart. That was it. He just said yes. I made more money, on par with men in my field, just by asking. I had stood up for myself, and in that moment I felt myself overcome a little more of my conditioning.

This positive experience gave me confidence in my abilities. I wanted my career to progress, but I realized that big jumps in salaries for someone technical like me usually came through a promotion or by quitting. The career ladder at my conservative IT company seemed to be through the management track, and I didn't want that. I never wanted to have a position of power over someone, and the manager-employee relationship repelled me in the same way the doctor-patient and lawyer-client ones did when I was choosing my university program.

As I pondered a more fulfilling career, I had a near-fatal accident. On a business trip to Michigan, my rental SUV hit black ice, skidded, and rolled over into a ditch off the highway near London, Ontario. It happened so fast, and I walked away without a scratch. For hours after, I picked safety glass out of my hair because the impact of the rollover broke the entire windshield. This accident made me realize how fast life can end and how lucky I was. It seemed to be a message not to take life for granted and settle for what's safe.

I started looking for jobs in the career section of the newspaper. This was long before LinkedIn existed. One weekend Tom and I were driving up to Sault Ste. Marie to visit his parents, a seven-hour drive north of Toronto. I used the time to look for jobs. One of the ads in the paper was for a project management role at a company called SciTech North, and as I glanced out the window, there was the building. I enjoyed the project manager roles I had at work because I loved planning and I knew I never wanted to manage people's compensation, an unavoidable part of the management track. It seemed magical how I had just passed the company location on the side of the highway as I read the ad in the paper. Even more impressive was that the company produced mass spectrometers. It fit perfectly with my studies, and it would leverage all the things my first job had given me — manufacturing experience and systems-engineering training. The ad said they wanted either an MBA or PMP (Project Management Professional) candidate. I couldn't believe it — I was planning to write the exam for the PMP certification in a couple of months. Being a professional engineer was also an asset for this job. It felt like I had conjured up this job by longing for something more. It felt like the universe had nudged me by giving me the newspaper to read at the precise moment the building came up on the drive and precisely when I would have the credentials under my belt.

I applied and went through three levels of interviews and even a psych evaluation to ensure I would fit the culture. The industrial psychologist, a middle-aged man, met me in a bright, airy office. He interviewed me, gave me several personality tests, showed me inkblots to describe, and timed me while I completed puzzles to match shapes.

If I got the job, I would be working on a project to launch a mass spectrometer designed with cutting-edge sensitivity. This new device could identify compounds from trace amounts and help life-saving research at universities and pharmaceutical companies. I really wanted this job. I was ready to leave the IT world behind.

Was SciTech North the next chapter? I felt like it had to be.

PART 2

Toxic Work

"The culture of any organization is shaped by the worst behavior the leader is willing to tolerate."

— Steve Gruenert and Todd Whitaker,
School Culture Rewired

CHAPTER 6

Physiological Burnout

SciTech North was a smaller organization with a more people-centric culture. It was clear from the interviewing process this company was looking for leaders with high intellectual and emotional intelligence. I was beyond excited to be chosen to be part of this team, but it was not an easy job I stepped into. They wanted a product that could ship in the fall for an important trade show. This mass spectrometer would be unveiled with a big splash. The big challenge was that we only had a fraction of the time in a typical product development cycle. Still, I was engaged and excited because the product was eagerly anticipated by scientists who wanted to make better medicines and cure diseases. My mind and heart were pulled into the mission at hand, and I landed in a company culture of support and encouragement. It felt so right.

A big part of my enjoyment at work was the people, who were not only driven like me but kind too. The company invested in training for all employees in the Six Thinking Hats process by Edward de Bono to help us think creatively to solve problems. I loved this process because it allowed me to ask people to keep on subject and time without them getting irked at me or overruling me. It saved time, saved face, and led to creative solutions. Takashi, the scientist, befriended me and gave me the insider backstory so I could navigate the business a bit better.

In a tech job, your manager is one of the most significant determinants of whether you enjoy your job or hate it. A great manager can make even a lousy workplace feel better. I was fortunate to have an exceptional manager to mentor me. He encouraged me to be a leader who "doesn't leave a path of collateral damage" in her wake. To me, this meant he didn't want people demoralized and stepped on to serve my success. From that coaching discussion onward, I've strived to support people I work with and leave them happier than when I came — never harmed. It was like he gave me permission to bring my caring nature to a highly technical role, and I quickly learned that people responded to my leadership style of being open-hearted. People appreciate niceness mixed in with intellectual capabilities. Being able to gather and unite people is something I learned from Mom. As a child, I saw her single-handedly plan gatherings of all sorts: birthday, anniversary, Christmas, and Hindu prayer. She tirelessly cooked, cleaned, and decorated so everyone felt engaged and loved. These are often considered female ways of doing things, but they are also essential ways of doing things — skills that are transferable from home to office, and that are sorely missed when they are absent. I saw that my role as a leader was to not just have a successful project but also tend to the emotional welfare of my team in a caring way. I had to get the job done, but not through bullying or manipulation. As an engineer, I had taken an oath to uphold the physical safety of the public. Now, as a project manager, I made a promise to myself to uphold emotional safety as well.

The report by the industrial psychologist who did my evaluation when I applied to SciTech North was a true gift because it told me my strengths and weaknesses for career growth.

My strengths were a "bright, active mind; can see the big picture and integrate detail into it; comprehensive, thorough, methodical; precise; good communication and interpersonal skills; inclusive; caring; honest; open; trustworthy; mature; productive; produces quality work."

My areas for development were that I "can be too tactful or nice; may need to be more direct and forthright; can take things to heart; may need to be less self-critical." This feedback let me see the unconscious challenges I faced as a minority woman leader. Specifically, it opened my eyes to the conditioning I had absorbed that I should be a "nice girl" and not "hurt people's feelings." It gave me a different way to unpack the self-worth issues I had started to see in the Quest empowerment seminar in 1995.

I used this report to embolden my voice at the table, trust my instincts, and not let self-doubt hold me back. Within a few months, my project hit its first significant milestone when we produced a prototype on time, within budget, and with the sensitivity the scientists wanted to see. Everyone was delighted, from marketing to sales to engineering, and they told me this success was largely due to my leadership ways. This should have been great news, but there was a downside to so much appreciation and expectation because I started to feel I could not fail in this job. There was so much to do to get a finished product ready for market in such a short time. I started to steal time from my personal life and sacrifice sleep and self-care to get all the work done. And the burnout cycle started.

My evenings and weekends were consumed with work or thinking about work. I had insufficient downtime. It didn't take long to feel like my body and mind were breaking down. Tom urged me to either slow down at work or find a different job. I refused either option because people expected so much of me, and I really liked the challenge. Even bursting into tears after work and constantly feeling out of control and obsessed with work did not strike me as alarming warning signs.

ALLOSTATIC LOAD AND THE STRESS PARADOX

The problem with psychological stress is that you can't see it. A workplace safety inspection might include checking the emergency exits, the first aid supplies, and the inspection signoffs of fire extinguishers. But how do you have a safety checklist for crying, anxiety, lack of sleep, poor nutrition, or work creeping into your unpaid time off? If I could have measured my body's physiologic response to this job stress, I would have seen chemicals called stress mediators, such as adrenaline, cortisol and epinephrine, produced to help me respond in order to survive. These mediators are a paradox because while they were intended to help me in the present moment, they were at the same time toxic to optimal health.

This idea of stress as a paradox goes back a long way. In 1936, the Austrian Hungarian Canadian endocrinologist Hans Selye put forward the then-new idea that stress can not only protect the body but also damage it. Then in 1998, Bruce McEwen published "Protective and Damaging Effects of Stress Mediators" in *The New England Journal of Medicine*. McEwen's research describes a process of *allostasis* in which the body adapts its physiology to cope with stressors, even if the stress is social in nature. Psychosocial stress is stress that can be perceived by the mind rather than by the body, such as a threat to self-worth, status, or inclusion in a social group. The process of *allostatic regulation* is what returns the body to a safe operating level from the effects of chemical mediators like cortisol and epinephrine. If the process fails, the effects of these toxic chemicals accumulate as *allostatic load*. Like a runaway train, the stress mediators can become dysregulated or chronically overused and can harm the body and mind. When people work too much, it can lead to more allostatic load than the human body can tolerate, risking damage to critical physiological functions such as the immune, cardiovascular, and gastrointestinal systems. This is why stress is said to be a silent killer. The allostatic load or overload develops over time, quietly, and symptoms can be subtle until they are catastrophic — heart attack, stroke, cancer, and mental illness to name a few.

I think my intense dream job exceeded my ability to cope and put me in allostatic overload. In the early phase, I was pumped up by the challenge, and the job stress brought out the best in me. I had enough time to rest while I was on the learning curve at a new workplace. However, once we passed the prototype phase and were given the green light to go full speed towards the production date, I started pushing myself to work without taking breaks, getting enough sleep, or eating well, and the allostatic load built up. It showed itself as crying when I left the office, feeling out of control, and attaching myself to the project's success as if my life depended on it. My body was never relaxed, I was not happy, and it felt like I would have a nervous breakdown.

The term "burnout" was first associated with job stress in the mid-seventies by Christina Maslach at the University of California, Berkeley and Herbert Freudenberger, a caregiver at a substance abuse clinic in New York City. Someone in poverty law used the term burnout to describe their difficult job to Maslach, who then incorporated it into her writing. At the drug clinic, burnout was slang for excessive abuse of drugs. Herbert Freudenberger found this term resonated for himself and his colleagues in their intense and demanding job as caregivers. It was like they had a bad relationship with their job, just like the addicts had with drugs.

Decades later, burnout is still being researched. In their recent book *Burnout: The Secret to Unlocking the Stress Cycle* Emily Nagoski and Amelia Nagoski say, "Work does not cause burnout. Our stress response, if stuck, causes burnout." Brené Brown, Emily Nagoski, and Amelia Nagoski discuss burnout in "Burnout and How to Complete the Stress Cycle" on the podcast *Unlocking Us* on October 14, 2020. They point out that unless the stress cycle ends properly, the damaging stress hormones keep circulating and can continue to do damage. Even after a stressful event *is over*, the mediators keep working until they get a clear signal that our emotional state has shifted. According to Brown and the Nagoskis, signals that successfully end the stress cycle include going for a walk, laughing, crying, and hugging. My body was intelligent enough to cry to deal with job stress, which helped it complete the stress cycle. However, I wasn't wise enough to stop working at that pace.

Some of these tensions and tendencies were flagged in my psychological assessment, which pointed out that the only risk to my being successful is that "the organization may be inclined to give [me] too much responsibility too quickly." Combined with my "readiness to please and accept challenge(s)," the psychologist predicted that I could "end up with too much on [my] plate too soon."

I did have a readiness — or a need — to please, and I did end up with too much on my plate. I didn't want to be a whiner, a complainer, or worst of all, an incapable woman. I didn't want them to question their decision to hire me. Instead, I worked hard and took on the stress of the aggressive timeline. I was never free of a stress cycle. I went further and further into burnout, and I don't think it was the organization's fault. I think I was driven because I had years of conditioning that conflated being a valuable person with getting kudos for my work. I felt valued and wanted by this company after going through its rigorous selection process. Being wanted was something that felt really, really good. It fulfilled a need in me that was integral to my identity. There was no way I was walking away from this job.

THE METAPHORICAL MACK TRUCK

When we don't listen to life's subtle cues, the universe sometimes sends a Mack truck to get us to pay attention. One morning at the office, I was hurrying down the wide stairway to the ground floor, which was in an open area. I missed the first step, went airborne, and fell. And just like how I tripped and fell into the pool in Guyana, I also landed hard and face-first at the bottom.

I awoke to worried co-workers around me who were relieved that there were no broken bones or visible damage. My arm reached out and caught between the railings, which broke my fall. A trip to the ER confirmed I was fine, but this accident showed me that I had a problem with overworking. I could have asked for less work, but it wasn't in me to do that, whether from cultural conditioning or my own issues to be a people-pleaser. I would just burn myself out if I stayed, and I'd sabotage the thing that enabled success — my mind. I needed to find a slower pace of work.

In 2000, technical project managers were in high demand due to the tech boom. There were hiring incentives at JumboTek Canada, one of the largest IT firms in the world, operating in more than a hundred countries and worth over 100 billion USD in market capitalization. Tom passed my resumé to a friend who submitted it under a referral bonus program, where employees were getting cash payouts for successful hires they brought to the company. I landed a job with a signing bonus, a 25 percent raise, a shorter commute, and work-from-home options, all with a short phone interview. It was sad to say goodbye to my dream job and good friends like Takashi. But I wanted to start a family and knew I needed balance and health for that next phase. I also didn't want to risk another Mack truck message if I didn't listen to what was important.

I reluctantly left SciTech North to start a new chapter of my career.

CHAPTER 7

The Spirit of a JTekker: Heart & Soul

I started at JumboTek Canada as a Level 8 Junior Project Manager. The cryptic job title meant little to me. I was more in awe that I had doubled my salary in five years out of university. After the burnout experience, I didn't want to rush up the career ladder at breakneck speed. Instead, the priority was having a good work-life balance and taking a break from being such an overachiever. I worked fewer hours with a shorter commute and better boundaries to keep work out of personal time. However, I did not stop being an overachiever.

The years 2000–2002 were difficult ones for the tech industry after the dot-com bubble burst. Where I was placed in e-commerce, however, the firm was busy with work. Customers like banks, insurance companies, and retailers needed solutions to service their online customers. I had learned a lot about bringing a team of people together under one vision and treating them with kindness. Clients and colleagues alike responded well to my leadership style, and my projects were successful. This was noticed and rewarded with awards, bonuses, and salary increases. But I wasn't practicing kindness on the job in a quest to fast-track my career. I was working this way because I identified as a JTekker, the odd term we called ourselves, and fell into the magic of the culture.

As a JTekker, I worked for intrinsic rewards, to feel the satisfaction of a job well done, deliver value to clients, and be part of a team. I received feedback that my "leadership and professionalism" were "key factors" in the success of the projects I worked on.

JumboTek's values of treating the customer right and providing value with a "one-for-all and all-for-one" approach became integrated with my values. Personally, the sense of teamwork and the gratitude from the client fueled me to keep going. I came to see that it didn't matter what the project was, I just loved being a project manager. Surprisingly, I was just as happy at JumboTek as I had been at SciTech North, even though I wasn't on the cutting edge of science. I also found satisfaction in helping my fellow JTekkers. It wasn't just external praise from a client that drove me; I also enjoyed going out of my way to break down silos within the company and sought ways to work as a cross-organizational team. My efforts were noticed by co-workers, who wrote messages like the following one I received after working for a year and a bit:

Subject: Thanks for making an exception and giving us the phone numbers

Sunita,

I wanted to thank you again for making an exception and giving us the phone numbers/pager for your folks. B _____ has been working a lot this weekend and could not have made the progress debugging the problems without having your guys step in and work along with him. We should be ready for Tuesday, or at least minimize the manual work if needed for a few days.

Thanks,
C _____

All-for-one and one-for-all. I didn't just absorb this culture out of thin air. My understanding of it came from the people I worked with. Just like at SciTech North, I had a great manager who assigned me a buddy. My buddy,

Luiz, felt like a father to me. He showed me the ropes and helped me understand what e-commerce meant (it meant we sold web hosting services to insurance companies, banks, and retailers.) My manager, Nikoli, was forthright and encouraged me to reach my potential. He was of Eastern European background and had warm eyes and a mischievous dimple when he smiled. He always had time to talk, and I knew our relationship was important to him even though I was one of the more junior people on the team.

In the first two years, I had work-life balance. The projects were given realistic timelines and budgets, and I could deliver value that made a difference. The client contract was the holiest of things to me. As the project manager, I was responsible and accountable for ensuring the client got the value promised in the "spirit" of the contract — not just the words. The client was paying top dollar for solutions, for people who would go the extra mile, for stellar reputation and client service levels.

My projects felt challenging, and there were bubbles of intense work that exceeded fifty or sixty hours a week, but I didn't feel drained. Clients appreciated my ability to bring positivity and results. Their feedback and my track record earned me top raises and bonuses. Even though I hadn't prioritized growing my salary quickly, it happened anyway because I had fallen in with a culture that said results get rewarded.

More important than the compensation I received was the energy I got from my job, which motivated me to take my health seriously. I began to exercise regularly and eat well. I lost the twenty pounds I had put on from university and early work life, where I overworked myself. I found a balance between feeling fulfilled at work and caring for my health.

What more could I ask for?

GREAT EXPECTATIONS

In March 2002, a new CEO assumed leadership of JumboTek and in June I was awarded stock options. The stock had dropped by almost 40 percent in the two years I had worked there and it was clear from the letter that accompanied my award that I was expected to help bring the stock price back up. Awarding stock options to employees made them more committed to working hard to raise the stock price and share in the financial reward.

That message was clear to me when my manager called me into his office and handed me a letter from JumboTek's CEO. I was told I was in a "select group of employees" to whom their management team had decided to award stock options. The letter continued to say JumboTek was making an "important financial investment" in me and in return the company had "expectations" for me to achieve the goals to win in the market. These expectations were my "continued support", "commitment to excellence" and "focus on disciplined marketplace execution." Lastly, the leader of our company ended the letter by telling me he was "proud" to have me on the team.

I was blown away by getting this letter. It made me feel special, but the expectations were clear, and they were big. The CEO seemed laser-focused on stock price, like a sports fan fixated on the scoreboard during a game. Clearly, the goal was to get the stock price up, and each quarterly reporting period was a season. While it was nice to be recognized, this award did not motivate me a great deal more because I was already motivated by the values of putting the client first and working as a team. My heart was already in the game, and I was a dedicated employee to the values and identity I had as a JTekker. But the letter did add to the pressure not to disappoint — by recognizing me, the stakes just became higher not to let people down.

The next year, on June 23, 2003, another letter followed, and more stock options were awarded. The stock had risen almost 40 percent in twelve months. At this time, I was five months pregnant and about to leave for a year of maternity time off, yet I was still recognized. JumboTek's culture was to treat people equitably — all minority groups, including women and people with disabilities. These values meshed with my values of treating people equitably, and I felt valued as a working mother to be recognized in what was a partial working year for me.

I felt I owed JumboTek my very best in return for their investment in me.

BABIES AND A CHANGE IN VALUES

With the birth of my first child, my drive to do my very best transferred to motherhood. However, a baby is not something I could control the way I was able to control the projects at work. I tried to tackle motherhood with an achiever mindset. The first big failure came within hours of bringing our seven-pound bundle of joy home, when I couldn't breastfeed her. Jessica couldn't latch, but I took this as a deficiency in myself, and I was determined to deliver the goodness of breastmilk and not fail my baby. So I rented double breast pumps and made repeated trips to a breastfeeding clinic to get it right, all while the baby was distressed for food. The first four weeks of Jessica's life were a misery because I could not perform this one essential task — feeding my child. Finally, after Jessica had lost weight instead of gaining, I listened to Mom and Tom telling me I had to put the baby first by adding formula to every other feeding. With this change, she finally became happy and slept better. Then I stopped the breast-pumping madness. I, too, became happy and slept better. I recognized I was doing with my baby the same thing I tended to do at work: allowing perfectionism to take over and cause me to lose sight of the fact that life is meant to be enjoyed, not conquered. I eventually recalibrated my expectations once I realized that the more relaxed I was, the happier Jessica became. I let my baby, rather than society or my own conditioned ideas, tell me what she needed.

Then unexpectedly, during the last few months of maternity leave, I became pregnant again. It was a shock, but we wanted two kids, and they would just be a little closer in age than we anticipated. The miscarriage came on Labour Day, of all days, when I was six weeks pregnant. I remember being in the utilitarian bathroom in the Emergency Room and wondering if I had lost my baby in the toilet. After a D&C procedure, Tom and I went home bearing this loss. But Jessica was there, and she needed us. I went back to my life loving one baby while grieving another. It was surreal how you keep going because life demands it.

After going through a healthy pregnancy and a failed pregnancy, I realized that I had to put life before work. Life was too unpredictable to do otherwise. Children could be taken away and lost forever. Success became about being a good mother, not a perfect mother. And being a good worker rather than a perfect one. And somewhere between being a good mother and a good worker, I still needed time for myself.

I returned to work and had to learn how to balance my job with a baby in daycare. It was not easy, but our family of three found its way and then I became pregnant again after a few months. I worried about another miscarriage, and so I asked for less-demanding roles, with a shorter commute and fewer late hours. JumboTek was very accommodating and gave me projects with manageable deadlines. I thought I had taken a career setback by asking for easier work but to my surprise my manager gave me a top rating for that year. Again, I felt valued as a working parent.

This time, I added another six months to my maternity leave so I could spend more time with the children while they were small. Within only a few weeks of Sophia's birth, I found being at home was not the idyllic stay-at-home Mom plan I had envisioned. Being responsible most of the day for a two-year-old and an infant was very difficult for me. In retrospect, I think I had postpartum depression, but I didn't know it. As I was focused on losing the baby weight, I started exercising, which I think alleviated my moodiness. With a clear mind, I saw that just because I wasn't good at taking care of two young children didn't mean I was a failure. It was about the quality of our time together, not the quantity. I had the option to return to work early and realized I would be better as a mother who combined paid work and work at home, or what used to be called a working mother (as though motherhood was not already work!). I would enjoy my kids more if I had some time at the office and wasn't exhausted by their caretaking.

When I returned to work, it was with a resolve to have a career that was balanced enough to allow me to give my best self to my family. But what I found was a workplace that had changed dramatically in how employees and clients alike were treated. Or perhaps it was my tolerance levels for what work could demand from me that had changed.

CHAPTER 8

Spiritual Burnout

In 2007, the focus on increasing the stock price of the company I was working for was pretty high. To compound things, my growing skills put me in charge of more work, and I found myself in difficult leadership positions that had me questioning my ethics — something I had been sheltered from as a young professional. Motherhood had also opened me up to a more profound way of caring about others, and I became more aware of the pain and suffering of the people around me. As a person with a high level of empathy and high standards for fairness, respect, trust, and truth, I felt emotional pain when colleagues or clients were treated unfairly. Putting clients first, working as a team, and promoting diversity were my core values, and they happened to be the same as my company's stated values and identity.

But those values would soon come under threat. Over the next few years, the pressure to keep the stock price growing quarter over quarter seemed to increase exponentially. That profit motive added pressure to the whole system and made it harder for me to live according to my values. The focus on measurement by numbers was so high that people were ranked at the end of the year as a 1, 2, or 3, which corresponded to exceeding expectations, meeting expectations, or falling below expectations. You had to be a 1 to be considered for the top awards, promotions and raises. But it wasn't always clear how fair the rankings were. These shame-based methods of motivating employees didn't sit well with me. These were triggers from my childhood that I didn't expect in my workplace, and this was a new challenge at work. Looking back, I can see a scared young woman in her 30s who was still terrified of having an authority figure angry with her as if she was facing a teacher with a ruler or something else buried away in lost childhood memories. However, at the time, the questions that surfaced for me didn't connect any dots from my childhood but rather focused on areas I thought the workplace was failing to deliver on.

I was faced with situations where I had to ask:

- Why were behaviours allowed, even rewarded, that were contrary to the stated values of our company?
- Was the emerging company culture that I interfaced with counter to my values?
- How could I work with colleagues who felt demoralized and still respect and trust my company leaders who said they cared about their employees?
- How could I work with clients who felt betrayed by my company?

I felt like there should have been an employee handbook from HR titled "How our company behaves and enacts workplace practices that can be soul-sucking." And yet I, like many of my colleagues, thought I had to suck it up and live under the toxic stress of excessive work and the threat to our values.

UTILIZATION RATE

One work practice that caused toxic stress was the utilization rate. This was a measure of how many hours were billed in a year. A high target of 87 percent could be assigned, meaning only 13 percent of working time was allowed for non-client activities such as training, internal meetings, vacation, holidays, or sick time. There was shame attached to this practice because no one wanted to fall short of the mark and be called out. There was also stress attached to the idea that you were being closely monitored. And nobody knew what the consequences of a low utilization rate might be. It was a badge of honour to have a high utilization rate and a constant source of worry and shame if you dipped below the target.

There was a feast or famine component to the utilization rate as well. If I could work extra hours, it was insurance for a rainy day when I might be on the bench too long without a project, or when hours might be lost to unexpected illness. There was also an approval component because you were highly regarded for exceeding this measure and, naturally, you wanted to keep that praise coming. And lastly, there was a fear component to this practice because if you didn't meet your utilization rate you could be rated lower, lose out on year-end financial rewards, or even be laid off. All these components added up to toxic stress.

I always thought about my utilization rate, even though it was in good standing. To fall below the target would mean not meeting my annual goal and, to me, that was like a failing grade from school days. I was trained to exceed expectations, not fall short of them. This practice exploited people like me who feared failure, craved approval, or measured their self-worth by their achievements. Even though I had done the internal work to heal these issues, I was still vulnerable to feeling driven by the utilization rate measurement.

Moreover, some of my colleagues were not in as safe a position as I was. I could feel their stress and worry about falling below target. I had a project team member who confided how worried she was about her utilization rate dropping because she would be off work for an operation for a month. She should not have had to worry about her job when surgery was worrisome enough. That kind of stress could hamper her recovery by encouraging her to return to work before she was ready to and by flooding her system with stress chemicals that inhibit healing. As a person who tends to take on the worries of others, I was vulnerable not only to my own stress around the utilization rate but also to second-hand stress from colleagues. Everyone was constantly looking over their shoulder, worried their utilization rate would threaten their job, and my own fear was compounded by the fears of others.

As time went on, it felt like the numbers mattered the most. I started to wonder if the company I worked for actually cared about people as much as they claimed to.

PERFORMANCE REVIEWS, QUOTAS & SALARY SECRECY

Another potentially psychologically unsafe work practice was the annual performance review and rating, which determined compensation such as cash bonuses, stock options, and salary increases.

Disclosing compensation was taboo at JumboTek. There was no written rule against it that I was aware of; it was something you just knew you should keep secret from co-workers. It was possible to have two people doing the same job and earning different salaries. For example, a newer hire could be paid more than someone who had been at the company for years. You had no way to know. Or one person might ask for a raise and get it while another person in the same role lacked the confidence to ask. Again, there was no way to know if you were paid equitably. I compared salaries with an ex-colleague after I left JumboTek. She and I had similar roles, so theoretically we should have had comparable salaries. However, my final salary was close to 80 percent more than hers, and she had more responsibility than me. It makes me ill to think about the unfairness of such a wide gap.

One of the most unfair practices at work involved the use of quotas to determine who got the top rating of 1. It should not have mattered if a team was full of top performers — everyone who exceeded expectations should have been rated as a 1. These ratings should have been earned based on results. But, like a bell curve in an academic setting, there were limits on how many top ratings could be given. You could exceed all expectations and still not get the corresponding rating because someone else was picked instead. Competing with your peers for a limited supply of top ratings can breed mistrust and excessive overworking, both of which are unhealthy. Thinking that you might have been shortchanged can affect your feelings of worth and trust in the company. That, in turn, can erode corporate culture. From the perspective of the manager who wants to be a fair and trusted leader, this can cause significant distress if their hands are tied when it comes to rewarding deserving workers.

QUARTER-END MADNESS

Our financial numbers were reported to head office every quarter with a focus on the impact on share price. This threw the company into regular quarter-end madness. Finance people were stretched at quarter-end. Sales colleagues could be in the same boat, trying to sign deals so they didn't fall short of their quotas to hit revenue targets. For project managers, we had to get work delivered on time to recognize profit from an accounting standpoint. Almost all parts of the business became hectic at quarter-end.

Quarter-end was a big stick to beat us with, and it restarted every three months. It was psychologically exhausting, and morale went down if actual sales numbers fell below target sales numbers. It's dumb to burn out people like this, but it happens nonetheless.

DON'T CONFUSE SALES WITH DELIVERY

The highest toxic stress had nothing to do with meeting numbers. It had to do with falling short of trust.

The saying "don't confuse sales with delivery" is a street term. Another similar term is "vapourware." It means that clients are promised the best during the sales cycle but then find those promises are not all lived up to once the contract is signed and the delivery phase begins. It was horrible to feel a client's anger or disappointment if they felt misled or deceived. If I happened into a project where the delivery dates were too aggressive, or the contract didn't include what the client thought it did, I felt it was on me to fix it. I went into overachiever mode, not motivated for personal gain but to make the client happy again. I was mentally strained if the client felt wronged, and I was anxious to repair the relationship. I hated walking into a situation with an angry client because trust is something I need in my relationships. Sometimes the sales team blamed the delivery team for not coming through because it was the sales team's word on the line. So I could feel anger and pressure from both our sales team and the clients to pull off miracles and meet cost, quality and schedule targets. Either way, it was a bad experience for me to feel so pressured not to let anyone down.

THE INSECURE OVERACHIEVER

Laura Empson defines the term "insecure overachievers" as "exceptionally capable and fiercely ambitious, but driven by a profound belief in their own inadequacy." One reason is that "some children grow up believing that they are noticed and valued by their parents only when they are excelling. This attitude may persist long after they have left home because they have internalised that insecurity as part of their identity."

Empson's book, *Leading Professionals: Power, Politics, and Prima Donnas,* describes how elite firms exploit such people. Chapter 6, "Leading Insecure Overachievers," explores "the dark side of social control and its most typical manifestation — overwork," asking "why do senior professionals 'choose' to exercise their autonomy by overworking to such an extent that they risk their personal relationships and physical and mental health?"

I think people who fit the profile of insecure overachievers, myself included, are at risk with these practices of utilization rate, salary secrecy, competition for scarce top ratings, and relentless drive to meet sales and profit targets every quarter. We were totally sucked into repairing and achieving good relationships with our clients. We were sucked into feeling valued when we met targets and shame when we did not.

PSYCHOLOGICAL HEALTH & SAFETY FACTORS

There is a standard that lays out the conditions for mental health at work and what happens when those conditions are missing. "Psychological health and safety in the workplace — Prevention, promotion, and guidance to staged implementation," or the "Standard" as it is called, is a free publication by CSA Group, a global organization for safety, social good, and sustainability originating from the former Canadian Standards Association. CSA Group describes itself as "one of the largest standards development organizations in North America — conducting research and developing standards for a broad range of technologies and functional areas." The Standard, which was published in 2013, lists thirteen psychosocial factors that are involved in mental health and explores some of the circumstances that can lead mental health to deteriorate. These psychosocial factors are:

1. Balance
2. Civility and Respect
3. Clear Leadership and Expectations
4. Engagement
5. Growth and Development
6. Involvement and Influence
7. Organizational Culture
8. Protection of Physical Safety
9. Psychological Competencies and Demands
10. Psychological Protection
11. Psychological and Social Support
12. Recognition and Reward
13. Workload Management

With recent increases in attention to the issue of mental health across a wide range of public and private settings, I can't believe there isn't more awareness of these psychosocial factors or more discussion of the best practices that companies and people can adopt in order to support mental health. I've given a brief description of each of the factors in Appendix A, and included links to the source material. Although everyone's case is unique and mental health is a complex phenomenon, I can't help thinking that I might have had a healthier level of stress if the Standard had been published during my first ten years at JumboTek, and of course I had somehow known about it. Given my particular vulnerabilities, I would have benefited from knowing about the following three specific factors, which are described on the Canadian Centre for Occupational Health and Safety (CCOHS) website as Psychosocial Risk (PSR) factors in the workplace:

- **Recognition and Reward:** "An imbalance between effort and reward is a significant contributor to burnout and emotional distress leading to a range of psychological and physical disorders."
- **Workload Management:** "Any system subject to excess load without reprieve will break. This is as true for people as it is for equipment. Increased demands, without opportunities for control, result in physical, psychological and emotional fatigue, and increase stress and strain."

- **Civility and Respect:** For safety reasons, we need a "workplace where employees are respectful and considerate in their interactions with one another, as well as with customers, clients and the public."

It was hard to run my projects and see team members and clients negatively impacted. I wanted to protect people from harm — not be part of a machine that caused it, and I felt lacking in integrity whenever I couldn't live up to this goal. This psychological stress was a new animal with sharper teeth than mere burnout. Anything that asks you to be part of an untruth, whether family or work, eats you up spiritually. It caused a slower burn to my mental health.

Why would any organization that cares about its employees treat them in ways that cause harm? A tech organization's most valuable asset is the brain capital of its employees. Why risk that competitive advantage and sabotage success? As an engineer, I'm trained to find the root cause of a problem. I believe an organization's embedded dysfunctions are the root cause of these undesired and dangerous health impacts. We must examine workplace dysfunctions to further understand the world's growing mental health crisis.

CHAPTER 9

The Organization is Sick

As a client project manager for over twenty-five years, I have wide-ranging experience with many organizations and cultures. I am not a business expert or sociologist, but I am an IT worker with first-hand knowledge of where organizations veer off their mission statement to treat employees with respect and equity. In my observation, the focus on winning in the stock market put in power people who prioritized results over people or who were good at showmanship rather than being authentic or kind. These people could appear emotionally intelligent and charming yet be ruthless behind the scenes.

I'll never forget the answer I received when I asked an investment banker whether he ever considered ethical investing. It was a financial information evening in the early 2000s, and I had privately bought into the fund this man managed. I know that wealth often comes from exploiting others, and that there is an unfair division of wealth in the world. I wondered how much human suffering came from making money, and how many degrees of separation stood between my personal profit and an illegal or inhumane practice. So, when the presentation opened for questions, I asked about it. The man in the power suit exuding confidence was not expecting this question, I could tell. He asked what I meant.

I said, "Well, what if the investment was in a country where people made a profit from corrupt government practices or used child labourers?" He looked at me like I was odd and replied, "If it makes money, I'd sell my mother." Everyone laughed at the joke, and the evening moved on to more acceptable questions. It didn't escape me that he never answered the question.

When success correlates to dominance and winning, it drives behaviour that can compromise values, ethics, and humanity. To compound things, how people are measured can cause them to make short-sighted decisions. For example, one year the board members of a client team decided to cut millions across all IT projects in order to maximize profits. This resulted in my project budget being shaved by 80 percent and caused us to delay ordering long lead time telecom equipment, such as the racks for the servers and network switches, until the following fiscal year when more funding was available. That decision almost guaranteed we would fail to meet the target timeline and risked costly penalties in extending equipment warranties and property leases. However, the board was more concerned about the profit statements in the current year than the future consequences. In fact, they seemed to have an unrealistic expectation that the team would figure it out somehow. Leadership like this fails to see the big picture and puts unnecessary pressure on the teams that support the organization. All of this is dysfunctional. The IT industry that I work in exists to support the other areas of the business, like sales and marketing. We are a service organization that enables the machine. When the machine is focused on business targets for competition and profit, it drives bad behaviour from top to bottom.

LETHAL LEADERS & VUCA – A TOXIC COCKTAIL

Lethal leaders are people who wreak havoc on the mental health of colleagues they have power over while pleasing the people who matter. Many big organizations have a small group of top executives, followed by a larger group of middle management, while the largest segment of the company is at the bottom. This last group consists of employees who have no one reporting to them. The organization is structured like a pyramid. The top is the smallest but has the most power. It only takes a bit of dysfunctional behaviour at this level to weaken the integrity of the whole organization.

One of the reasons for this is explained in *Snakes in Suits: When Psychopaths Go to Work,* by Dr. Paul Babiak and Dr. Robert D. Hare. They document how, faced with constant change and stiff competition, modern businesses look for leaders who can "shake the trees, rattle the cages, and get things done quickly." They suggest that a psychopathic person's ability to appear charming, confident and calm can be a perfect fit for companies that need to cut costs and increase their market share. Depending on how a company recruits and promotes its top leaders, it could enable a toxic culture.

Stanford University's Professor Robert I. Sutton made destructive personalities in the workplace the focus of his colourfully titled 2007 book, *The No Asshole Rule: Building a Civilized Workplace and Surviving One That Isn't.* This book grew out of an article Sutton wrote for the *Harvard Business Review,* in which he detailed his department's effort to avoid hiring toxic employees. As Sutton described it, his small department was happily free of destructive personalities, unlike so many other academic departments, and he and his colleagues wanted to keep it that way. To maintain the supportive and congenial work atmosphere that they had carefully cultivated, they needed a strategy for avoiding hiring people who would turn out to be toxic. Sutton's work resonated widely and revealed that having to work with "assholes" is a painful and all-too-common experience. Such people are rightly referred to as "smiling assassins," "spin doctors," and "sharks" when they manipulate others with ease and skill. Moreover, in my experience, such toxic employees rarely face the consequences of their decisions and are often rewarded for duplicitous behaviour, as long as it leads to profits.

Even if an organization's leaders are generally egalitarian, low on ruthlessness, and prefer not to compromise ethics to win, they can fall prey to what's known as VUCA and act in ways that are dysfunctional. VUCA is a military term to describe the chaos of the post–Cold War era, and it stands for "volatility, uncertainty, complexity, and ambiguity." In business, chaos can come from such things as downsizing, mergers and acquisitions, going public, social change like the #MeToo, BIPOC, and LGBTQ+ movements, technology disruptions, war, and natural disasters. VUCA is a reality of the tech industry, which is marked by rapid and constant change. In these conditions, good and bad leaders alike can react in unmindful and uncompassionate ways that can cause toxicity in the workplace.

Wherever power hierarchies are well-established, as in big tech, academia, and medicine, organizations can become sick because of power dysfunctions. I see three power dysfunctions that wreak havoc on employees' mental health and wellbeing: (1) white-glove treatment, (2) glory and domination, and (3) the double bind of winning vs. ethics. The combination of power dysfunctions, a VUCA world, and a few bad apples at the top make for a toxic cocktail.

POWER DYSFUNCTION #1: WHITE-GLOVE TREATMENT

In general, executives at the top of an organization are treated as the more important people. They tend to be treated like rock stars or divas whose time can never be wasted. Those from a lower position of power walk on eggshells to avoid causing displeasure or go to great lengths to please them. Special treatment can extend to high-priced perks like elite medical diagnostic testing costing tens of thousands of dollars, large offices, enormous compensation packages, and generous "golden parachute" termination packages. These VIPs wield a kind of power over people who fear triggering their wrath. The white-glove treatment they receive is a symptom of a two-tier class system where people at the top stress out everyone else in the organization by being demanding and scary at the same time.

The phrase white-glove treatment refers to the gloves worn by English butlers and servants when they served their superiors, people who were addressed as Lord. This outdated practice of treating top officials like royalty infects the organization with a spiritual illness. There should be no two-tier system in an organization when it comes to psychological safety. Everyone deserves equal protection. When VIPs are revered and feared it can lead to them being given a free pass on wrongdoing or immoral behaviour. This sends a message that their well-being and happiness trump those of the so-called rank and file employees below them.

I was in a meeting where the team had called off a deadline because they were burned out, and there was too much risk of delivering untested code to production if they tried to pull out all the stops. After this healthy decision, a top executive called for an escalation and pushed the team to work through the weekend. He said he valued work-life balance but needed to not disappoint the customers. I had to make sure I was on mute when I laughed out loud at this contradictory statement. But really, no one was willing to say no, so there was no choice. He was given the white-glove treatment at the expense of people's well-being.

Examples of this kind of top-down behaviour can be found in almost every sector, from private companies to government. In July 2021, CTV News broke the story of then Governor General of Canada Julie Payette's resignation amidst accusations that she had been a toxic leader. It was alleged she had bypassed the vetting process for the position because of her celebrity status as a former astronaut. Employee statements in the independent inquiry told of allegations of yelling, screaming, aggressive conduct, demeaning comments and public humiliations at work. A workplace like this would be toxic with these kinds of dysfunctions.

Similarly, a culture of fear and control has been implicated in the Volkswagen diesel emissions scandal of 2015. In this scandal, the company was caught equipping its cars with software that could fool an emissions test and then switch to another mode for road driving, with higher emissions. The software could figure out that the car was in an emissions test if no steering was detected. If steering was detected, then the software knew that the car was actually being driven and more emissions were allowed, for a better driver experience. This intentionally engineered system was known as a "defeat device." Martin Winterkorn, who was CEO at the time, resigned shortly after the scandal broke, saying, "Above all, I am stunned that misconduct on such a scale was possible in the Volkswagen Group." In 2017, the US Department of Justice charged six VW executives with alleged criminal activity. In a piece about the scandal titled "The Fish Rots from the Head Down" by Otto Scharmer, an MIT-based lecturer, posted on *HuffPost* in 2015 and updated in 2017, Scharmer explains that deception on a scale like this comes back to leadership. "Its top-down and control-based leadership culture, once a source of success, now prevented leaders from reading and recognizing information that, in a culture of fear and control, no one ever wants to communicate upwards — thereby preventing the company from learning as a system."

As out of date as the servant's white glove is, this kind of special treatment is a reality in most sectors, and continues to give VIPs a free pass to behave in ways that are toxic to organizations and rank-and-file employees.

POWER DYSFUNCTION #2: GLORY & DOMINATION

Dysfunction can be found whenever leaders justify immoral and unethical tactics in order to dominate the competition and bring glory to the company. Yet these practices have been so normalized within corporate culture that they don't even seem dysfunctional until we unpack their origin.

Two authors wrote about rising in rank, beating your enemy, and being glorified across the land. This was well before modern business came about. Yet, these two ancient treatises — *The Art of War* by Sun Tzu, fifth century BC, and *The Prince* by Niccolò Machiavelli, sixteenth century AD — continue to influence business tactics and modern notions of successful leadership. Sun Tzu and Machiavelli argue that the end justifies the means and that domination over others is the end game. It should be disturbing to everyone that these books are bestsellers and used in college curricula. That's part of the problem.

Viewing employees as foot soldiers who can be given little choice but to burn themselves out to be competitive is a brutal tactic. Believing you can conquer a subordinate sexually, financially, or emotionally is a sickening abuse of power. Denying the knowledge of wrongdoing to avoid looking weak or vulnerable while valuing transparency is dysfunctional.

A common thread here has to do with saying one thing and doing another. Most of us would not hesitate to call out open hypocrisy from friends and family, but when corporations use it to gain an advantage, we call it good business. It's not. It's dysfunctional.

Jonathan Vance was a senior leader in the Canadian military in charge of a campaign known as Operation Honour. The name was shortened to Op Honour and its purpose was to reduce sexual harassment in the ranks. Canadian Minister of National Defence Harjit Sajjan and Prime Minister

Justin Trudeau claim they were never aware that Jonathan Vance himself was accused of sexual harassment. The lower ranks of the Canadian military had dubbed Op Honour as "Hop on her," indicating either that no one took the investigation seriously or that attacks on women were a well-known reality, or both. This seems like an obvious sign of dysfunction when people at the top do not know — or say they do not know — what is common knowledge among people at the bottom. Sun Tzu might approve of the commanders denying knowing anything when it strengthened their position.

The consequences can be deadly if people try to win at any cost, as with the coverup of the Boeing 737 MAX flight control system change. The United States Department of Justice said these important changes were discovered in late 2016 but concealed from the FAA (Federal Aviation Administration). Because of the deceit, the control system was not flagged for pilot training and played a role in the deaths of 347 people on Lion Air Flight 610 in 2018 and Ethiopian Airlines Flight 302 in 2019. "Boeing's employees chose the path of profit over candor by concealing material information from the FAA concerning the operation of its 737 Max airplane and engaging in an effort to cover up their deception," said Acting Assistant Attorney General David P. Burns of the Justice Department's Criminal Division.

Abuse of power, when tolerated, breeds more abuse. We don't make the world a better place by following these old treatises on winning and looking good at any cost. As my manager at SciTech North told me, we need to succeed without leaving a wake of collateral damage.

POWER DYSFUNCTION #3: THE DOUBLE BIND OF WINNING VS. ETHICS

Some leaders try to lead ethically and morally, even in disastrous situations like those faced, and caused, by Boeing and Volkswagen. There are good people who may end up behaving unethically because of a double bind.

Leaders are driven to ensure the corporation succeeds, gains market share, doesn't lose face, and stamps down the competition. That is more or less their primary mandate and often their legal fiduciary duty as officers of the company. There can be secondary mandates like following the company values and putting people first. But if those human workplace practices come at the expense of profit or market share, it's quite possible for secondary mandates to be overridden. To ask these officers to put things like a healthy workplace that fosters human needs or social and environmental initiatives on par with their corporate duties to grow the company puts them in a clear double bind. The imperative to win or stay powerful is strong, and collateral damage is often acceptable. It's easy to see how good people could make decisions to keep their companies successful and delude themselves that they are not harming anyone because they are doing their job.

An example of putting profit first is to lay off a part of the workforce to cut costs. But it gets unethical if it breaks laws about selection based on age. At JumboTek, we were told that downsizing was not done based on age. Yet my colleagues and I still wondered if it was about getting rid of higher-paid older employees and bringing in younger lower-paid ones or taking those roles to countries like India, the Philippines, or Colombia, where wages are far lower. Downsizing was a common practice in my industry that heaped psychological stressors on people — the managers doing the firing, the employees left behind to pick up the workload, and the clients wondering what happened to people they trusted. But it could be devastating to the people who were told they were valued their whole career and then just tossed away as redundant. Some people who were let go could become depressed, deeply hurt, angry, or even suicidal.

Jorgen Lohnn from Bridgeport, Connecticut worked for IBM, another tech giant whose layoffs routinely made the news. He was only fifty-seven and had worked for IBM for fifteen years when he took his life after being let go. His widow, Denise Lohnn, filed an age-discrimination lawsuit against International Business Machines Corp. in 2021, where she "alleges that Mr. Lohnn lost his job as the result of IBM's discriminatory efforts to systematically reduce its employment of older workers in order to build a younger workforce, pushing out thousands of older workers while hiring younger workers (which IBM often refers to as 'Early Professional Hires' or 'New Collar' workers), in order to better compete with younger technology companies, such as Google, Facebook, Amazon, and others." Mrs. Lohnn's lawsuit references an executive communication in which the author "describes his plan to 'accelerate change by inviting the "dinobabies" (new species) to leave' and make them an 'Extinct species.'" It is chilling how this memo is worded, and Mr. Lohnn's death was tragic. Winning in the market is a primary duty of any company, but it can lead to cold-blooded decisions that put employees in harm's way.

I felt the double bind even as a project manager. I felt squeezed by the pressure to finish a project and the feeling that I was exploiting the offshore team's tendency to never push back on work. Workers from India have a reputation for being willing to please; they are known to work hard and de-liver results, and can even be pushed into working on religious holidays. The Canadian workforce would rarely be asked to sacrifice a religious holiday. A Latin American colleague once told me, "You have Indians on the project, and they never push back on work. You're lucky." He was referring to the company we hired that supplied offshore technology services from workers in India. Did he not realize I was South Asian, and that this was an inappro-priate comment? Yet I know it to be true that offshore people will take more shit at work, and offer less resistance, than onshore people.

The power dysfunctions that are built into organizations can create psychological hazards in the workplace. These hazards show up as mental and physical illnesses in the psyches and bodies of employees. But the source of the disease is the "fear-and-control" and "win-at-all-costs" mindset that drives many companies. Mental health at work will improve when white-glove treatment, winning at all costs, and unethical actions are challenged.

I soon faced a situation where I had to challenge a leader at JumboTek in order to stand by my ethics.

CHAPTER 10

Integrity vs. Work

In her 2021 book, *The Way of Integrity*, Martha Beck defines integrity: "It's the idea that we can put our lives into integrity the way an airplane can be put into structural integrity. If all the millions of pieces are functioning together, the plane will fly. If the parts are out of kilter, the plane will crash. Our lives work the same way. When we're able to stay in integrity (the word simply means 'whole' or 'intact'), everything in our lives works better."

One thing I started to see in the years of juggling a career with a young family was that I wanted to be in integrity in all areas of my life. I couldn't be in integrity if I was teaching my children values and then went to work and compromised these same values. I couldn't raise my girls to be secure and brave while I was insecure and out of kilter at work. I couldn't be in my own integrity if I said I valued quality time with the girls but got sucked into working too much.

OPERATION PLAN-FOR-FUN

Tom and I took a hard look at our lives and the dysfunction in our workplaces and realized that if we wanted to have a joyful, fun life and bring that energy to our children, we had to plan for it. We routinely found solutions at work to impossible problems, so with that mindset, we came up with Operation Plan-For-Fun.

Tom created an elaborate spreadsheet to calculate how much we needed to save for retirement and university costs, and we agreed to spend the rest on fun. We then made a list of what "fun" would be. On the list was an RV so we could unplug from work, restore our spirits with nature, and be with the kids without the TV around. According to the cash flow model Tom created, we didn't have a lot of disposable cash, but we went in with another couple and bought a used 1978 Aristocrat RV. Our investment was only $1,000 each. It had brown shag carpet, orange upholstery, and a spotless, functional bathroom, which was my must-have.

We packed up the kids and all their stuff, including the highchair, and headed to Cedar Beach Campground in Aurora, only a thirty-minute drive from our home. The resort had two pools, a sandy beach, majestic old trees, playgrounds, and lots of open grassy fields for the kids to run in. It felt like we had escaped to another world.

We loved the RV lifestyle so much that we upgraded to a used twenty-eight-foot Ford Class C motorhome built by Triple E. It had a bed for the girls over the driver compartment, giving us more space. This RV could also tow our car, giving us more travel range. We excitedly planned a two-week trip to Yellowstone National Park. The RV and camping brought a sense of freedom to our lives that I didn't think I would feel until retirement. Operation Plan-For-Fun was working because it gave us something to look forward to while we worked in jobs that didn't feel fun anymore.

I tried to make work less of a priority and focus on fun, but work continued to prioritize me. I discovered that I was in some pipeline that was designed to promote women and diversity in the workplace. I won an award for minority women "who have demonstrated exceptional achievement in their workplaces and communities and inspire other young women to succeed." I was invited to a national conference in Atlanta, Georgia, for women of colour in STEM (Science, Technology, Engineering, and Math) to receive my award. It was my first time away from the kids, and it was fun to be in a hotel and not worry about the relentless cooking/clean-up cycle, bedtime routines, or harried mornings getting ready for daycare drop-offs. Listening to inspirational talks from other women of colour was nourishing.

When I returned from the conference, I was met with other news. I had been promoted to Level 9, Advanced Project Manager, with a raise. I remember being upset that I was promoted. I wanted to stay at Level 8, Junior Project Manager, and not feel the pressure to do more and more. The money was not worth the time away from the kids for the extra work demands it brought. I even asked if they could reverse the promotion, but it couldn't be done.

PROTESTING MISINFORMATION

I soon found myself on a project where my integrity was on the line. I enjoyed this project and my colleagues, who were all the A-team. We went out after work, laughed all the time, and formed a high-performing team. But my integrity was soon tested when I saw an error in the contract caused by someone else's mistake that could cost a lot of money to fix. I had to bring this to light, but being a whistleblower was stressful. Still, the emotional load was worth it to be truthful rather than silent. Due to this mistake, I found myself with a highly complex project instead of the simpler one I had signed on for. It meant a lot of extra hours. But I decided I wanted to rise to this challenge and learn from my colleagues. I used Operation Plan-For-Fun as a guiding principle and hired a live-in nanny. She took over the mundane tasks at home and allowed me to work longer hours but still spend quality time with the girls, playing dress-up, reading, and making crafts. And then my integrity was challenged once more when I was asked to conceal something from the client.

Partway through the project, a special task force was invoked because the client was unhappy with the delays and challenges. I was asked to review the plan and come up with an earlier delivery date to regain the client's confidence. However, I couldn't align the dates to the timeline the client expected. During a big meeting, I realized the senior leader was not communicating the schedule that my analysis supported. I had a choice to make. I could sit and say nothing, thereby endorsing the message, or I could speak up and confront the leader at the front of the room. Neither of those options worked for me. I just stood up and deliberately walked out in the middle of the presentation. It was a pronounced exit, and the message was clear to the client that I did not support that plan. It was the first time I had defied authority in such a bold way.

Trust in my company was further diminished when I was told that while I did an above-and-beyond job on this project to mitigate risk and contain costs and reputation, monetary rewards were for people who helped the company grow revenue. This was the best job I had ever done, and I was rewarded the least. I poured all my talents into turning around a dire situation and minimizing millions in losses. Negative revenue was not my fault, but perhaps there was a black mark against me for walking out of that presentation.

Years later, a female colleague told me my actions were discussed as a bad thing behind closed doors. She told me walking out of a meeting was brave and said she was sorry I didn't receive more support. Psychological Protection is Factor #10 of the Standard for psychological health and safety. When it exists, "employees feel able to put themselves on the line, ask questions, seek feedback, report mistakes and problems, or propose a new idea without fearing negative consequences to themselves, their job or their career." I put myself on the line, and I do not feel I was supported or recognized because of it.

Speaking up for truth was the right decision. It built trust with the client and, as a result, improved our relationship, and we worked better together. What upset me were the dysfunctions I had to work around in order to speak the truth. It was not right that senior leaders wanted me to compromise my values. That made me angry and added to the cumulative stress of working under corporate dysfunction.

THE FROG IN BOLING WATER

Organizational Culture is Factor #7 of the Standard. "Culture sets the tone for an organization — a negative culture can undermine the effectiveness of the best programs, policies and services intended to support the workforce. An unhealthy culture creates more stress, which lowers employee well-being. A culture of profit at all costs and constant chaotic urgency can create an environment in which burnout is the norm."

I had overcome physical burnout, but now I was experiencing spiritual burnout. It came on slowly and stealthily. I was like the frog in the story where the water gradually heats up, but the frog doesn't realize the danger and stays in too long rather than jumping out.

The IT industry was gradually becoming more driven by profit and power and less caring about people. There were so many pleasant and satisfying experiences at work, and I truly enjoyed my work and the fantastic people I interacted with. I appreciated the recognition and felt supported as a working mother. But the three power dysfunctions got worse over the years. The culture was becoming dangerous to psychological safety and thus mental health. Like the frog, I didn't think I was in any danger. But I was most definitely immersed in the conditions for disease to arise while thinking I was safe.

Not everyone has the same values and thus may not be as psychologically stressed as I was when I saw unfairness or dishonesty at work. From a neuroscience perspective, the threat/reward system varies from person to person across five domains — status, certainty, autonomy, relatedness, and fairness (SCARF). NeuroLeadership Institute co-founders Lisa and David Rock developed the SCARF Model to help organizations assess differences in social motivation. In it, they point out that "some people are more sensitive to status threat and rewards, others to certainty and relatedness." Understanding how people are motivated can help organizations drive engagement and retention. When I took the SCARF online quiz, I scored high in the areas of fairness and relatedness. So when things are not fair, or when relationships are compromised, it's not something I can shrug off the way others might be able to. It feels like a threat to my integrity and sense of self.

Like the frog, I had a choice to make — stay and perish or make a change. I wrestled with the question, "Should I stay, or should I go?" I had financial goals — paying down the mortgage, saving for retirement and university tuition, and having enough money to enjoy life while I had health and my young family. I had strong cultural drivers to be a hard worker and not walk away from a well-paying career that could support my family. I knew I could end up somewhere that didn't support working mothers as well or didn't allow the flexibility of work from home. I still had traces of my childhood needs to overachieve that compensated for my low self-confidence. The culture of another tech company would likely be just as unwholesome for me as the one I was in. Switching workplaces might not get me out of the hot water.

It became urgent for me to figure out how to solve the integrity vs. work problem.

PART 3

Jailbreak

"There is no jailer powerful enough
to hold Spring contained.
Let that be a lesson.
Stop holding back the blossoming!
Quit shutting eyes and gritting teeth,
curling fingers into fists, hunching shoulders.
Lose your determination to remain unchanged.
All the forces of nature
want you to open,
Their gentle nudge carries behind it
the force of a flash flood."

—Maya Spector, "Jailbreak"

CHAPTER 11

A New Relationship with Work

Although I had said I was done working in an unhealthy way many times before, it was a pivotal moment to take a stand and walk out of that unethical meeting. Being in work-*spiritual* balance was a more vital force than being an overachiever to get praise and recognition. Other questions started coming up for me in the wake of that moment. Maybe that's how integrity works. It spreads from one area of life to another.

Tom and I started to feel an urgency not to waste our lives. In the last few years, three of my uncles had died suddenly from heart attacks, one in his 40s, one in his 50s, and one in his 60s. It was a tragic and sudden end of life for hard-working, overachieving people with loving families. The abrupt loss of life seemed to wake me up to the importance of not putting things off to the distant future. I wondered if this was the mid-life crisis I had heard about, calling me to do something drastically different with my life.

Work used to feel like a key component of a meaningful and fulfilling life. Now it felt like a chore. Tom and I were coming home depleted after the workday. Between long hours at the office and long commutes, the kids were getting the leftovers of us. We fantasized about quitting our jobs, selling the house, and travelling in our RV while homeschooling the girls. We wanted to feel excitement at being alive. But we could see that that would not be fair to our kids — they liked their teachers and friends, and we knew the social atmosphere of school was important to good mental health and their development. We still daydreamed about going further west than Yellowstone National Park. We spent a lot of time on Google Maps charting an adventuresome course from the grandeur of Denali National Park and Preserve in Alaska to the jungles of Costa Rica.

In the spring of 2010, we both felt we were at a breaking point and had a gnawing feeling that we were squandering time that would be better spent enjoying our family. Out of this despair, an idea came. If we just took time off unpaid, we could keep our jobs and do a mini-trip during the kids' eight-week summer vacation.

It seemed impossible to afford such a trip, but things started to fall into place. I realized we would save thousands of dollars on summer camps for two kids. Tom found out his client would accept it if he didn't renew his contract on July 1 but instead pushed it out to September 1. I found out from the HR website at work that JumboTek offered something called a Sabbatical Leave, meaning I could take up to eight weeks off unpaid. We did the math to determine what the trip would cost in fuel, food, accommodation, and excursions, how much income we would lose by being unpaid over those weeks, and how much we could offset it by not paying for camps. The final number on the Excel budget sheet was breathtaking, and not in a good way. I think it was close to $50,000. But we knew this was an opportunity of a lifetime, and we went for it.

We planned out a route that was 10,000 km roundtrip from Toronto to the Pacific Northwest, then down Highway 1 to San Francisco, and back home through the American Southwest. We were committed to the idea of *not* waiting until retirement to enjoy our lives. And we wanted that feeling of freedom while we were young and while our kids still needed us. Jessica was almost seven at the time, and Sophia was nearly five. We realized that our jobs afforded us the privilege of pausing to give more of ourselves to our two girls, so we took advantage of that. We would be hitting our bucket list of places *and* making our kids happy simply by being with them. Work was no longer our main driver in life; it took a back seat to fun and family.

We packed our 300-square-foot motor home with food, supplies, and enough clothing to get us through summer and cooler mountain weather. We even managed to stack all four bikes on the back of the "toad." In the RV lifestyle, the car towed behind the RV is called the toad. We were vibrating with joy as the departure date came up. Mom and Dad came to wish us goodbye and safe travels. And we were off.

I sat with the girls at our dinette, colouring, reading, and playing games. DVDs were a lifesaver for all of us, with Barbie, Dora the Explorer, and multiple Disney princesses coming on the road with us. I created bingo cards with things we'd see out the window, like a red car, an airplane, and a yellow sign. The girls were delighted to get prizes. I surprised them with McMommy meals — I had bought kid's meal toys from McDonald's for weeks to create lunches like peanut butter sandwiches that came with a toy. When they had to go to the bathroom, we didn't stop driving. I would help them walk to the toilet and keep them steady over bumps and turns. I had a multiplication times table chart on the small bathroom wall, and we would practice the two times table while patiently waiting for a poop. Tom did his share with the driving and setting up camp. We were a good team.

For the first time in a decade, we had enough sleep. I didn't have all those stress hormones being triggered by email, unreasonable demands from superiors, the commute, and too many meetings in a day. I was able to complete the stress cycle described in the podcast with Brené Brown and the authors of the book *Burnout: The Secret to Unlocking the Stress Cycle*, Amelia Nagoski and Emily Nagoski. I had more patience with the girls and a childlike wonderment at the scenery and wildlife, sunrises, and sunsets. And we were suddenly getting much more exercise. I traded a sedentary desk-job lifestyle for hiking, biking, and walking. The camper was tiny, and we tried to only sleep and eat there. We had to spend our time outdoors if we didn't want to get on each other's nerves. And being in nature was good for all of us. We were filled with joy, curiosity, and excitement at each stop on our itinerary. A whole new physical world opened up as we crossed mile after mile. And I opened up spiritually in response.

A REVOLUTION OF SPIRIT

We, of course, saw many wondrous things. The stark barrenness of Badlands National Park, the rocky ice caves of Craters of the Moon, and the quiet stillness of the fourteen-story redwoods of Jedediah Smith Redwoods State Park delivered peace and wonder.

I felt a spiritual connection to the land, relating to the trees, rocks, and rivers as if they had their own sense of being. On a hike near Mount Hood, I saw a rotten tree stump. I was dazzled by the blackness of the wood next to the greens of mosses and leaves. At this point in the journey, I had seen a lot of forests. But it was like that stump spoke to me, the delicate leaves as joyful as puppies in a basket. I had the sense they were conscious and delighted to exist and to be in communion together. I stopped in my tracks with the sheer magic of it. As Maya Spector says in her poem "Jailbreak," these moments hit me with "the force of a flash flood."

The furthest from home we drove was 4,400 km to Oregon Dunes National Recreation Area. We parked the RV to climb some of the world's tallest dunes and walk to the Pacific Ocean where it was miles of shoreline with no other people. It felt so majestic and pristine. My spirit flowed out and mingled with the natural world around me.

Feeling this sense of oneness and loss of my boundaries was new territory for me. I had been very much in my head so far, all about getting things done and how knowledgeable I could become. Going around feeling plants talking to me and having out-of-body experiences on a deserted beach was a new way to relate to the world.

Merriam-Webster defines revolution as "a fundamental change in the way of thinking about or visualizing something: a change of paradigm." My paradigm change on this trip was that genuine human relationships were what I wanted at work. It was a new way of thinking for an engineer like me — that my spiritual needs mattered and were a fundamental part of my human existence. I was a non-practicing Hindu and did not believe in traditional church or prayer. But I had come close to death a few times in childhood, from drowning and seeing the "light" to being on by-pass for hours during my open-heart surgery when I was eleven. Perhaps those experiences made me a little more open to the supernatural. In any case, I was starting to define spirituality as something different —something intimate and without any kind of hierarchy. Years later, when I heard the onset of menopause discussed as a time of spiritual awakening for many women, I thought, "Aha, that makes sense." I had turned thirty-eight on this trip, just on the verge of perimenopause.

Another breakthrough for me on this trip was that I saw that the world was safe. Besides freedom from work, this trip was freedom from fear. The never-not-be-afraid worldview from my childhood began to ease off. We had breakdowns on the side of the road, but we got help from kind strangers. We had walked on paths that warned us of rattlesnakes, mountain lions, grizzly bears, scorpions, dying in the desert if we didn't take sufficient water, and the lack of guardrails at the edges of the Grand Canyon. At Yosemite National Park, we saw a park ranger walking funnily as we came out of the camp store. He was looking for a black bear that was hiding in the bushes. We were carrying bags of food with a bear nearby, yet we were okay.

Without work on my plate, I had time to pause and think about the bigger picture. I saw that the harmful ways of the corporate world were here too. Many of the parks were established to preserve the natural world for generations to come because we had taken too much from the Earth. At the visitor centres, I learned how the first peoples of North America had been protectors and stewards of the land, only to be displaced and erased by a colonial-settler-conqueror mindset

There were stark reminders of how progress in technology has a darker side. Because of my studies in nuclear engineering, we gravitated toward nuclear tourist attractions. In South Dakota, we went to a silo designed to launch a Minuteman II missile. This was breakthrough technology because it could launch within one minute and drop nuclear warheads on multiple enemy targets with intercontinental range. I walked in Arco, Idaho, the first city to have its power grid run on fission energy. At the National Museum of Nuclear Science & History in Albuquerque, New Mexico, we stepped into the 1940s, retracing the historic decision to drop atomic bombs on Hiroshima and Nagasaki. We saw the casings of Fat Man and Little Boy, as the bombs were nicknamed, and marvelled at how small they were. All of that destructive power could easily have fit in the back seat of a car.

When I returned to work in September, I was no longer the same person. I had a bigger worldview that included interconnection, spirituality, and relationship, even across space and time. I likely would not have studied nuclear engineering if World War II had not fueled the research. I can only live on this land because the first owners were displaced in the name of conquering and taking. My life is barely anything in the cosmic timeline, yet it has meaning, connection, and continuity.

I came back feeling like I carried the planet inside of me, etched from the experiences, from walking on the Earth, and with the understanding gained from many park visitor centres of the people and animals who walked here before I did. I understood both how small and impermanent my life was and, at the same time, how magnificent it was to be alive. As a teenager, I kept a poster of Albert Einstein on my walls. It was that iconic image with his tongue sticking out and his long, white hair standing on end. He was a role model for me because he didn't worry if people thought he was different. He embraced magic, miracles, God, and science alike. Einstein is quoted as having said, "There are two ways to live your life. One is as though nothing is a miracle. The other is as though everything is a miracle." He also held, "If you don't believe in any kind of magic, or mystery, basically, [you're] as good as dead."

I had heard Einstein's "woo woo" quotes many times before, but now I had lived experience of the truth of his words. My inner world could feel the magic and miracle of the outer world. I returned from this journey more open to the sacred. I came to see, much as Einstein did, that we must balance technological advancement by evolving our sense of humanity to keep up. This trip immersed me in the natural world and removed me from the world of technology. I felt an awakening that although I had exceptional training in engineering and years of experience in delivering technical projects, the most advanced knowledge was to be found in what I couldn't read in a book or be marked on in a test. The most advanced knowledge was what could be learned wordlessly from the natural world, from spirit.

BEING VULNERABLE WITH A TOUGH GUY

For a few blissful weeks after our trip, I remained inside the bubble of that new worldview. Even as I returned to 40-hour-plus workweeks and the gruelling pace of juggling work and home life, I felt calm and connected. Eventually, of course, that calm faded, and the stress of daily life and work crept back in. After a few weeks of emails, meetings, and morning routines, including endless lunch packing, my body felt like it had never been on an extended vacation. But the feeling of connection stayed.

I started my next assignment committed to bringing integrity and humanity to work. While carrying this mindset with me, I soon met Marco, a client with a tough-guy demeanor who was fed up doing business with JumboTek. When we first met, I was smiling and eager to introduce myself. He smiled too but said bluntly that he didn't believe I'd be any different than the rest of the people he had met from JumboTek. Marco had been through a few cycles of broken promises as a JumboTek client. He hated that his company was stuck in a multi-year contract with us. He wasn't unprofessional, just candid. I sensed so much disappointment and frustration. Marco was one of those rare leaders who let you know if they think you're full of bullshit, but it was not offensive because it was delivered in such a direct and genuine way. Meeting Marco was my call to action to put integrity into my work relationships.

Kim Scott's 2017 book, *Radical Candor,* teaches people how to create a "culture of compassionate candor" in the workplace. Scott encourages leaders to solicit criticism to improve their leadership and shows them how to give guidance that helps others grow. She says effective business conversations can show that we care personally (the love part) while still challenging directly (the truth part). She points out that we're conditioned in childhood to stay quiet if we don't have something nice to say. Then, when we start working, we're told that we should be professional, which can mean suppressing emotions and acting like a robot. I didn't know about Kim Scott's book when I met Marco, but instinctively I knew that I needed to have a direct conversation with him.

I invited Marco to coffee and asked him to tell me, with no sugar coating, about the most significant pain points in his organization's partnership with JumboTek. I promised not to be offended. Marco needed no other invitation and laid it all bare. I listened, paraphrased, asked if I got it right, then asked if there was anything more. Once I saw Marco's face relax, after he had been invited to speak the truth, I asked him to let me make him a promise.

I said, "I don't have the power to address everything, but it's in my power to deliver projects with realistic dates. Or at least I can be honest if the dates won't be met, even if I have to risk my job. I can't have relationships where we're bullshitting clients."

I knew Marco valued this. In return, I asked him to keep being candid with me about what wasn't working. It was magical what happened after I established trust with Marco. I realized being radically candid was the best way to counter the damaged situation I had walked into.

I had found a new relationship with work, one I could live with.

CHAPTER 12

The Woo Comes Calling

I extended the radically candid way of communicating to the client's project managers (my customers) and they found my transparency refreshing. Yulia, impatient with all inefficiency, was a straight shooter. She told me she was fed up with missed commitments. Liam had a wicked sense of humour. Despite being easy-going, he wanted excellence in the solution design and didn't tolerate what he thought of as incomplete work. Patrick was so friendly and would never say anything offensive, yet I could tell he was stressed if we were late, because it made him look bad as a project manager. Ben, who had anglicized his Asian name, was empathetic, but he too seemed to be at the end of his patience. I think they opened up to me because I listened and cared. We had genuine conversations and together overcame the main challenge of corporate bureaucracy — lack of transparency. They were a close team and welcomed me as one of them. Just like Marco, this group was forthright and caring. I found a team where I could be human at work.

Yulia, Liam, Patrick, Ben, and I opened up communications on the back channels. We would smile at each other in meetings if we heard something that sounded pompous or a little too slick. We knew after the meeting we'd get together and figure things out. After work, we'd go for drinks, vent our frustrations, and laugh out the stress. I also worked with colleagues within

JumboTek to find their pain points, and through candid conversations we found ways to make things better. The architects on our team were committed to honesty and building excellent solutions. A new executive joined who was caring and took on the big issues directly.

Slowly, with both JumboTek and client allies, we formed working relationships that were less tense, and more filled with camaraderie and respect. These genuine relationships made the workplace stress less damaging to my mind, body, and soul. It was still hard to see when wrong was done, but I no longer felt trapped by the dysfunctionality. I had a measure of control by choosing not to play games with this client and by bringing honesty and caring to the workplace.

POURING LOVE ON JAPAN

Sometimes embracing inner truth invites more truth in unexpected ways. On March 11, 2011, I had an experience that was literally out of this world. I had a dream where I was asked to urgently help. The asking wasn't done by a voice but came across more like a wordless feeling. I remember I was compelled by the intensity of the plea for help, and in the dream I felt fully awake. It was as if Tom had awoken me because one of the girls was sick. I would have snapped fully awake and been ready to go to them. That's how I felt inside the dream. I was being called to help, and I deeply cared to go. Then in an instant I was hovering in space, looking down onto the Earth, and it was beautiful, like a blue-green jewel on black velvet. I had no fear at all of being so high up and just drank in the sight of it. Then the same feeling gently guided me to golden lights floating up out of the Earth.

It said in its wordless way, *Send love.*

It was as if I had slipped into a place that was neither the sleeping world nor the awake world. I put my heart into sending love to those lights with as much intensity and focus as I could generate. It felt like love poured out of me like a river, and even as it poured out, I was filled with joy. And I had the sense it was hard work, like when you hit the zone in a workout, and you're giving it your all, and then you dig deep to find more energy to keep going. I think I woke up briefly wondering at the lucidity of this dream. Usually, I struggle to recall details of my dreams. This was like I'd just watched a movie. Glancing at the clock, it was way too early to wake up — maybe 3 or 4 a.m. — and I went back to sleep, grateful for the limitless feeling of love and beautiful images this dream had left me with.

Later that morning, I heard about the tsunami in Japan that took so many people's lives. I remembered my dream, realizing that it would have been around the same time. Had I been part of those souls' journey after they left their bodies? Was it the divine, the Creator, who had spoken to me? Was love so powerful it could connect people across the planet and across life and death? I don't have the answers to such questions. But I do know that it felt like I'd slipped into a world that works on the flow of love. A world that is intimately and instantly connected. If this dream was somehow a reality, it was the miracle that Albert Einstein talked about. If this dream was a meaningless coincidence, that didn't matter because I had the experience of love pouring out of my heart, one I will never forget.

GOING PART-TIME

Summer 2011 was approaching, and the freedom of the summer 2010 trip was still in my body. Tom and I wanted more of the family time we'd had on that trip. With Sophia entering Grade 1 and Jessica in Grade 3, our daycare costs were about to drop massively to just after-school care. That would give us back a couple thousand dollars a month, which, at our tax bracket, was about four thousand dollars of income. We could do a lot with that money because we were already used to living without it. We thought about investing it. That would be great for the far-off retirement phase. But we would be shackled to the grind of full-time work, rushing home to get the kids out of daycare, then making dinner and having barely any fun time with them. Again, they would get the leftovers of us.

I didn't want to advance at JumboTek, but I still enjoyed having a career, especially with my current working group. A possibility of feeling freedom before retirement presented itself again. The client fully funded my role, but what if it was split so that I focused on program-level work, while a lower-cost project manager did the bulk of the smaller routine projects? I could do my work in 80 percent of my hours or thirty-two hours a week and become a part-time employee. At 80 percent, I would still have benefits and my pension. The reduction in pay would be offset by not paying for after-school care. The other eight hours could be used to fund a lower-cost project manager to pick up the work I funneled off.

The account executive was fully supportive, and the client too. I had proven myself to be dedicated and trustworthy, and I don't think this arrangement would have worked without their blessing. In fact, they wanted to support me in balancing family and work. Yulia in her direct yet loving way said she didn't want to see one email from me after 2:30 p.m. With their support, I felt I could overcome my workaholic tendencies to work after hours. I applied to go down to 80 percent part-time, and it was approved to start in August.

The thirty-two hours were spread across the whole work week, from 8:10 a.m. to 2:35 p.m., Monday to Friday, aligned with school bells. I soon realized that while I had given up only 20 percent pay, I'd gotten back way more time because of how many weeks I had worked more than forty hours for free. Tom and I knew it was the right thing to prioritize family over money. It was such a joy to close my laptop for the day, pick up the girls from school and just focus on spending quality time together. I saw that they were miracles and that they had much to teach me.

A PICTURE TO ARREST MY HEART

Jessica is the big sister and has a quiet personality, whereas Sophia never keeps quiet whether she is mad or sad. So, when it came time for Meet-the-Teacher night, we were excited to hear about how Jessica was doing in Grade 3 and how Sophia was doing in Grade 1.

Jessica's teacher had the children fill out a booklet on their first day to share their likes and dislikes. The booklet was on each child's desk on open-house night, and Jessica was eager to show Tom and me. She led us through the school, to her classroom, and to her miniature desk. She carefully read the title to us: "This book is about me. It tells who I am, some of the things I like, and some of the things I do not like. Some things about me I like a lot. Some things I want to change. But, I AM GLAD TO BE ME!" I smiled at this because good self-esteem is so important.

Her answers were so endearing. The question "I hope I will never..." in the section WHEN I GROW UP was finished with "go to jail," printed very neatly. In the section SCHOOL, it was clear to see what she liked and didn't like:

> My favourite subject in school is: reading.
> The subject I think is the easiest is: reading.
> The subject I dislike the most is: math.
> The thing I dislike most about school is: math.
> The thing I like most about school is: reading.

Her Grade 3 teacher had written in, "I hope I can change the way you feel about math!" and given her a star sticker. She was so excited for us to turn the page because this next section, HOW I FEEL, included drawings she had worked hard on. There were two questions about when she feels happy and when she feels sad.

The first question was filled out, "I am happy when I: draw." That made a lot of sense. If she wasn't reading, she was drawing. She had even drawn a picture of herself sitting at her desk, drawing. Her tiny drawing inside the drawing was of a tree, with the sun shining down from the top right corner of the page.

The second question was filled out, "I am sad when: I get yelled at." But it was her drawing that stopped my heart. It was a picture of me yelling at her, lines of anger shining out of my mouth, like the rays of sun in her tiny drawing within a drawing. But instead of a tree receiving that energy, it was Jessica, crying and sad, receiving my anger.

Write it :

I am sad when
I get yelled at.

Draw it :

I still feel like there is a stone in my belly when I look at this drawing. My throat hurts, and my eye sockets feel heavy. I didn't want these vulnerable children to feel this way. I didn't want to be a scary authority figure. But I did yell when I got stressed and lost my patience.

As I spent quality time with the kids, I saw I was training them in how to please me and behave so they didn't disappoint me or anger me. I saw that careless actions on my part could give them life-long issues about their self-confidence and self-worth, like I had as a young working woman when I went through the Quest empowerment seminar. The drive for approval and not feeling safe emotionally were the last things I wanted to transmit to my daughters. I had to go deeper and unravel those things in me because I had a gut feeling that if I wasn't in integrity then I couldn't be the mother I wanted to be.

I set a new intention after seeing Jessica's drawing. I had to be a loving person in my words and actions, not just my thoughts and dreams. It was a confusing part of life as I confronted my failure on the job that really mattered — parenthood. It was like I was feeling around in the dark for something, wanting something different but not knowing what. There was something for me to learn here that the guilt and shame wanted me to see.

A journey of inner work started, and I became aware of simple places to start, such as bringing ease and fun into the moments before dinner prep. I was vibrating with stress during the pre-dinner time, like a drill sergeant running an orderly household with no room for mistakes, messes, or disobedience. And I often lost my temper if things went awry, which they regularly did. I knew if I could be more present and easier going, it would make my kids feel more joy and less stressed, and I would be aligned with my values. As I paid more attention to my intention, I could catch it when I screwed up and seek to do better next time. It was like Jessica's drawing put me on notice of what to pay attention to.

CORPSE POSE – A DEATH OF SELF

I was turning forty in 2012 — a big transition — and I wanted to do better all around. When I got a $40 Groupon offer for a month of unlimited hot yoga, I thought this was a nudge from the universe because it matched my upcoming birthday. Turning forty felt empowering, and I wanted to be stronger physically and mentally. Although I'm South Asian, with yoga squarely in my ethnic background, I had never tried it and was a complete novice. I picked the first class on Sunday, April 1. I'll never forget it because I was so intimidated. The room was suffocatingly hot, and it was an advanced flow class, which meant I put my body into forty poses flowing in quick succession. I tried to keep up by watching the people around me covertly, and I was always a move behind. We held challenging positions, and I had to use all my focus to pay attention so I wouldn't topple over.

The sweat was dripping into my eyes, and each pose gave me different sensations. I visualized the area being stretched, sent my breath into the muscles, and then breathed out the locked-in tension. I had never experienced my body like this — section by section and with such intense focus. There was no clock to watch, but I finally made it to the last pose, Savasana, also known as the corpse pose. I was blissfully happy to be done with the moving part. Even the heat wasn't so oppressive anymore. This was the first time I was so single-minded for such a long time. I think the class was seventy-five minutes in total. My mind didn't have a chance to worry, plan or daydream. This last pose, also the least physically demanding, has been called the most difficult one because it forces a do-nothing state, something the mind doesn't often get to experience in our fast-paced culture. I just melted into the bliss and energy of the pose as I lay on the warm floor.

When others started leaving, I did as well. After showering and putting on clean clothes, I drove to my parents' house for breakfast and a Sunday morning visit. I exited the highway on autopilot, having made this trip many times. As I drove up Garden Street in Whitby, a flood of joy coursed through my body as I seemed to dissolve "Sunita" and expand into "everything."

It was a drab spring day. The landscape was covered in muted browns, and the sky was an overcast grey. The Earth did not look pretty; in fact, it looked a little beaten up as it emerged from wintertime. Yet everything seemed to pulse with energy and be vibrant in a way that flooded my five senses. I saw the world as interconnected, joyful, and a place where energy danced. The feeling in my body was bliss — a type I had never experienced even when my babies were born and placed on my chest. It was like there was no more me.

I had a sense I could feel every living thing around me, including the insects under the earth. We were all one network, and it was the most joyful feeling. I was in this euphoria when I walked into my parents' kitchen, where my dad and brother were arguing. It felt so silly that they were angry and thought of each other as different entities. My mind couldn't process it.

The feeling lasted a bit longer, but slowly I returned to my usual way of looking, listening, and feeling the world around me. I've never experienced such a total loss of self since that day, and I can only recall a faint glimmer of it.

This experience was wild but I didn't want to hang on to it. I had practical things to do in life. There is no room for a mother who has all her judgment suspended, her ego dissolved, and who talks about interconnecting all living beings, including insects. Who would plan the meals and book medical appointments if all I did was live in the present?

I do trust that there is more to reality than I can know and I've always been drawn to the "woo." My Grade 8 science hypothesis was to determine if ESP existed beyond statistical probability. I constructed a machine to light up if, hidden from each other, people could make a match between five symbols. That same year, I had an eerie experience with a Ouija board when my friends and I held a seance. We scared ourselves silly when the board started moving, the window blew open, and the candle flame blew out. It seemed there were other spirits in the room with us, and we put the board away, not wanting to tangle too much with the unknown. In university, quantum physics made me realize you have to accept uncertainty in all things. I was stunned to learn that physics estimated that *everything we know* is less than 5 percent of *everything that is*. The unknown part is roughly 68 percent dark energy and 27 percent dark matter. Rather than considering this a depressing hypothesis, I found it wildly exciting that we have so much yet to understand.

Now life had given me some space with a part-time job, a good salary, and kids old enough to do things for themselves. I felt called on to live a more authentic life, one where I was a better mother and more connected to the mystery that seemed to be calling on me. And the woo side of me was returning. I cued the universe that I was ready to know myself, and the universe answered by waking me up with the pouring-love dream, Jessica's drawing, and the dissolving of self. These experiences were a sign that I was on a more authentic and connected path.

However, I was still feeling my way along this new path. Integrating my spiritual side to work and family life was going to be tricky; I needed to find ways to follow this path without freaking people out. The questions of "Who am I?" and "What is my purpose?" evoked an intense desire to explore. The notions I had been taught to value — status, achievements, praise — all of a sudden seemed immaterial to living my best life.

CHAPTER 13

Life Class Begins

My mind was hungry to understand myself, and I thought about coaching as a career that would be more fulfilling than project management. I researched Gestalt and Adlerian psychotherapy because they seemed professional, well respected, and deeply insightful. However, I was a long-time fan of Martha Beck, and I would read her article first when *The Oprah Magazine* arrived every month. I devoured her books and felt connected to her way of figuring out life more than I resonated with more traditional coaching programs or psychological perspectives. But I worried that Martha Beck was *too* woo, and that I should be obtaining more recognized credentials if I was to change careers.

I took a two-day coaching intensive for managers at Toronto's Adler Institute of Learning to see what it was like. I learned how to ask open-ended questions and saw the power of deep listening when one of the participants made a breakthrough. Yet, I struggled with the idea that Adler would be a safe path. I wanted the wild path, the one my heart called for instead of my brain, which to me was Martha Beck.

A nudge from the universe seemed to come in the form of an email on September 20, 2013, informing me that there were two spots available in the Martha Beck Life Coach Training program starting in just two days. The spots had come open because of cancellations. I emailed Tom:

Omg! I would love to do this, but
A) don't know if it's "too weird" and un-marketable
B) if we can afford $7k US right now
!!!

I had never felt this zing of excitement with any other coaching program and by that feeling alone I knew it was what I wanted in my secret heart. Tom supported me immediately and said to go for it, and yes, we could afford it. Martha Beck's self-help books brimmed with integrity and magic, and I couldn't believe she could be my teacher. It was the right decision because this training gave me two truth-seeking tools, one called Shackles-On/Shackles-Off and the other called The Work of Byron Katie.

SHACKLES-ON/SHACKLES-OFF

This tool simply lets your body's intelligence guide you on which things bring joy and which ones don't. I learned that scanning my body gave me non-verbal feedback. When I had joyful experiences, my body relaxed and felt open, regardless of whether I was thinking about something from the past, experiencing something in the present, or anticipating experiences in the future. If an experience was not enjoyable, whether it was a painful memory, a real-time overwhelm, or anxiety about the future, it correlated to a tenser body.

Once I figured out how my body worked and learned to read the signals, it became easy to calibrate my life for joy. It required mindfulness and body scans, but I learned these skills and slowly adapted my to-do list accordingly. I made lunch prep more enjoyable by buying pretty and functional bento box containers that went into the dishwasher. I made my week more enjoyable by tasking the girls with cleaning their own washroom, a change that was doubly satisfying because it taught them an important life skill while getting me out of something I hated doing.

In this way, by tuning into my body's way of knowing, I was able to decrease the dread and increase the joy I felt every day. It was amazing that

I was just learning to read my body's intelligence after all these years. It was like a treasure map I didn't even know I had.

THE WORK OF BYRON KATIE

Byron Katie had an awakening that suffering came from believing her own thoughts and the way out of suffering was to dissolve her thoughts by asking four questions of each painful belief. Her process is also done in a meditative mindset and is just as simple as the body inquiry. It starts with identifying a painful thought or belief and then asking:

1. Is it true?
2. Can you absolutely know it's true?
3. How do you react, what happens, when you believe that thought?
4. Who or what would you be without the thought?

The first and most enlightening question is "Is it true?" As I asked the other three questions, I could feel painful beliefs get lifted away. I carried less mental weight with every thought I changed. These thoughts were things like, "I'm an imposter to be a coach," "I'm a bad mother," or "Tom disrespects me." The slow and deliberate process of interrogating each thought revealed how untrue they were and replaced them with much better ones: "I'm an imposter not to be a coach," for example, or "I disrespect Tom" (which I did when I contradicted his disciplining of the girls).

This process of interrogating my beliefs was challenging at first because I had to admit that some of my own beliefs — including ones that didn't serve me well — were wrong. I had loved being right my entire life because it validated me and made me feel safe and worthy. Being less right and more honest in my thinking put me in more integrity than I could have imagined. I came to love this process because it unfailingly dissolved what disrupted my peace.

EMOTIONAL INTELLIGENCE — POSITIVE AND NEGATIVE EMOTIONAL ATTRACTOR (PEA/NEA)

That same fall, in 2013, I signed up for a Massive Open Online Course (MOOC) called Inspiring Leadership through Emotional Intelligence. It was taught by Richard Boyatzis, Professor of Organizational Behavior, Psychology, and Cognitive Science at Case Western Reserve University. The time commitment was intense, but I did not feel strained because I was fascinated by the subject of positive psychology. It felt like I was in flow and my energy was stoked by my curiosity. But still, taking a course like this was only possible because I worked part-time, the girls needed a lot less attention, and Tom was an equal partner on the home front.

The best thing I learned from this class was how to observe Positive Emotional Attractor (PEA) and Negative Emotional Attractor (NEA) in people around me and myself. To practice my observational skills, I had to interview someone and ask them about their life. My objective was to watch the facial expressions, voice tone, and mannerisms and note whether the person was in PEA or NEA. PEA meant they were in the parasympathetic nervous system, or rest-and-digest mode. NEA meant they were in the sympathetic nervous system, or fight-or-flight mode.

One evening after the kids were in bed, I practiced on Tom by asking him to tell me a story of a mentor who'd helped him. As I observed, I saw he demonstrated signs of PEA, such as smiling and relaxing his posture when he told me about a great teacher who believed in him. Then I asked what he regretted or a dream he never fulfilled. It was clear he had switched to a NEA state as he reflected and told me he dreamed of being a pilot, but that just didn't fit our priorities. His face was sorrowful as he described a dream I hadn't known about during our seventeen years of marriage. I wrote up our interview for my homework and thought about Tom's dream for the next couple of days. I realized being part-time meant I could take on extra childcare duties so Tom would have time for ground school, the first phase of flight training. We could afford it if we put off some house renovations. Within a few weeks, Tom was in pilot training at the Oshawa Airport. I saw a joy in him I'd never seen before.

This homework assignment showed me that when we are attuned to each other emotionally, we can bring things to the surface and understand people better. It's no wonder that emotionally intelligent leaders who lead by creating a safe and positive atmosphere outperform their colleagues who rule by fear and intimidation.

MIRROR NEURONS & CONTAGION

A part of Richard Boyatzis' research on emotions that stuck with me is that emotional states are contagious and can be transmitted from person to person, unseen, like a virus. Scientists think emotions are contagious through cells called mirror neurons that fire when we mimic one another. I decided to run an experiment with the kids and Tom to see how this contagion worked at home.

I set up visual space on the fridge door, which is our information centre. I picked four magnets, one to represent each of us, like game pieces. The board was a green sheet of paper for PEA and a red sheet for NEA. The object was to peg someone as PEA or NEA, and if they were NEA, to switch them to PEA. The prizes were coveted candy, even before dinner time. This motivated the girls greatly. It turned out to be a learning experiment for all of us.

I had taught the girls that you could look for clues like body language — a frown if we were grumpy or a smile if we were happy. I'd come home from a tiring day and commute, and Jessica would put my magnet on the red NEA paper, but then she'd offer to help with dinner because I was tired, and my face would beam at her kindness. She would move my magnet back to the green paper and take her prize. Not to be outdone, Sophia would wait for Tom to come home. If he said tensely, "Who left all these shoes at the front door. I can barely get in," she would offer him a hug and say she could help put away the shoes. She also would get candy before dinner.

It was an important lesson for all of us. We saw our emotional states on the fridge door. We realized how the rest of the family could pick up on our body language, tone of voice, and facial expressions. PEA and NEA became household phrases. We said things like, "Don't make me NEA," and, "Are you in NEA or PEA? I can't tell."

The kids picked up on it so quickly. It made me realize how much my NEA state impacted them, even if I didn't yell. I had to truly be in a positive state to put them at ease. This simple experiment changed our family and gave us a new vocabulary. I took that lesson right to work and started noticing when someone was in NEA and then slowing down to meet them where they were before I sprung things on them. Or I was a little softer and less reactive to someone's NEA state or harshness to me.

When I told my work friends about how much PEA/NEA changed my ability to tune my emotions, Julia said I had to give a lunch talk about it. I was skeptical about what busy technology professionals would think of a presentation about emotional intelligence, but they loved it. I got the real sense that talking about stress, emotions, and humanity at work was something people wanted. This kind of connection and conversation was desired in the workplace, and it certainly was not coming from top management.

As I practiced these new mindfulness strategies of questioning and changing my thoughts, observing my body language, and tuning myself to more positive states, home and work became less stressful. But there was more here than managing stressors in my environment. Compassion for others and myself was growing in me with these trainings, and that was a game-changer.

COMPASSION AS A SUPERPOWER

Compassion has been defined in different ways. Buddhism views compassion as a virtue that should be cultivated to free others from suffering. His Holiness the Dalai Lama says, "When you have great compassion, you'll have the fortitude to help others overcome their sufferings." Leaders can be compassionate, according to Richard Boyatzis, when they empathize or understand others' feelings, give a person a felt sense of being cared for, and then respond to the feelings that emerge. The clinical psychologist Chris Germer simply says, "When love meets suffering and stays loving, that's compassion."

My clients told me it was refreshing to work with someone who was not just driven by business results. Like Sulley in the Pixar movie *Monsters, Inc.* who realized that joy was more powerful than fear, I realized that the greatest power comes from those who can generate the Positive Emotional Attractor state around themselves. This brings good things to others — colleagues and family alike. It brings success — to work projects and home life alike. From the teachers my path took me to and my own observations at home and at work, I came to see that being soft and caring from the inside out is the most effective way to lead.

CHAPTER 14

Flipping the Script

As I followed this path of truth and compassion, I finally felt the security that had been so elusive in my life. It felt like I was developing a different part of my intelligence through the coach training and being coached by the other students. I was sensitive to the emotions around me at work. I was attuned to whether I was being a compassionate person to those I cared about, including myself. And I needed that compassion because I could see how often I failed at my goal. When I lost my patience or judged harshly, I knew it more quickly, which meant I could also fix it quickly. It seemed like I could watch myself more from a neutral and wise place and see more clearly.

Work brought some challenges, with people leaving and the rest of us needing to pick up the slack. A short burst of extra hours to overcome a challenge was not an issue. But our team culture suffered when a new leader arrived, one who didn't elicit anywhere near the same level of trust, positivity, or hope as our previous leader. The project managers, Yulia, Patrick, Liam, and Ben, and others on my client team, like Marco, were frustrated and very vocal that they were not getting the expected service levels. The JTekker mentality was to care about client satisfaction, and I couldn't understand the attitude shift. After six months and working well beyond my part-time hours, I saw that I would burn out because it was becoming a hopeless and toxic work environment. I was attuned to being flipped to the Negative Emotional Attractor state a lot more, which was a contagion to my family and deteriorated my health. I had data points from the science I had learned. Thus I had confidence that I wasn't being irrational.

I documented the issues in a detailed email and expected the higher-ups at work to care. But what I got back was denial and hubris. All of my examples were brushed aside, and it frustrated me as I realized nothing would change. To take a stand, I refused to endorse a project intended to cut delivery timelines for new servers that our client needed in days, not weeks. It seemed we were saying we could do it to keep them happy, when in reality we could not meet their expectations. My transparency and my objections to the "company narrative" caused friction with my bosses on the account. I was commanded to be a team player and support the project, but I couldn't do so and maintain my integrity. My professional competence was on the line, and I wasn't about to compromise it. Even a couple of clients were skeptical and mistrustful about our ability to deliver. I made a formal complaint to do the right thing for the client and also to protect JumboTek's reputation and potential for new business with this customer. We were risking client confidence, trust, and mutual respect, all of which were values we held dearly at JumboTek. It was risky to make a formal complaint, as I'd seen from my last experience of taking a stand, but I believed the upper leadership would care. I believed I needed to do this to be in my own integrity and uphold the trust of my clients.

I was called to a meeting to discuss my email complaint. There were two or three people, including a senior woman who had encouraged me to speak up. The others could have been from HR, though I cannot recall. Throughout the entire session, even though people were signalling in friendly ways, I picked up negative emotional states. There was minimal eye contact, and the body language was not welcoming. At one point, one of the attendees swivelled their chair around so their back was to me. It was a clear signal to me that what I had to say was not welcomed. I felt deeply disrespected by that single action.

Still, I hoped that even if my arguments were not believed, it was still the right thing to ensure senior leaders knew the situation. They would at least have the information to pay attention to the client's needs so we would not lose trust and possibly future business. I believed I could safely express a dissenting opinion.

After I had my say and they questioned me, they said the matter would be investigated further. I waited for the outcome, hoping the emotional burden of going through this process was worth it.

It was not.

A PROFOUND DISAPPOINTMENT

After looking into my concerns, they found a problem — with me. I had created a short cartoon video using Powtoon for a training meeting. The JumboTek leaders found the video posted online and asked me to remove it because it included the client's name. At the time, this little cartoon was met with chuckles because it was cute, but I could see that it was a valid concern, so I removed it immediately. But I didn't see anyone take responsibility for the serious client issues I had raised in my email and discussed in our meeting.

As the new year started, I learned from my annual performance review that I was a "profound disappointment amongst the team members" because I was expected to accept work without any pushback. I was a senior manager who should remain "engaged." My previous annual performance review had given me the highest rating, with glowing feedback, including, "Sunita understands the JumboTek business control requirements and ensures she is working within them executing within the appropriate processes." In just twelve months, I did not change my ethics. I worked to the boundaries I knew were appropriate, and I questioned the authority figure when I saw fit. But that resulted in me being the problem.

I finally had the confidence to speak up, something I had heard many men do in the tech world when they disagreed. The last thing I expected was a double standard. It didn't even dawn on me that I didn't have the privilege as a woman to push back on work. I especially should have been supported to not take on extra work out of respect for my being a part-time employee. And my strong connection to the client should have given me credibility. But it was clear from the comments in my year-end review that I was not respected.

A few weeks later, my leader, the subject of my complaint, asked to have a meeting with just me. As I sat alone in a small meeting room with this person, I could feel the tension. He smiled in his suave way, and then he told me he couldn't have anyone on his team who wasn't a team player. He said I must leave. I got the impression I was inconveniencing him by forcing him to make this decision. It was clear that this was not about the business's needs but his needs. The conversation felt so slimy, with fake concern and nice words. His eyes crinkled in a smile, and he reached out a hand to squeeze my shoulder to convey his best wishes as I moved on. I felt no warmth. My body just shrunk back, and I wanted his hand off me. I didn't trust him, he had power over me, which he had just clearly demonstrated, and he was making physical contact. Somehow that combination caused my body to react with fear of its own volition. I left the room, not even regretting being told to go because staying was no longer an option.

THE GOOSE STORY – A TEAMWORK LESSON

Yulia, Patrick, Liam, and Ben were outraged. They told me I took one for the team, and their appreciation and validation comforted me in my shock at being dismissed from the account. Liam cancelled his afternoon meetings, and we went to the Path, the underground walkway in downtown Toronto, and found one of the best remedies for being screwed over — tequila. After four shots and a good amount of venting, I felt better.

To celebrate new beginnings and good friendships, these friends arranged a proper goodbye at Pravda Vodka Bar on Toronto's scenic Wellington Street. As we sat cocooned in a red velvet booth nestled behind curtains, we toasted our friendship over vodka martinis. The warmth I felt from the group was exactly what was missing from the senior people at JumboTek. It was disconcerting to just be dismissed, but I was left with these great relationships when the job fell away.

As a going-away gift, they gave me a framed story that still stands on my desk today. It tells of how geese support each other in times of need. One line reads, "People who share a common direction and sense of community can get where they are going more quickly and easily because they are traveling on the thrust of one another." That is what we had been doing for several years, but now we'd be flying in different formations as I moved to a new work group. They signed the area below the story, and their words, like the honks geese use to motivate each other, remind me that it's worth doing the right thing, even at personal cost.

Their inscriptions tugged at my heart:

"All the best. Thanks for being part of the team." —Ben

"It's always a pleasure working with you. I'll be your wingman anytime." —Patrick

"This is so apt!! You stood up for us despite all odds. We'll see you around." —Yulia

"Thank you for all you have done for us. I very much value this time spent working together." —Liam

This evening out and their gift was a rite of passage for me, to help me say goodbye, but let me know we were a team always, even if we didn't work together. We were a group of people connected through shared values. We had created a community where we could speak the truth and vent frustrations, which helped counter the stress of a toxic workplace.

The goose story reminded me from that day forward that I couldn't divorce integrity and truth when I went to work. Someone might dismiss me for it, but I'd have failed if I compromised those values. My heart no longer had a compartmentalizing option to park my values and keep quiet at work.

Strangely, it was liberating to hear the words I had strived my entire life to avoid: "Sunita, you're a profound disappointment." The insecure over-achiever version of me would have been mortified to be called a disappointment and would have carried that hurt in her heart. But I wasn't crushed. My true achievement was in words inscribed under a flock of geese, not those in a Sunita Alves file somewhere in JumboTek's HR system.

I had learned that it was okay if someone in authority didn't like me, disapproved of me, and found me to be a horrible failure. JumboTek was the profound disappointment, not me.

LISTENING TO THE INNER VOICE

I had seen that visualizing a dream can really work. Tom had almost finished flight training and had his own plane now, a 1970 Piper Cherokee. This was beyond his wildest dreams, and it started during a coaching session with a vision of what would bring him joy. I think we each have a blueprint for happiness that we must uncover and dig down to find through the magical process of pausing, quieting, and stilling to self-reflect. My blueprint was pointing me to coaching and mindfulness. I started to awaken to a purpose that involved bringing kindness to people.

Many of the wake-up calls that got me to change direction were harsh, like the near-death accidents involving stairs and a car rollover on the highway. Jessica's Grade 3 drawing made me realize I wasn't the mother I wanted to be. But it was the training I did to become a coach that showed me how to work, how to show up authentically, and how to maintain humanity. I had this distinct feeling that people needed me in my workplace. I asked myself, "Who am I to think I should be helping people?" As soon as I asked the question, I received a reply. The voice I heard was the same wordless feeling that had asked me to love the lights that were leaving the Earth on the night of the tsunami in Japan. This time it said, "Because people need you."

At first, I rejected this idea because it felt so self-important. Yet, I couldn't be both a skeptic and a seeker. If I was on the path of seeking, I had to suspend feeling stupid or self-important and trust this wordless feeling was my inner Voice.

I started coaching people as a side business. I was still unwilling to be a full-time entrepreneur. I wanted to have time with my kids and the financial security of a job. But I was unsure how to stay at JumboTek and find meaning in my work.

A few months after the Pravda outing, I did an exercise with a friend from my life coach training cohort. It was meant to get to your true self's voice. I don't remember the question, but I wrote the answer in my journal. It felt like my hand was writing from a source that was indeed my inner Voice.

April 24, 2016, Journal Entry: *I am going to stop working at my job. I will not quit. People need me there. But I will stop working and only play. From now on.*

I felt the truth of these words like a lightning bolt of clarity. I could redefine where I put my effort at work to focus on what was important to me. I had things to give that people in my workplace needed. Right or wrong, I decided to stay in the same company, *but not to stay the same*. I would flip the script. I would change my mission at work to bring light to the workplace, my clients, and co-workers. My core duties would get done with just enough effort.

I resigned myself to being a "good-enough" employee if it meant being more human at work. This decision felt like freedom. I was going to play and have fun and get paid for it. It seemed like an impossible and flippant statement, but it resonated with me.

I realized the worst-case scenario was not being fired; the worst-case scenario was dying suddenly of a heart attack or stroke, or reaching the end of my life and realizing I hadn't spent enough time on what mattered. I called this "zero fucks to give," or, without profanity, "my bad work attitude." When I shared my new outlook with close colleagues, some were skeptical of this new Sunita's ability to follow through on not being a star employee, but I think most cheered for me.

I was about to see that the universe responds powerfully when you listen to your inner Voice like this. Things started to happen beyond what I could have imagined, as opportunities to make work more aligned to my values started to come my way.

CHAPTER 15

Wholehearted at Work

A close friend, Greta, who I had worked for before and bonded with over being a working mother at JumboTek, asked me to transfer departments and work for her in a different business area. I could not believe it. I found essentially a new place to work without quitting, keeping my pension and vacation weeks. But best of all, Greta was a warm and kind manager who cared for me and looked out for me. Under Greta's leadership, there were no shenanigans about the truth, so I didn't have to accomplish any heroics at work to fix unrealistic promises. I didn't need to stand up against toxic people or work practices because it was a safe working environment with team members who were kind and fun to be with. Without work demanding excessive hours or causing greater stress, I had time and energy to explore some of the benefits a big company like JumboTek offered its employees.

Employee interest groups are voluntary for employees to join to feel more connected at work. JumboTek supported many official groups focused on different interests such as culture or sports. Two groups attracted me because they improved the mental health of employees: the Mindful@Work Pod and the Coaching Pod. Mindfulness is about cultivating awareness in the present moment. Coaching is a way to help people navigate work challenges and grow in their careers. These were grassroots, employee-led groups without anyone from management setting what we needed to accomplish. Participation was based on common interest and was not part of our paid work. It felt like a breathing space to be at work and not be driven to achieve targets. As such, the two communities were filled with people who were seeking what I was seeking — a better, more human way of working.

In the Mindful@Work Pod, I learned I had colleagues who led mindfulness practices during the workday across the globe — in the UK, South Africa, and the US, to name a few. A JumboTek engineer brought mindfulness meditation to our workplace in 2008. He led teaching and practice sessions for his colleagues in the building cafeteria. He recorded the sessions and posted them in an online community on our internal employee network. Finding his recordings was like finding treasure. I remember thinking, *Wow, here is a template for practicing mindfulness in the workplace. I want to do this.* This groundbreaking employee had left the company, so I couldn't speak to him, but I listened to the recordings, followed his breathing instructions, and felt peace and joy. It opened a new dimension of work.

The other group, the Coaching Pod, consisted of employees trained as coaches who supported JTekkers struggling with work or personal issues or wanting to grow their careers. This community had monthly meetings where members shared their knowledge, and I loved attending these and being with like-minded people.

I was so inspired by the people leading the Mindful@Work Pod and Coaching Pod. They were passionate, wholehearted leaders navigating the corporate landscape to effect changes with a grassroots movement. Until I got involved in these groups, I had no idea the same workplace that broke down my mental health could also help build it up.

FREE AT CADES COVE

I felt more relaxed than ever and comfortable in my own skin that summer. With this newfound sense of freedom, I went on summer vacation, another epic camping trip in the RV. That year, Operation Plan-For-Fun involved camping in the Great Smoky Mountains National Park, then on to Nashville, then a visit to the National Corvette Museum in Bowling Green, and finally a stay in Mammoth Cave National Park, a UNESCO World Heritage Site and International Biosphere Reserve.

It's always a fun moment for our family to roll up to the National Park sign of our destination, and the Great Smoky Mountains park did not disappoint. We were awed by the lush Tennessee greenery as we drove into our campsite in Cades Cove campground, 518 meters above sea level. I felt the magic I always do when the RV setup activities are finished, and I paused to take in my surroundings. The air was fresh, and the trees surrounded us like curtains. I said hello to yet another personality of Mother Nature, and we greeted each other like old friends.

The name Cades Cove is most likely due to a Tsiya'hi leader known as Chief Kade, yet there is a more romantic theory, though discredited, that it was named for Cherokee Chief Abram's wife, whose name was Kate. European settlers arrived in the 1820s to settle this valley and hunt its abundant deer, elk, bison, and bears. The next day we set out to explore, and the park ranger recommended a moderately difficult eight-kilometer round trip hike to scenic Abrams Falls. The trail was covered in needles and framed with the thick dark leaves of rhododendrons. It was a beautiful summer day, hot in the open parts of the trail but cool where the trees created a ceiling of green overhead. It was a pleasure just to feel my body moving in nature and to be together as a family. It took about an hour to get there, and we were rewarded with the steady roar of the water as it fell seven and a half meters, like a bridal veil flowing down. We had snacks, and the kids climbed around as we kept a watchful eye that they didn't slip on the wet rocks.

As we prepared for the walk back, suddenly I just couldn't be in my shoes any longer. I felt this pull to be free of them and to feel the earth with my own body. I told my husband I wanted to walk back barefoot. As any sensible person would, he said it was too dangerous. The ground had sharp rocks and roots. When I looked down, though, I didn't see the danger. I only saw a beauty that coursed up and wanted to feel me too. I took off my running shoes and then my socks and took a few tentative steps. The ground was cool and hard. My feet felt alive as they contacted the earth without any barriers. As hikers came the other way, with their hiking poles and proper hiking boots, they gave me funny looks. But all I could do was grin. Each step took me deeper into joy. It was as if the world was humming with energy as it revolved and orbited the sun, spinning through the galaxy at incredible speeds, and I had just tapped right into that.

My feet did not want to walk. I told my family that I wanted to run ahead and that I would catch up with them later. Holding my shoes and socks in case common sense descended upon me, I started running. By their own intelligence, my feet avoided rocks, slippery bits, and gnarly roots. I watched them with amazement. I expected to do this for a couple of minutes because that's all I could ever run at home without gasping for breath and feeling pain in my shins. But as I ran on the trail, I didn't get out of breath. In fact, it felt so easy to run that I seemed to bound effortlessly. By now, the people I passed were really astonished, but they only had seconds to see me coming before I was gone again. Usually, I'd never want people to stare at me, but I didn't care about that either. It was as if I'd dropped my Sunita self and melded my consciousness with the forest.

Without interference from my mind, my body seemed to have the endurance of an athlete. I didn't even have the common sense to question what I was doing. It was like the part of my brain that would say, *this is crazy and dangerous,* or *people are staring,* was offline. I finally stopped for my family to catch up. After all, this was a family activity. When they arrived, Tom was worried he'd find me with a twisted ankle or cut up foot, but I was fine. I went to put on my shoes, and one sock was missing. The kids said they noticed a sock lying in the mud just after I had started, but didn't know it was mine. I thought about it and said I couldn't leave a sock in such a pristine place. It was disrespectful and wrong.

So, I told them to wait for me. This time I left my shoes and sock and I ran back to find the lost sock. I should have been tired, exhausted, muscles on fire and screaming in pain. But I wasn't. I asked people as they came the other way, "Did you see a sock?" I don't know what they thought when they saw a barefoot brown woman running at them. Many of them smiled, likely in response to the sheer joy and grin on my face, and everyone I encountered at first said no. Then as I got closer, people started to say there was a sock and then I saw it. Without any fatigue yet in my body, I started running back to my family, sock in hand. As I passed the same people, some of them gave me cheers and I waved the sock. Tom and the girls were waiting patiently in the shade. They knew how much I trusted the body's intelligence based on the body scan exercises we had done as a family, so I think they accepted this strange version of me.

I don't know where the energy came from on that hike or what overcame me. I was not fit by any means and did not work out regularly. I should have had days of soreness from an out-of-the-blue exertion like that, but in the days that followed, I felt fine. Great, even.

Since that time, I've never felt the need to run like that. It felt like I had joined up with the forest the way horses join up with people. I lost my sense of self. But this time it was not a calm feeling of love. It was a surging, barely contained power of love. It was another version of "the force of a flash flood" that Maya Spector describes in her poem "Jailbreak."

FIND THE INNER PATH AT WORK

The power of that love showed me that I could be simultaneously vulnerable and strong; I could peel off the layers of protection I had donned to feel safe in the world; I could trust that life would not harm me as a result. It taught me to follow my heart, quiet my inner critic, allow fear to exist without dominating me, and trust my body's wisdom to carry me through. It showed me that I would miss out on so much if I took the safe way. It showed me that I was powerful and that it was okay to accept that fact. It was also okay for me to be a bit odd relative to what society or common sense deemed acceptable. I came away with the realization that I would need to be wilder, not tamer, if I followed the call of my true self. With the most intense level of inner power I've ever felt, I returned to work.

I set an intention and tweeted on September 15, 2016: "My Intention: Find the Path from Inner Knowing to Outer World Action." It was a public declaration that I would take what I knew to be true inside me and transform it into real-world action. As if that intention manifested something, my career as a project manager transformed into roles at JumboTek I never imagined possible.

***

The Mindful@Work Pod was growing, and I stepped up to lead an in-person training session in Toronto, much like what other JumboTek offices in countries such as Brazil had done. I created a poster, got permission to post copies of it around the office, and started to receive RSVPs. I felt the discomfort of doing something not widely understood or accepted in the workplace. It was not the culture of our fast-paced workplace to slow down like this. I also felt the imposter syndrome because I was only self-taught by joining other practice sessions at the workplace. However, my experience at Cades Cove was still fresh in my mind, and I just went with the mantras "feel the fear and do it anyway" and "all will be well."

I'll never forget the first session I led. A man named Anders, who was about my age but tall and blond, had a breakthrough moment. He worked in sales, and I knew he led a Christian prayer circle at work, so he was clearly comfortable in his religion, but he seemed to be one of those highly positive people who just loved learning. During the session, I drew a stick person standing on the Earth on the whiteboard and explained that mindfulness is "bringing your attention to where you are in the present moment, most likely somewhere on Earth." I pointed to the stick figure and asked the attendees to "imagine this is you, and you are on the Earth at this exact spot." Then I told them that, "Mindfulness practice is to bring your mind into the present moment — what is happening now." I drew little bubbles from the stick person's head. In one, I wrote "The Past," and in the other, "The Future." I said, "If your mind is wandering around the past, or wandering around the future, then it's not where your body is — right here."

Anders put both hands up and exclaimed that he could see how his thoughts were not his mind. I could see the wonder on his face as he beheld his consciousness as a larger part of himself, separate from the thoughts that ebbed and flowed in his mind. His enthusiasm for mindfulness energized all of us. I guided the diverse group of about eight men and women to sit, bring their awareness to their feet on the floor, and scan their body all the way upwards. I said it was okay to have their minds wander off, like in the stick person picture, but I told them to notice whether they could catch that moment and gently bring their mind back to their body. I said the mind naturally wanders around, and that this gives us opportunities every few seconds to return to the present moment and experience it anew.

Week after week, the sessions got more comfortable both for the participants and me as a leader. We relaxed our bodies and supported each other through our learning curve of slowing down a mind that races around all day. We had the felt experience of ourselves beyond the thoughts we had. The first time you realize that you are not your thoughts is a profound moment.

I loved the connection I felt with people in the group and I started to lead video conference practice sessions across Canada. I also bravely introduced a mindfulness minute in my "day job" at a senior management meeting with about ten people. As strong leaders, I knew they had different viewpoints, but I wanted to show them that they each had good intentions. They were game to follow their breath for a minute, then state what outcome they'd like to have after our one-hour meeting. We went around the meeting room table, and each person had a slightly different want. But the exercise meant that we understood each other's needs upfront, and that focused the meeting. In less than thirty minutes we finished our business, with everyone feeling satisfied. Usually, we would have wasted time on posturing and countering opinions. The mindfulness minute had cleared a space for everyone to be more intentional, and that made us more efficient.

Becoming someone who would lead groups of employees to do body scans, breathing practices, or just talk about the mental and physical benefits of mindfulness required that I let go of my need for control, approval, and perfection. This was all about trial and error, and we were experimenting. Mindfulness was not a common office word at that time. While one part of me was jumping up and down in anxiety, another part of me was able to calm the first part down and say, *Hey, these are good people. No one is going to yell at you if you don't do things perfectly.* With each practice session, I was able to let go of a little more self-doubt, low self-worth, and low self-esteem. This unholy trinity's hold on me was getting weaker all the time, and it felt so very good.

Before the end of the eight-week mindfulness session, I was offered a formal role to co-lead mindfulness for JumboTek Canada. It would be part of my paid job function. To my knowledge, this was the first time in JumboTek worldwide that such a role was formally identified. I was doing what I loved, what felt like play, and a job came of it. Amazing.

***

The next opportunity blew my mind even more. JumboTek had created an initiative to help disadvantaged youth graduate with a free college diploma. The program was called J-Academy. The initiative involved partnering between a high school, a local college, and technology partners like JumboTek to design a curriculum that qualified for high school and college credits. Students graduated with a post-secondary diploma in a high-demand technology field and with work experience at the corporate partner, all free of charge. They could then enter the workforce or go on to more education. In Canada, there is a push to have more Indigenous students graduate with a post-secondary degree. JumboTek Canada's Corporate Social Responsibility department wanted to help by giving Indigenous youth a pathway to jobs in tech where they could make good incomes. They were looking for a project manager to bring together Indigenous and provincial secondary and post-secondary schools as well as provincial and federal funding sources to make the first J-Academy in Canada a reality.

I would have never heard of this role if a work acquaintance, Vinnie, hadn't sought me out to encourage me to apply. He was part of the team looking for the right person to join them, and he thought of me because we had been introduced by chance just a few months earlier, and I had impressed him. He said I was the perfect fit because I was a female engineer, a minority, and I could be a role model to these students. I also had the soft skills to build trust, and I had the complex project management skills required. I applied and got the J-Academy leader role in Canada. Greta was disappointed I was leaving her team, but she supported me in this once-in-a-lifetime opportunity and gave me her blessing.

One benefit of this new position was that I would finally be unshackled from maintaining a utilization rate of billable hours. I could hardly believe my luck. Within a couple of months of declaring my intention to bring my inner strengths to work, my career at JumboTek had had a complete makeover. Both roles felt like they were charted by my heart to align work with my inner path.

BETWEEN WORLDS

They say that life is what happens when you're making other plans. My mother called, as broken as I've heard her in my life, and told me that my younger brother was being taken to the Emergency Room at Ajax Hospital. It was a genuinely frightening time because he had had a stroke, was paralyzed, and couldn't speak. Those next few hours were going to be critical to how well he recovered. Internally, it was like the world stopped, and I was living from moment to moment. My sensitivity to emotions heightened. I could feel the terrified energy of my sister-in-law and my parents. But when I saw my brother lying on the hospital gurney, I tried to centre myself and look into his eyes with calm energy. It was the only way he could communicate.

I got the sense he was confused and scared with all the commotion. I became sensitive to the discordant energy of one nurse in particular who was angry that there were so many of us near him. I recalled Jill Bolte Taylor's TED Talk, *My Stroke of Insight.* When she had a stroke, she could feel others' negative emotions. I had no idea if my brother was feeling like Jill, but I decided to be an island of calm for him. I willed all the fear, confusion, and stress out of my energy field. With the absolute knowledge that this is what my brother needed, I found whatever determination I needed to drop my fear for his life, so that fear-energy would not transmit to him in his vulnerable state. I did it through mindful breathing and calming my body. It was like I had only one mission: Bring calm.

I spoke up quietly but strongly to the nurse and said that raising her voice was not acceptable. I explained that that kind of energy was not good for my brother. I had learned this from my daughter Jessica's picture of me yelling at her. It showed me how someone powerless feels if there is an angry authority figure. I also knew that negative emotions are contagious and that that is not what someone who is hurt needs to feel. I told her that she should treat people in distress with more humanity. I said if she didn't immediately behave more professionally, I would report her. She stopped harassing us and left us to another nurse to deal with. He was much nicer to us and confided that her attitude was not appreciated by the other staff either. He thanked me for saying what I did.

With my ability to be calm and manage my fear, my family wanted me to be the one to remain in Emergency. I went to work like I did in the dream the night of the tsunami in Japan. I poured calm, loving energy, and nothing more. I visualized the medicine he was given doing its job perfectly. The doctor had shown us a picture of the clot, and in my mind's eye that clot was going away.

I communicated with my brother non-verbally, through soothing sounds, loving touches, and healing thoughts. I stood at the foot of his bed and rubbed his feet under the blue hospital sheet. Deep in that visualization, an image of our ancestors appeared. As I sat in stillness, it came to me how much Nani and Mom loved us and how much Indian women loved their children. Male children are especially celebrated in Indian families. The devotion between mother and son is a trope in many Bollywood movies. I had seen this my whole life — how a baby boy is born and becomes his mother's life. It dawned on me that there would be countless mothers in our ancestry who would have wanted their sons to live, who prayed daily for the well-being of their children. I realized that although those ancestors were not here, their love was still alive.

To the very beginning of time, I called on all the mothers of all the sons in my lineage. I told them their prayers were needed now. I asked these maternal ancestors to do what my inner Voice had asked me to do in the dream I had during the night of the tsunami in Japan: *Send love.*

In this visualization, my ancestors appeared around my brother. I filled in the circle with mothers of mothers until my brother was surrounded by Indian women, all dressed in green, red, pink, bright blue, and yellow saris. These were women whose DNA coursed in his veins. They were overjoyed to be invited to this healing space, and I could feel peace, joy, love.

I looked at them in the circle, and I told them, *This is your son. The energy of Mother is needed to heal him.* And love just poured out. I'm not sure how long I stayed with this visualization. I do recall looking at them in wonder at being able to see my ancestors. They were young and slender, old and plump, fair and dark. They felt real to me and not like figments of my imagination. It was as if they had popped out of some other realm to spend some time with us. We were between worlds but connected as if time didn't matter.

ALL THE FORCES OF NATURE

It felt like all the forces of nature were opening me up with magic and mystery to something much bigger than I could experience with my knowing mind. The land at Cades Cove had been a force like no other. The force of my ancestors felt like it opened a connection to transfer energy between my brother and the mothers in our lineage. The force of pouring love on the world during my dream of hovering in outer space showed me the power of love. The force of the dissolving of my ego after yoga showed me that we were all one. The force of community and colleagues at work connected me to meaning.

Mindfulness practice was full of gentle realizations of how demanding and harsh my self-talk was to get meditation "right." As I trained myself to be more accepting, more compassionate, and more kind in these moments of stillness, I was training myself to be that way in general. My kids didn't want a perfect, overachieving, controlling, insecure mother. They wanted one who was with them in the present moment and who was relaxed, easy-going, and fun to be with. My children told me that I was a better mother to them, nicknaming me "Zen Mommy." They encouraged me to meditate because it made me kinder and more present.

Jessica's Grade 3 drawing of me yelling at her had been a wake-up call to say that how we feel, and make others feel, is more important than what we get done. I heeded that call to change into a more loving, compassionate, and kind person. Then a path of learning opened so I could do just that with coach training.

My brother recovered his health rapidly, and it felt like a miracle to us who had seen him so immobile just a few days earlier. He was young and healthy, apart from the stroke, and the speed at which the medicine was administered was a significant factor. I believe he would have gotten well whether or not I was practicing mindfulness with him, calming him and sending him healing energies from another world. However, the practice of mindfulness was my support during this time — it helped me remain calm, which is what my family needed from me. It helped me be fierce and stand up for my brother's rights when a nurse brought negativity into his presence. Mindfulness gave me the clarity to be calm when I needed to be and confrontational when that was what was needed. It allowed me to read the energy in the room and do what was needed.

All of these forces reduced my attachment to overachieving in my career and strengthened my intention to bring my inner power to the outer world. There were many times I thought, *Who am I to be leading corporate programs like J-Academy or mindfulness? I'm not an expert on Indigenous Canada, the secondary education system, government policies, or mindfulness.* I didn't study sociology, politics, history, or philosophy. But, I recalled what Marianne Williamson said in her book *A Return to Love*: "Our deepest fear is that we are powerful beyond measure. It is our light, not our darkness, that most frightens us. We ask ourselves, Who am I to be brilliant, gorgeous, talented, fabulous? Actually, who are you not to be?" With this in mind, I thought, *Who am I not to be leading these programs?*

Over twenty years had passed since I had sung "The Best" to the other empowerment seminar attendees at the Travelodge in Oshawa. I was then a young professional starting her career as an insecure overachiever. Now I was mid-career and standing in my own purpose. It had been a long road to let go of doubt and fear and see myself as worthwhile and good enough, to even glimpse myself as part of the miracle that Albert Einstein said was everywhere. Sometimes a jailbreak of that magnitude takes years.

The jailbreak wasn't to jump out of the boiling water and search for better circumstances like in the frog story. The true jailbreak was to get still, tune in, and find the course charted by the spiritual being inside of me. The power of spirituality, connectedness, and compassion was the transformative force that created the better life I was seeking.

I looked to 2017 with excitement and anticipation of working wholeheartedly.

PART 4

Heartbreak

For Rosie

*"Sometimes when things get taken away from you it feels
like there's a hole at your centre where you can feel the
wind blow through, that's sure."*

— Richard Wagamese, *Medicine Walk*

CHAPTER 16

Dark Shadows

I had zero experience in education funding, creating a curriculum, or establishing mentoring programs for youth. A key foundation of the new J-Academy school was the technology curriculum, and I felt the pressure to become familiar with the topics. One of those was Java programming, which the students would be taught. I was way out of my comfort zone and grateful to learn that the man who had recommended me for the role would be mentoring me. His name was Vinnie, and he was in his mid-sixties with a large build. He had an air of snobbishness about him that seemed to suggest that the Corporate Social Responsibility department was for the chosen few. The rest of my team did not have this attitude. They felt humbled to be part of a team that did wonderful things like supporting communities through innovation, volunteerism, charity, diversity, equity, and inclusion investments.

Being an open person, I told him I was unsure of myself, but he assured me he would teach me everything I needed to know. We spent a lot of time together while he shared his expertise. When I felt insecure about something, my response was to learn as much data and facts as possible, so I appreciated his time. He was very enthusiastic in his compliments, which I think was to reassure me but ended up making me feel like he gave me too much attention. The things he did seemed innocent, yet I started to be tense around him. I began to feel like a toy he liked playing with. He praised me too much, there was too much charm, and his looks were too penetrating. Some warning system within me had gone off, saying this was crossing the line of professionalism.

Having practiced mindfulness meditation in business settings, seeking to reach a state of calm or ease with my groups, I was very aware that my body was not at ease during our lengthy meetings. My muscles tensed, my vision focused, and my breathing became shallow. I noticed my mind racing to rapidly figure out why I felt so weird in his presence.

Breathe, I said to myself. *He's just an odd duck.* Vinnie told me a few times that he was eccentric and that people sometimes didn't get him. It seemed he was building a persona to make excuses for his oddities. It felt like I owed him friendship for how he helped me get this job, yet I couldn't warm up to him because he put others down, and his humour was dark. I didn't like any of these traits.

I could watch the thoughts come through my mind in my mindful state:

Why is he so excited about me? Is he attracted to me? No, that can't be.

Does he just lack social skills, like knowing good professional boundaries? He does act like a bumbling scientist.

Why would he say such mean things directed at women? Is he a sexist? It feels like he wants me to only like him.

Is he a narcissist? Why is he talking about how great he is so much?

I should have been thinking that I had a right to a more psychologically safe workplace. I should have been looking for ways to directly address these issues. But I wasn't sure if my unease was justified, or if I was imagining things. Another thought came to me. *He has power over me. I'm new, and I can't rock the boat here. I just have to put up with this so I can focus on the job.*

When he got too personal, I steered the conversation back to business topics, hoping he would pick up on the subtle hint. I thought, *I am a professional, and I can manage this situation.*

I tried to put things into context and figure out how to deal with this. He clearly lacked empathy for the way he judged others and tried to poison me against our team, especially the other women. I told him not to disparage the other team members during our meetings because it wasn't respectful.

I thought that would work, but he continued to share his intimate confidences, and I became increasingly uncomfortable being alone with him.

Maybe he got the wrong message because I was naturally open and warm. Perhaps I had laughed at his jokes out of politeness, and he picked that up as a more intimate connection than I intended. He was just a difficult relationship I had to deal with to meet the tight timelines to launch the first J-Academy school in Canada. Working backward, the curriculum had to be set, partnerships confirmed, and press releases initiated in the next few weeks. I knew how to get things from the idea stage to reality as a project manager, but I needed his help to be successful in such a short time. So, I carefully navigated this work relationship, as draining as it was. I soon learned that I wasn't the only one who found Vinnie difficult.

ROSIE

"Sunita, I'm so glad you're on the team," Rosie said as she hugged me. We had met a few times through our mutual volunteer activities at work. She was a warm, caring person. She wore her grey hair in a bun, and her eyes crinkled when she smiled. She loved children and was excited to be working together with me at the J-Academy school. "I love all children," she would say. "I have my two daughters, but these students will also be my kids." Her heart was big enough to include an entire school full of kids.

But she said something that gave me a twinge of unease. She said, "I feel better with you here."

I was sensitive to her body language and could see that she had switched into the negative emotional attractor state. Her spirit, which was so uplifted when she talked about the students in the school, suddenly seemed heavy.

I asked her what she meant, because this department felt like the epicentre of caring at JumboTek — the one that did good and was unconcerned by the relentless drive to make profits. As we walked down the hallway, Rosie put her arm in mine and found a quiet spot in the cafeteria, far away from the other tables. In hushed tones, she told me a chilling story of how she came back to work after almost dying from sepsis, to find an email with a picture of a skeleton's hand at the bottom. She said that email made her wonder if her job was safe, and she felt like maybe the person who sent it didn't want her to come back at all. Vinnie had sent it, likely as a joke. But to Rosie, this odd and cryptic email left her feeling unsure of her standing on the team.

Although it had happened in the past, Rosie was still visibly shaken by this event. And I could see she felt insecure. This was no way to live in peace. I knew this kind of day-to-day stress build-up was unhealthy and that it could pose a health risk. My heart broke for Rosie, who was a good person and didn't deserve this treatment. I told her that I would be her friend always and that if ever I saw any wrongdoing, I would speak up. She lit up at that, having switched back to a positive emotional state now, and called me a lifeline.

Rosie shared her worries about what bothered her the most at work: being treated as inferior and feeling forced onto the margins. I stood up for her whenever I could, reminding people that she was part of the team and sending her emails that didn't include her but should have. To be excluded is a painful experience. It bothered Rosie to not know the reason. She wondered, *Why am I not good enough?*

Watching out for myself and watching out for Rosie added psychological stress to my work life. When Rosie felt the pain of disconnection, I felt it too. My heart was heavier for her in a way it was not for my own situation. I didn't want to feel sad because I knew it affected my mood and thus my family life. But it was not an option for me to compartmentalize and not care. Mindfulness and coaching work provided a sound support system that helped counter the stress I was feeling. So again, I thought I was managing the situation.

A TRAGEDY AT WORK

Just a few months into my J-Academy assignment, a co-worker came to my cubicle and said in an upset voice, "Sunita, don't go into the hallway. I think someone jumped."

The hallway windows overlooked an outside terrace, and someone had jumped off the roof and landed there. My co-worker moved on to warn others, and I felt disoriented and full of shock.

As my emotions flooded me, I started to slow my breathing and feel my body on the earth. I grounded my feet and felt the floor and then the support of the chair and the arm rests. I brought my mind to the rise and fall of my breath. Slowly the emotions calmed, and I was able to open my heart and then visualize this person as a golden light. I sent love to their soul like I was called to do in my dream the night of the tsunami in Japan. I imagined this person as a golden light and sent love to them across space and time, as well as love to their family, friends, and the first responders coming into the building.

After his body was removed, I couldn't even walk by where he had landed. It felt so awful to know someone alive that morning was no longer here. Some of my colleagues and I wondered why he jumped and if it was because of work. We could not know, but we agreed that JumboTek had become a heavier workplace in the last few years. Counselors were on site to help anyone who needed to talk. It was mindfulness I turned to for help with the painful emotions. One of my colleagues asked if I would lead a group mindfulness practice to process our shared grief. When the time came, the room was filled to capacity.

Because emotions were high, we started with mindfulness of the breath and body. Then, for positive energy, we did loving-kindness, or *Metta,* a practice from Buddhism. We repeated phrases to send good wishes to all people, and it generated a warm-hearted feeling. Initially, the phrases were to ourselves and our loved ones. Then we sent love towards our colleague who had passed and all the people grieving. Finally, we directed love to all people in the world.

We repeated, "May they be safe, may they be healthy, may they be happy."

The feelings of kindness and friendliness at such a dark time fostered a sense that we could share positivity even during the sadness. Doing this guided heart meditation felt good and helped us process the confusion and grief while we still had to go through the motions of work. We had a few of these sessions, which brought light to the workplace.

SISTERS IN SPIRIT

I connected with another amazing and warm-hearted woman at JumboTek who was the leader of Indigenous Relations. I sought a meeting with Rachel because the J-Academy school would focus on Indigenous youth, and I wanted to learn from her. Rachel and Rosie were already long-time friends, having travelled to Indigenous communities across Canada to host technology camps for the kids. I was the new one, but we bonded instantly and came to call each other Sisters in Spirit. We were that connected and same-hearted.

I was thrown when Vinnie — the man Rosie and I had issues with — spoke badly of Rachel. It almost seemed like Vinnie tried to poison my mind. But Rachel was an astute businessperson, elegant and poised. I realized that I needed to be wary of anything Vinnie said because it didn't match reality. He seemed unhinged, and I realized I needed to stay as far from him as possible.

Rachel introduced me to two things that I needed to learn about. One was the UNDRIP, and the other was the TRC. The UNDRIP is the United Nations Declaration on the Rights of Indigenous Peoples. The TRC is the Truth and Reconciliation Commission, established in Canada to investigate Indigenous history and the next steps for repairing the harm done. Perhaps because of my engineering background, my first step when tackling new things is to gather all the information and take it in. This is what I did.

The UNDRIP is eighteen pages and has forty-six articles listing the rights of Indigenous Peoples "as a standard of achievement to be pursued in a spirit of partnership and mutual respect." For example, Article 3 holds that "Indigenous peoples have the right to self-determination. By virtue of that right they freely determine their political status and freely pursue their economic, social and cultural development."

The eleven TRC reports, published in 2015, are thousands of pages, and the summary includes ninety-four Calls to Action to government, religious, and business sectors in Canada. I printed the first four documents to flag things I wanted to remember. The dining room table was the only surface big enough in our house to accommodate the binders, and it seemed I highlighted or added sticky notes to every other page.

For about four weeks I walked by five hundred years of brutality and inhumane treatment of children documented in those pages. Reading the survivor stories, I had so much empathy come up for the abused children, the parents who had their children stolen, and the children of the abused children. I came to understand how the current child services and justice systems continue to inflict a cycle of harm. I woke up to the fact that I was a treaty person, and that there are over six hundred sovereign nations in Canada. How did I not know this? And many of the treaties are not honoured to this day. It changed my view of myself as a Canadian. My sadness grew as I contemplated that my Canadian identity was built on brutal harm to others and stolen rights.

I know I became too consumed with the TRC documents, but I felt it was my part of reconciliation to know more of this truth. The sadness was heavy, and compassion meditation helped a lot. Talking with Rosie and Rachel helped too. Rosie and I reached out to the Native Women's Resource Centre in Toronto to understand more. They invited us to join them in making lanterns for the candlelight vigil for missing and murdered Indigenous women. We visited their centre, which was in a stately Second Empire heritage home in Toronto capped in a black roof with what looked like eyebrows over the tall windows. Rosie and I hot glued ribbons and flowers to mason jars for the lanterns all day, as people came through to get lunch. There was a big posterboard in the space, with hundreds of pictures of women and girls. Although lost, they were clearly not forgotten.

We joined in a simple but delicious meal, and the room felt warm and connected as people poured in and took a seat. I watched a mom help her daughter get ready for the ceremony. The girl was about eight or ten years old, wore a bright beaded dress, and had neatly braided hair. People took up the lanterns as we headed out for the ceremony.

I felt the strength of their spirit as I joined elders and beat on a canoe that had been turned into a drum. I saw a continuity of strength as we lit our candles and listened to the words of a people who never give up hope for their lost women and girls. I saw that spirit as the little girl and her mom held the posterboard up with the faces of missing girls and women. The little girl struggled just a little bit under the weight of her end until her dad came and helped her.

Rosie and I had so many conversations that day and learned people's stories. We huddled with an elder of the community under my umbrella when it started raining. She told us that she would be so lonely without the Women's Centre. When it was time to go home, Rosie gave me a look that said, *We can't take the umbrella away from her.* I asked our new friend if she would like to keep the umbrella because we had raincoats with hoods, and she gratefully accepted.

I'm so glad I went and joined in on the meal and the celebration, rather than just reading the reports. The reports described reconciliation and spoke of the resilience of spirit of the survivors. But on this night, I was in the presence of that resilience. I saw that reconciliation was Indigenous and non-Indigenous peoples coming together in mutually respectful, healing, and joyful ways. I was now excited to look to the future with this school project because education was the way out, just like my ancestors had always valued it. The J-Academy school became more than a charitable project. It fully sank in that it was a reconciliation project for future generations.

WORKPLACE HARASSMENT – TO GO OR NOT TO GO TO HR?

The situation with Vinnie escalated rather than going away as I became more capable to lead the school project without his training sessions and spent less time with him. He had started telling me about sexual experiences he'd had, and I was on the alert if he reached out and touched me in a friendly gesture on the arm or back. I was constantly tense and on the defensive. This had to stop, and I wasn't sure what to do, so I leveraged my support network. I asked other senior women what they would do. I was shocked to hear other women sharing stories of men grabbing their breasts on a business trip or taunting them to come to sit on their lap. I couldn't imagine things like this happening at work, but they obviously do. Going to HR or speaking to his boss were two options, but my previous experience of speaking up, where I ended up being investigated and removed from the account, had taught me not to trust the process.

This issue was not worth jeopardizing the school launch, which had such a tight timeline. I did not have time to deal with Human Resources and launch a formal investigation. Also, I wasn't sure who would be believed. Vinnie had told me how close he was with his boss and that he was essential to the team.

To test the waters, I opted to meet with an HR representative for a hypothetical discussion. When I explained the situation and asked if I could deal with it directly or file a complaint, the representative told me I could work it out on my own in this situation or file a complaint. It was up to me.

I had not heard of the #MeToo movement. Though I knew Ontario had just introduced Bill 132, with more stringent definitions of sexual harassment, I didn't know any details. I was just relieved to know I didn't have to report this, which would be awkward and embarrassing. What if Vinnie's manager didn't believe me? My manager, Maeve, seemed to like Vinnie as well, and I wasn't sure if she would support me, the new person. From the last two experiences of speaking up against wrongdoing, I had learned that it only caused career setbacks. I didn't want to go through the experience of being seen as a problematic employee or not being believed. In the end, I chose to handle it directly because the HR person didn't seem shocked, and anyway, my complaints weren't nearly as serious as the stories I had heard from other women.

Tom wanted to support me in whatever decision I made. He could understand why I did not want the stress of a formal inquiry. I recalled the saying in our industry that HR works for the company, not you. I wasn't interested in justice here. I just wanted it to stop, so I could focus on my job.

I decided to confront Vinnie directly. I dreaded this conversation more than any I could remember, but it couldn't be avoided. And I needed to be prepared. I wrote out my points on note cards the girls used for their speeches at school. I made the call from my kitchen before the kids came home from school. I launched right in. I told him, "I need you to stop doing these three things. Stop touching me, stop disparaging my co-workers, and stop talking about your sexual life." I had limited my points to three because I had learned that that was an effective number for people to retain in a presentation. His response was one of surprise. He said he hadn't meant to do any of those things, apologized, and assured me it would not happen again.

But the stress wasn't over. I had to continue to work with him, and it was awkward. He did change to a purely professional relationship, and that was a relief. But I was still a bit wary of every interaction, and I worried about possible retaliation. I had already been stressed dealing with this for weeks. Then I had been stressed about finding someone in HR to talk to and deciding whether to file a formal complaint. Then it had been stressful to prepare and have that conversation. The stress kept layering on.

The harassment, the situation with Rosie, the grief of losing a colleague violently, and the realization that so much harm had come to pass in my country's history felt like an emotional storm. It was like I became aware of how much pain there was around me, and I breathed it in, and it became something I carried, like thick, heavy smoke.

As the old man in Richard Wagamese's novel *Medicine Walk* said to his ward Franklin Starlight, "It feels like there's a hole at your centre where you can feel the wind blow through." This sadness grew in me like a hole at my centre. But I had faith our project with the school would do good things, and that kept me going.

CHAPTER 17

Some Highs and a Big Low

The first meeting to draft our agreement with the Indigenous school leaders started with a young man who wasn't even going to stay for the rest of the meeting. He stood up at the front of the room and spoke for fifteen minutes. That is a long time in a business meeting for anyone to listen. But we were not meant to listen with our ears as much as our hearts.

He relayed the Haudenosaunee Thanksgiving Address, Greetings to the Natural World. Gratitude is given to people and is extended to the Earth, the elements, the natural world, the celestial world, and the Creator. Each section ends with, "Now our minds are one." If ever there was a way to pour love on the world, it is with this greeting. As I sat on my chair I practiced mindfulness of breath, so my mind didn't wander as the young man spoke. I wanted to let his strong, clear voice, which seemed to be echoing generations of voices, reach me fully. I smiled because I'd never thought to thank the fish in my gratitude meditations. I don't have his exact words, but an online version states, "The Fish: We turn our minds to all the Fish life in the water. They were instructed to cleanse and purify the water. They also give themselves to us as food. We are grateful that we can still find pure water. So, we turn now to the Fish and send our greetings and thanks. Now our minds are one."

It was good to initiate this meeting by connecting our minds as one. We came from worlds of Western business and Indigenous education. We were coming together as one group to improve the high school experience for students in the community. We were at the school's conference room table, but this agreement needed to fulfill the needs of those not at the table — the students, their caregivers, and perhaps even social workers supporting the families through trauma. We were meeting as one, including the people who were not in the room. I felt so fortunate to be part of this project.

EDUCATION AS A PATH TO RECONCILIATION

That visit to the school was about establishing trust. We could not show up as the big company doing the school a huge favour or come across as superior. Based on the Indigenous beliefs I had learned about in the TRC and UNDRIP, we needed to show respect and listen more than we spoke. My mother and grandmother had taught me to be respectful to others, even to lower myself in service. Rachel, Rosie, and I had discussed beforehand our concern that we not come across as arrogant. I saw how clients reacted when JumboTek showed up for a meeting with twice as many people as the client had or when JumboTek did most of the talking. It was a power move, and if there was a sense of superiority, it made the meeting hard to take. If it came across that JumboTek didn't care about the client's requirements, it fostered distrust. I had seen how these behaviours had disappointed people like Marco, Yulia, and Liam.

One of the school leaders, Stacey, was a direct and challenging person who reminded me of Marco. She didn't have the same tough-guy look as Marco, being a petite person with hair in a simple ponytail. But she gave off the same no-bullshit energy.

At my initial meet-and-greet with her, she was kind but made it clear that there had been challenges. It was clear there was something here to repair, and I needed to understand things from her point of view. When I asked her for the pain points, no sugar coating, she was just as direct as Marco had been. She wanted me to see I had made an error.

Stacey said, "You come in here and want to help, yet don't take the time to learn about us as a First Nation."

She continued on to express some of the key principles of Indigenous education that were important but that we had not understood. As I listened with openness and equanimity, the truth behind her words hit home. Although I had read the UNDRIP and TRC, I knew little about this First Nation. They were a sovereign group of people, just like any country. Would I think that France and Spain are the same in their view of education? Of course not. So why hadn't I been curious to explore the history and culture of this First Nation I'd be working with?

I asked her what she would suggest, and she smiled and winked as she said, "Google it." She pointed me to a website that had a short video to explain the beliefs of the First Nation, like the *Dish with One Spoon*. I checked in on Stacey's body language throughout that initial meeting to see if we were in resonance or dissonance. It felt like resonance, and I often asked if I understood things correctly and fully.

By the time of the big group meeting, I had watched the videos and understood more. As the Thanksgiving Address finished and the young man left the room, I ensured all the needs were brought to the surface and understood. There absolutely could not be any trace of power-over tactics here.

As Rachel explained, this school agreement had to be aligned with Indigenous ways of making agreements and partnerships, not the ways of the corporate world anchored in colonialism and power hierarchies. The J-Academy school model had been created and rolled out globally in a highly successful manner. Yet, that successful model could not just be dropped into an Indigenous community as-is. There had to be a process to examine the needs of JumboTek and the needs of the school leaders and ensure the final solution met all requirements. Otherwise, we would repeat a past of asking Indigenous peoples to give up their right to self-determination.

Stacey and other school leaders wanted this school to be open enrollment, meaning they would not turn away students who didn't fit the "disadvantaged" criteria. As I understood the requirement, it was that only by including all racial, ethnic, and economic sections of the community could the school population come together as one. Segregating the school in any way was not an option.

It was also important to the school to give students, especially those who had a hard time learning through traditional Grade 9 classroom "sage on a stage" methods, a more engaging and hands-on learning experience. They wanted the students to be the leaders too, and not just have the teachers be the leaders. It was an essential requirement for the students to have access to technology, like computers they could tear down to see how they worked, V.R. kits like Google Expeditions and Oculus Rift, Xboxes, and other enticing tech. This would prepare them to understand how technology works and for the dual credits that started in Grade 10 towards their tuition-free college software engineering diploma.

The school was also revolutionary because Indigenous education is funded by the federal government, whereas public education is funded by the provincial government. Two levels of government would be coming together to support the tuition.

This was truly a first-of-a-kind hybrid solution, combining college and high school curriculum; federal and provincial funding; Indigenous and non-Indigenous students; and academic and non-academic learners. This was a lot to take in, but I saw how the Thanksgiving Address at the start of the meeting set the stage by repeating, "Now our minds are one." We went through the meeting, going over the agreement line-by-line with track changes so everything was transparent.

As we drove back to the office, Rosie, Rachel, and I felt good about the connection and collaboration that had just happened. The meeting had been respectful and inclusive, just as we had all wanted it to be.

FAILURE TO LAUNCH

I was very proud of the draft agreement we had created together and how we had gathered to develop it. However, that feeling soon evaporated when I learned there was a big issue that could jeopardize the agreement. The next step was for JumboTek to sign the agreement, and we needed the blessing of our parent company in the US. They, however, were not happy we were proceeding to partner with the school without a commitment from the Ontario Minister of Education. The model was firm that we must have public funding, not the private kind raised so far. In addition, open enrollment also went against the J-Academy tenet of offering the program only to kids in need. Here in Canada, the open enrollment approach was non-negotiable because the Indigenous leaders saw integration as a path to reconciliation. The partnership was in big trouble.

We needed more time to figure out these mismatches, and there wasn't time before marketing materials had to launch. It became a "go/no-go" moment. The "go/no-go" is a meeting that IT projects have just before a launch or cutover—a rapid changeover from one phase of a business system to another. This term originated with US navy aircraft carrier pilots and astronauts with a "go" meaning they were cleared for liftoff and "no-go" meaning all the checks were not in place for the launch. Without JumboTek US agreeing to sign the agreement, we could not go forward with calling the school a J-Academy. It would be a no-go to have the first J-Academy school in Canada.

The school leaders were disappointed to not have the prestigious J-Academy name, but the school was still a go. They pivoted to rename the school so the marketing materials could go out on time. They chose the name STEAM, which stood for "science, technology, engineering, arts, and math." It was a good name for this innovative school. The school leaders demonstrated strength and spirit to not let our withdrawal impact their launch plans. But there was a distaste in my mouth about not following through on our intention. I felt sick in my stomach like we had played games in this relationship. I took it really hard.

The local leadership in JumboTek Canada also felt some heat from the JumboTek US parent team about going as far as they did with the agreement. I must have discussed my fears with my family because the girls surprised me with a campaign button they created, written in pink marker, "#SaveMaeve2k17." They chanted "hashtag save Maeve 2 k 17" around the house and told me to wear the button to work and start a campaign to save my "good" Canadian boss, Maeve, from the "bad" US bosses. Clearly, they had simplified the story to fairytale terms, but I found it endearing that they cared so much about the idea of this school and they thought Maeve was the heroine here for championing the school.

This was not at all a light issue in my heart though. I was feeling ashamed of my company's lack of flexibility and integrity to work through the issues and sign the agreement in time. We were JumboTek, for heaven's sake. I felt like we had crossed a line with this relationship by putting the company's needs ahead of the school's. Everything felt out of control, and it scared me to see the depth of my own feelings. As I breathed through and tried to come to the present moment, one message came through loud and clear. I had to go there, in person, and apologize.

FINDING A MIDDLE WAY

From the TRC, I knew that speaking the truth and apologizing were essential components of a relationship. I went to Stacey in person and apologized for what I came to think of as stringing the school along and acknowledged that it was our fault for getting as far as we did in our discussions. Stacey thanked me for this. She saw how I was taking JumboTek's decision personally. Her eyes twinkled as she told me not to worry so much just because JumboTek US pulled the plug on allowing the school to be called a J-Academy. As a STEAM school, they would fulfill their vision.

The determination of the school leaders was an inspiration. Our JumboTek Canada team pivoted as well to help the school in whatever capacity we could with volunteering and community grants. We also created a full-year program to support the Grade 9's with mentoring and workplace visits, similar to what a J-Academy school would have done. It was a bit of a rogue move, for sure. But Maeve was a fearless leader. I told her about the button the girls had made, and she laughed.

One of our Technology Wednesday school visits had the students coding to demonstrate how sensors monitor African wildlife. A student shyly asked me for help because he didn't know how to do the copy that was part of the exercise. I explained he could select the code with the CTRL+A key combination, copy it with the CTRL+C keys, and paste it with the CTRL+V keys. He asked me where the CTRL key was. I realized that not all students have access to computers, and a coding class takes a level of familiarity for granted. A few students were done already. From this boy's point of view, I could see that it would be easy to compare and then despair of catching up. By having so many JumboTek volunteers, we gave each student the level of attention they needed, so no one felt left behind. I showed him where the control key was on his keyboard, and after the select, copy and paste commands, he ran the compiler, and it worked. Watching your code spit out the right results is one of the best feelings ever. It was a win for him and the school. As an engineer and mother, this work was very close to my heart.

Even though it was not a J-Academy, JumboTek was still vital to the school. Full-time people organized their work so they could travel to the school. Indirectly we showed students the tech world was diverse just by the mix of JTekkers who came. The volunteers got so much out of this relationship as well. It was a win all around.

NATIONAL MINDFULNESS

While I navigated the ups and downs with the school, mindfulness continued to help me keep the stress at bay. To have some formal training, I enrolled in the Applied Mindfulness Meditation certificate at the University of Toronto (U of T). It was nurturing to be with compassionate teachers and a community of like-minded people. The mindfulness practices and breakout discussions in the classroom helped me through a lot of my stress at work. We came from different sectors such as the corporate world, teaching, and medicine. It was really fun to be novices together in the meditations we learned. An ex-airline executive started laughing because we all looked like Zombies as we walked mindfully around the hallway. We were timing our steps to a slow in-breath and a slow out-breath, so it was like walking in slow motion. I was worried I'd topple over or step on the person's heel in front of me. A big group of slow walkers would have been a frightening sight.

The facilitators embodied mindfulness and showed me, by example, how to be a teacher of mindfulness in a Western business setting. This program helped me with imposter syndrome when I had to stand on stage and lead a meditation at one of our all-company meetings. I was in person at headquarters in Ottawa, Ontario, but the session was live-streamed to offices across the country. It might have been the first time employees meditated on a scale like this in our history. To centre myself, I went into the Mindfulness room and played "The Best" on my iPhone. Singing the lyrics the way I had learned in that long ago Quest empowerment seminar helped me drop some of the fear. Sophia rewrote my cue cards in artist markers with cute illustrations to inspire me. I went on stage, spoke to a few slides, then closed my eyes in front of everyone to meditate. One time I thought I'd fall off the stage. But mindfulness of my emotions helped calm me, and I was able to complete the meditation practice. So many people approached me afterwards and thanked me or said how great they felt after meditating. It was a really good feeling to overcome my fears to help others.

SAWUBONA

One day, I joined a Webex video conference with a group of coaches from the Coaching Pod. The word *Sawubona* was on the screen. The organizer explained that today's meeting would start with the Zulu greeting. There were about twenty of us on the screen, each a little rectangle from many different countries. We were diverse in appearance and common in humanity. We had come together to create a new coaching program at JumboTek to train employees to be coaches so we could support each other more. All of us were volunteers. That is how caring JTekkers can be.

Today was a status meeting to check in with trainers and discuss any challenges. Our fantastic leader, a Black woman from JumboTek US who led with her heart, explained Sawubona to us. It was a simple but profound practice. One at a time, we picked someone, looked into their eyes, and said, "I see you." They replied, "I exist." Then that person would do the same to another until everyone had been greeted with the two phrases.

Orland Bishop, a community leader at the Global Oneness Project, explains Sawubona "as an invitation to a deep witnessing and presence. This greeting forms an agreement to affirm and investigate the mutual potential and obligation that is present in a given moment.... This 'seeing' is essential to human freedom."

Looking into the eyes of another human to greet them was freeing and loving. Many of us had tears come to our eyes. We said essentially the same thing as the Haudenosaunee Thanksgiving Address, Greetings to the Natural World — "now our minds are one." It is a gift to be able to connect to people like this at work. These communities of mindfulness and coaching helped make the uncertainty at work and the disappointment of not partnering with the school less hurtful.

CHAPTER 18

Yard Sale

Although I had my share of close calls, I never confronted death as a real possibility. I don't remember the childhood accidents of breaking my arm under the falling bookcase or passing out after hitting my head on the bottom of the pool. I wasn't scared of the open-heart surgery or being in the hospital because the staff at SickKids made it so much fun. On a business trip to Kalamazoo, Michigan, I hit black ice and rolled an SUV off Highway 401 near London, Ontario. I barely had time to recognize that the car was airborne after skidding into the snowbank on the shoulder of the road. When I opened my eyes, I was in the ditch, thankfully right side up. A few months later, I walked down the stairs at work and missed the first step, again going airborne. I woke up face down at the bottom of the concrete staircase with co-workers all around me. Both of my work accidents happened too fast for me to think, "I could die right now," and both times I walked away without even a scratch.

That changed in 2017 when I had an accident in the middle of the night in my own home. "Yard sale" is a slang term used by skiers and snowboarders. It's used when they see someone on the slopes who crashes, wiping out in the snow. Upon such a spectacular fall, their gear goes flying. It looks like they are having a yard sale of poles, mitts, hats, and goggles spread out all over the ground. People who witness this from the ski lifts or coming down the slopes yell "yard sale" to acknowledge the crashed person.

As the strain at work built up, I had insomnia and digestive issues. I would wake up at two or three in the morning, worried about whether the school partnership would be cancelled. Or I would get upset about how Rosie was treated, thinking about how I could do a better job of standing up for her at work. Sometimes I would literally get an upset stomach in the night. Then I had my own yard sale, which ended in a call to 911 and a trip to the ER.

That night, I woke up and was unable to fall back to sleep. I went downstairs to make a cup of tea, felt my stomach gurgle, and went straight to the toilet. I sat there, nothing happening except for painful cramps. I felt lightheaded, then blacked out. I can only guess that I fell forward and hit my forehead on the powder room vanity.

When I woke up on the bathroom floor, I was face down and confused. I didn't know I had a concussion and couldn't think clearly. I saw vomit mixed with bright red blood and assumed it meant imminent death. I didn't know the blood was from a deep cut on my forehead because I didn't remember hitting the counter.

That was the moment I confronted my death.

It was urgent for me to say goodbye to Tom. I dragged myself out of the bathroom into the hallway to call for him. I didn't want him to find me dead when he woke up and it was too late. I was driven by this need to say goodbye, and I yelled, "Tom! Tom! Tom!" until I heard him reply at which point I slumped back into my daze.

Tom walked into my yard sale of blood and vomit, with me toppled over, unable to hold myself up against the wall. My nightgown had rolled up as I dragged myself to the hallway, and my underwear was still down around my knees. He literally found me as a mess on the floor. Tom told me later I wasn't coherent and couldn't tell him what had happened. I would not cooperate to get into the car to drive to the hospital. He had to call 911 to get me out of the house safely. Later I thought about what I would be going through if I had to dial 911 for someone I loved. It would be a terrifying experience, one I hope to never have, but it's one I gave to Tom.

Jessica had just turned fourteen and was about to get up for swim practice. Tom woke her up and told her to cancel with the parent who was doing carpool so she could be there when Sophia woke up. My family tells me I was very agitated because it was Sophia's birthday, and I was distressed not to be there. I kept asking Jessica to tell her I was sorry as I was taken out of the house.

THE VAGUS NERVE SPEAKS UP

The cause of the fainting, I was told at the ER, was likely a vasovagal syncope. According to the Mayo Clinic, a vasovagal syncope occurs when you faint after your body overreacts to certain triggers, such as the sight of blood or extreme emotional distress. The trigger causes your heart rate and blood pressure to drop suddenly, which leads to reduced blood flow to the brain and loss of consciousness. The doctor recommended I follow up with a cardiologist, especially given that I'd had heart surgery. He told me to go home and follow a list of activities for concussion recovery.

I had the makings of a one-inch scar over my eye from a cut that they had glued shut, and my head hurt a lot. The vomit and blood had dried in my hair, and all I wanted to do was go home and shower.

When I called my parents, Mom was shocked that another accident had happened. Dad was sick with worry and told me that I should never go downstairs in the middle of the night — just stay in bed where it's safe, he implored.

I followed up with my family doctor, Dr. Joshi, who explained that the vagus nerve ran from my brain to my torso. If this nerve is overstimulated, it can cause blood vessels to dilate, especially in the lower regions where I was feeling the cramps in my stomach. The heart can temporarily slow down and stop feeding oxygen to the brain, which can lead to a loss of consciousness. Dr. Joshi asked me a few questions to ascertain why this happened. When she asked me about work, I didn't connect my upset stomach to the stress at work.

"Are you still working with the Indigenous community?" she asked. I don't know how she remembers these details from past appointments, but it makes me feel cared for.

"The school just launched last month," I told her. "It's been so much fun to be in the classroom with the students, and we have a school trip planned for them to visit the JumboTek offices soon. I'm also leading mindfulness at work which has been amazing."

"Meditation is so beneficial. Keep doing that. And how are the girls? And Tom?"

"They're all good. Just all the normal stress of family life and raising teenagers."

Dr. Joshi referred me to a cardiologist to ensure there wasn't an underlying heart issue. In the meantime, she explained I should not drink caffeine in the evening or during the night as it can stimulate an upset stomach. Instead, I could try a herbal tea like chamomile. Lastly, she said if I felt light-headed to put my head between my knees to prevent another fainting event.

I bought chamomile tea for the first time and stayed in bed when I woke up in the middle of the night, even if it meant hours of just lying there. I had really scared Tom, my kids, and my parents. I needed to get better for them and also to get myself back to work.

THE HEART SPEAKS UP

The first day back, I was not coping well. I was a bundle of nerves, sensitive to anything emotionally distressing. I didn't know it consciously, but I was not emotionally strong anymore. It was like I had no resilience. At home, I could blow up if Tom said something wrong. I think he walked on eggshells around me. Then at work, I blew things out of proportion, spiraled, and struggled for control.

In one such occurrence, I became distraught when Rosie wasn't invited to a team appreciation event. The only thing I could think about was how unfair and callous it was for the team to exclude her. I didn't want to go to the event but still did. I recall sitting at the table in the restaurant and becoming so sad and trying to hold the tears in. I could feel them well up and hurried to the bathroom before anyone saw me openly crying. I wet the coarse brown paper towel sheets in cold water and put them under my eyes to lessen the redness. I swallowed down the tears because I knew at one level that my reaction was way over the top. The intensity of my emotions and my lack of control frightened me. When the tears finally stopped, I went into a numb emotional state to get through the rest of the evening. I went home early, and from that moment on, I could not shake off the heavy sadness I felt.

The cardiologist appointment came up. I told the elderly white-haired doctor about my brother's stroke, and he said my fainting was likely unrelated, but he wanted to see me annually. "Your heart is strong," he reassured me after listening to it and reviewing the ultrasound. But he told me my blood pressure was high and said I should see my family doctor about it. My blood pressure had always been low, so that did seem odd to me.

When I saw Dr. Joshi, she suggested I wear a monitor for twenty-four hours to find out if my blood pressure was high consistently or just when I was in her office. I wore it even at work, and it took a reading every twenty minutes. My results were a hypertension diagnosis. My heart was talking to me, telling me something was very wrong. Even with the group practices and meditation, which strengthened me and added positivity to my life, my heart was not working as it should. Yet maybe without the meditation and the loving communities I was part of, the vasovagal syncope could have been a heart attack or stroke. Perhaps one part of my work protected me while another made me ill. However, the part that made me sick was taking the lead.

CHAPTER 19

Broken

Going back to the workplace with a hypertension diagnosis had me on edge, as I was worried about my health now. Then multiple things started happening on the job that made me feel like I was going to lose my sanity.

Since my unpleasant phone discussion with Vinnie about his harassment, he had stayed out of my way for the most part. It wasn't unusual to cross paths, so I wasn't expecting it to be an issue during a routine department meeting. But as soon as I saw him in my more fragile state, his presence seemed bigger and more oppressive, even though he had not approached me or singled me out. We were in one of the new meeting spaces, with glass partitions, sleek white bar-height desks, and brightly coloured walls. It should have been a happy, open, creative space. But I felt trapped.

Get it together, I thought, as I started to panic unreasonably. I focused on calming my breathing as everyone took their seats. I saw a few people between Vinnie and me, which made me feel better.

An announcement was made about an upcoming reorganization. I scanned the hierarchy diagram on the PowerPoint slide to see where I was. That's when I saw my name and his name, together on a small team. It would be too intimate. I freaked out internally, though I just sat there. There were murmurs as others took in who would be where in the department now.

I didn't dare look around to meet anyone's eyes because I didn't know what to do with the panicky feelings. I was already jittery just being in the same room with him, and now we'd be working together as part of a small team? The woman beside me tugged at my elbow and whispered that I was now going to report to the JumboTek US department in charge of managing the J-Academy schools. This threw me for a loop because our Canadian team had a different, kinder, and more polite culture than the US counterpart. I didn't want to change bosses and lose Maeve. I felt like my working team had changed for the worse. I felt confused and knew I didn't have the mental faculties to deal with this level of stress.

I went home and hoped the weekend would give me perspective. That following Tuesday, I was emotional because the then minister of Indigenous services the Honourable Jane Philpott was visiting the STEAM school, and it was a proud moment for the school. JumboTek could not be there formally, but I drove to the school to show my support. As I watched the students give their speeches, I had mixed feelings of happiness and anger. I felt so strongly that JumboTek should have been there in a more official role, publicly supporting the school with the government and school leaders. It was depressing to see this turn of events, and I wanted at least to have my presence there as a silent show of support.

The sadness in my chest grew bigger. After all of the time I had spent connecting with my body through mindfulness, I knew something was not right. It scared me much more than the fainting/concussion incident when I thought I was about to die. This time it was my mind that was going. A departmental reorganization and politics were nothing new, but I was not myself. I called and made an appointment for the next day with Dr. Joshi.

MY SUPERWOMAN SELF UNRAVELS

As I waited in the exam room, I wondered what to tell her. How could I explain my feelings of detachment or my sudden loss of motivation? How could I explain that there was a Shadow Sunita now, a woman who lacked all of the can-do attitude that had fueled my overachieving ways since I was a young child?

Dr. Joshi entered and greeted me warmly yet directly. "Tell me, Sunita, what's going on?"

I searched for how to put these messy feelings into words. I told her about the anxiety and about how I dreaded every workday, and had trouble even stepping foot into the office. I told her that I was crying at work and at home. I admitted that I was having horrible, dark moods and that it was hard on Tom and the kids too. I told her that even with meditation, I was worried that this had gone beyond what I could deal with on my own.

She asked me to say more. I told her they were small things, but as I struggled to put them into words, I could see they were not small at all. I told her I had been getting more and more anxious for months, wondering if I would be ordered to drop the partnership with the Indigenous school. I felt like I was part of a lie and my sense of honour, truth and integrity were under fire. Not just with the students who I had met in orientation and gotten to know at various school events, but with the adults, like Stacey, to whom I had given my word. I could not bear to go back on a promise of this magnitude. I could not bear to betray any relationship, much less ones that had been betrayed in our shared history in Canada. I felt intensely that the way JumboTek treated the school was a continuation of the patriarchal and colonial mindset that had caused generations of trauma. And I was distraught to have been part of it.

I told her I thought these were overblown emotional reactions but that I wasn't sure how to stop them. I told her I hated that my company put out this perception that integrity, transparency, and respect were priorities, when I could see firsthand that it wasn't that way behind the scenes. And I couldn't take it anymore. I'm sure I was all over the place trying to convey what was in my messed-up mind. Yet she was giving me the space to let it all out.

Through my tears I explained how it felt to see Rosie being treated in a way that hurt her. And I talked about Vinnie and how panicky I was to even be near him, despite the fact that there were no more issues. I said I was at the point where I could feel my heart start to race as soon as he entered the room, and how my body just froze up in his presence. I told my doctor that it felt like I was always close to tears because my emotions were so amped up and I couldn't control them, while at other times I felt totally numb.

I was so confused pouring out these thoughts that I'm unsure how she understood anything I said. But she looked kindly at me. And in the silence,

I said the thing I didn't want to say. I admitted that I didn't know if I could do my job any longer.

And with those words, it felt like my identity dissolved.

A STARK CHOICE: HEALTH OR JOB

After listening to me unload everything that was wrong with my work life, Dr. Joshi gave me a stark choice. She said, "Sunita, you have to choose between your health and your job." This pierced my brain fog, and I became alert. Somehow, when she said it, it became real.

Dr. Joshi had me fill out a short questionnaire designed to measure depression and anxiety. I answered the simple questions about how I'd been feeling over the last two weeks, which put me as mildly depressed. For the next steps, Dr. Joshi did not want me to go back to work and worsen the depression. She suggested I take two weeks off work, which I could legally do in Ontario with a sick note from her. She also said I didn't have to talk to anyone at work, explain my medical diagnosis, or justify my absence. I sent an email to Maeve, with a photo of the note attached, explaining that I would be off starting that day, February 7, until February 16. I would return after the Family Day holiday on February 20. While my mind was conflicted about leaving so abruptly and without explanation, I was relieved to have this time. Unlike when I'd taken time off to recover from the concussion, I did not want to hurry back.

HEALING WITH KINDNESS

I slept and meditated and cut off all contact with work. After a few days, my blood pressure was normal. I was amazed to see that a condition like hypertension could ease off outside of the work environment. I felt better with meditation and being away from the stressors. I didn't have the dread hanging over me of thinking about stepping into the office, and that alone relieved me. I was feeling calmer and more centred than I had been for a long time. I had a sense of being capable again in my life.

Rosie sent me a bouquet of pink and white carnations, a symbol of sisterhood. Her card read, "In the cherry blossom's shade, there's no such thing as a stranger. By [Kobayashi] Issa." Rosie adored flowers.

Anders, the man who loved my stick drawing of mindfulness, emailed a prayer he had written for me. He said the entire group was praying for me. I printed his beautiful words and put the prayer on the fridge where the whole family could see it. He wrote, "Please bless Sunita, Tom, Jessica, and Sophia on their wonderful adventure together.... And let your love flow to them, and through them, to each other to create a truly incredible family beyond their wildest dreams, bursting at the seams with great love, faith, joy, generosity, selflessness, patience, forgiveness, laughter, peace, fun, adventure, and then even more love, faith and joy all over again!... In Jesus' amazing name we pray, Amen." At the time, I could not fathom ever feeling joy like this again, but it meant so much that someone else had faith in us as a family.

I could feel the outpouring of love when I walked into my kitchen and saw the flowers and the prayer. These were gifts filled with positive, healing energy that seemed to flow into me.

***

As my first day back approached my anxiety built up. On the holiday Monday, I had a panic attack and lost control of myself and my breathing for a few seconds. Still, I felt strong enough to return to work and figure out the new organizational changes. I felt certain I could do it.

I was wrong.

THE END OF WORK

I parked in the covered garage and walked to the stairs leading up to the main floor. When I got to the garage door, I felt a dread creep into my body and slowed down. Just being close to the office seemed to make the strength I had gained during my sick leave evaporate. I had walked this path thousands of times in eighteen years. I usually bounded up the stairs to the main elevators, impatient to get to my desk. But as the elevator ascended and I forced myself out, panic weakened my body. I got to the turnstile that allowed entry one at a time to prevent tailgaters, but I didn't want to step in. It seemed what was on the other side was going to swallow me up.

My breathing felt constricted. I tried to lift my badge to the security pad, but my hand wouldn't budge. I knew right away that it was dread that was stopping me. I was trying to force myself to walk into a toxic environment, and my body was putting up a big Stop sign. Finally I took a breath and pressed my access badge against the electronic lock. As I crossed over into the office, I wondered if people would ask me about my time off. I felt intensely private about my sick period. I didn't want to explain myself because I just didn't have the energy to do it, and I was afraid of how they might judge me. Would they ask to hear details? What could I tell them? My mental health wasn't fully functioning, but I didn't want to disclose this to management.

As it was these fears came true almost immediately. Within the first hour, a senior manager tried to persuade me to talk. It was like he discounted my preference not to talk about it. He wanted to know, and that's what was more important. I felt like he violated my right to privacy. This triggered me to feel unsafe, and the feeling of wanting to get out of the building rose up in me. The tears seemed to be right at the surface. I didn't want to cry, and the only way to avoid that was not to talk about it.

I escaped to find a desk in the maze of cubicles open for those visiting the office and hid there the rest of the day. I tried not to cross paths with anyone from upper management. Finally, it was time to go home and walk the opposite way back to my car. This time I felt relief on exiting the turnstile. I knew for sure I didn't have the will to enter the office again.

But I was heavy with worry and guilt about abandoning Rosie, my mindfulness and coaching roles, and most of all, the STEAM school. I called Rosie to let her know, and she promised she would be fine and said she would take care of the current students and plan for the upcoming Grade 9 cohort. Rosie was worried about me and assured me that she and the school would be fine. She said she would miss me there and had always felt protected when I was around. She thanked me for being her friend at work.

The next day, I drove to the school to let the principal know in person I was leaving work. My mind was swirling with thoughts about how I was yet another person to let the Indigenous community down. In that distracted state, I had a close call on the highway. It reminded me of how narrowly I had escaped my other accident with the SUV rollover on the way to Michigan. I was shaken that my emotional state could lead to poor driving.

I knew with this sign that I had to stop work because I couldn't function properly anymore.

The kind principal sat with me, much like Dr. Joshi had, and listened as I poured my heart out. I was in tears because I didn't want my going to negatively impact the school's success. He said he fully supported me in putting my health first and that my kids needed me. He told me I had done so much, and it was time to focus on my health now. I said goodbye to him, his kindness and compassion staying with me.

Having ensured the people I cared about knew why I was leaving, I made an appointment with Dr. Joshi. I told her about the panic attack and the close call on the highway. I told her I didn't feel safe at work. She agreed I needed to stop working and start a disability leave and wrote me another sick note. I was so incredibly relieved to be out of the workplace. With this decision, I fully accepted I wasn't going to be fixed in a few days. I sent the note to Maeve and let go of my work life.

It was time to accept that I was unwell. It was time to figure out how to live with a broken heart and broken mind.

CHAPTER 20

Surrender

If I could describe the depression, it would be as a grey numbness that buffered the sharpness of hurtful things. From the perspective of a healthy mind, I now see my nervous system was on fire from the turmoil of the organizational changes and the uncertainty of our business direction with the school leaders.

Going on disability leave was like a permission slip to drop all the balls I held up in the air. I was exhausted, drained of all energy. In meditation, the phrase "be the watcher" means to move your attention to a zone that watches your thoughts flow by. The watcher observes what is unfolding in terms of sensations, feelings, and thoughts. Before I got sick, I remember my mind being busy planning and thinking ahead. But now, as I watched my mind in its depressed state, it was dull and didn't care about things. Before the depression, my mind was like a city packed with streets, buildings, and people, running around, getting stuff done. Now it was a ghost town.

I no longer felt capable, motivated, or in control. Not wanting to be in control and not having the next thing to achieve was how I knew I was no longer *me*. I had turned from a positive, can-do person to one who saw little hope. The vibrancy of life was just gone. I could smile on the outside to my family and make lunches, do laundry, and go grocery shopping, but apart from taking care of the necessities, I lay around in apathy. Tom would come home, and I'd still be in my pajamas, lying on the sofa or working on a puzzle at the dining room table.

My ability to regulate my feelings was gone too. I was emotional, irrational, and overly sensitive. I got upset with people and made drama where there didn't need to be drama. It was hard for Tom and the girls to deal with such a sad, deadened version of me. They loved me and hoped I would get well, though I didn't have the energy to explain to the girls I was suffering from depression. It wasn't because I had a stigma about being depressed. I had learned about mental illness at work. JumboTek had even sponsored me to take the Queen's University certificate in Workplace Mental Health Leadership. I knew this was a real illness, not something to be ashamed of. However, I didn't tell my kids, parents, or brothers because I didn't have the mental energy to explain it or deal with their emotions, questions, or well-wishes. I just wanted to retreat into my shell, where it was dark, safe, and empty of all relationship load. Looking back now, I wonder if depression hormones are something my body triggered to ease emotional pain. It felt like a depressive state of mind was a much safer place than the real world.

FINDING PEACE IN DOING NOTHING

Being the watcher of my depression during meditation helped both to ease my depression and let me also notice that it was easing up. Jill Bolte Taylor, the same scientist I thought of when my brother had the stroke, says an emotion lasts roughly a minute and a half when you watch it. I told myself that the worst pain could only exist for ninety seconds before it would shift into something different. Ninety seconds was all I had to get through before things changed, and that seemed doable. As I watched my mind, I greeted each feeling or thought with, "I see you," the Sawubona greeting. After a week or so of just sitting around while the house was empty of my family, and having no energy but to be the watcher, I could feel myself coming out of the fog and wanting to be better. As in Orland Bishop's description of Sawubona, watching my mind opened a potential in the present moment for better things, and reminded me of an obligation to my highest value, which was to love my family. A part of me spoke up in the stillness and said I needed to find help and get back to a life of joy.

My journal entries show I was seeking to be happy again. Just giving up control and admitting I wanted help was an important step. Asking for help was a big lift out of the depression because the seeker mindset is more open-minded and action-oriented. I think it was grace that answered my call for help. It was the same grace that I encountered in my dream of Japan, in the hours after my first yoga class, on the hike at Cades Cove, and in the hospital with my brother. This time, grace came with friends, and brought the right people to help me.

FINDING PEACE IN WALKING ON MOTHER EARTH

One of the people who showed up to help me was Thich Nhat Hanh. I had heard about Thich Nhat Hanh from other mindfulness leaders at JumboTek, but I didn't know much about his way of mindfulness. During my sick leave I decided to listen to his audio book *Peace Is Every Step* because one of the things I did do was go outside for short walks. Walking meditation practice pays attention to the ball of one foot coming down as the heel of the other lifts up while breathing in sync with the movements. This is the same kind of meditation that had my friend laughing at our University of Toronto class because it does make you look a bit like an extra from *The Walking Dead*. I remember walking around my one-kilometer block following the instructions to walk mindfully. It was a still grey February morning. The street was empty, so I didn't worry about terrifying anyone with my stilted walking. I could feel peace from just touching the earth in the space between those one thousand steps and breaths. Step by step, my mind narrowed into the present moment of a foot touching the ground, leaving the ground, and connecting again. My mind was soothed like it was being rocked by the repeating movements. Thich Nhat Hanh said this kind of walking connects you back to where you came from, the loving energy of Mother Earth. Walking meditation became a daily practice where I could find reprieve from my heavy mind.

FINDING PEACE FROM COMPASSIONATE LISTENERS

As I opened up to needing help, I remembered JumboTek's Employee Assistance Program. I had told JTekkers of this benefit many times during mindfulness talks or coaching sessions. I explained my situation to the agent when I called the toll-free number and asked if they could help me. The answer was yes, they could.

The agent suggested a couple of books to help with diet and exercise, which can support mental wellness. They sent me, free of charge, *YOU: The Owner's Manual* by Michael F. Roizen, M.D. and Mehmet C. Oz, M.D., and *10 Steps to Healthy Eating* by Leslie Beck, R.D. The agent also offered a career counselor to help me find a job that would make me happy. Lastly, based on how sad I was feeling, I asked to talk to a professional to see if there was a deeper issue that mindfulness and diet could not address. I'm a big believer in mindfulness, but I also believe that therapy could be needed as well. The agent helping me said they would pay for sessions with a licensed psychotherapist. I asked for a female therapist because I didn't feel safe around men after that last year at work, or at least safe around dominant male energy. I was told that there would be a long wait for a woman and that if I wanted something sooner, I would need to meet with a man. I reluctantly agreed.

My plan was to practice mindfulness, start therapy, get well through diet and exercise, and find some hope again for my work identity with the career coach. It was a multi-pronged approach and a lot to take on at once. But I told myself I would slow down if I got overwhelmed; I did not want any more yard sales, or Mack trucks, by going too fast and not heeding my body's signals.

I was inspired by the two books and changed my diet to more fresh food and less sugar and salt. The career counselor and I met over the phone. He was empathetic when I told him how much stress I'd felt. I think I saw him as an expert in the world of work, and his validating my feelings and responding with compassion helped me feel seen. Although his coaching services involved administering career aptitude questionnaires, his true help was to recommend *Man's Search for Meaning* by Viktor Frankl. He said he found inspiration in this book and hoped it would resonate with me too.

The book did resonate because it was a story of losing things held dear and finding out who you are without them. Frankl chronicles his experiences as a concentration camp inmate and uses those experiences to develop a new branch of psychoanalysis that he called logotherapy. This is a psychotherapeutic method for finding meaning in all forms of existence, even terrible ones, and thus finding a reason to continue living. I wrote in my journal that the prisoners lost their name, health, possessions, loved ones, dignity, and social status. I wrote, *What is left? What has permanence and consistency of perception? The Observer is all that is left. In conditions of suffering, when all of value is gone — body, wealth, identity is stripped away, the Observer has access to joy. To choose a better action. To believe a kinder thought.*

Viktor Frankl's words reminded me that the watcher I connected with in meditation is the one constant in life and my path to joy. I started focusing on things that brought me joy, one of which was the purple pen I wrote my journal entry in.

Then it was time for my first therapist appointment ever. I drove to the small plaza Google Maps directed me to, hesitant about whether I could trust a stranger. I found a warm and compassionate man who spoke with a soothing Nigerian accent. I instantly felt he was a good person, and my body relaxed. He even asked me if it was okay that he closed the door. Maybe he sensed I was skittish and nervous. In the end, he was the perfect person to have come into my life. As a Black man, he knew the inequality with which a minority culture can treat men and women. I talked about the unfair treatment of women in my family, about women like Rosie at work, and about the power tactics at work. As the words and tears left me, he compassionately witnessed this pain. I felt lighter with each visit.

Thich Nhat Hanh, Viktor Frankl, the career counselor, and my therapist were teachers who showed me the way of compassion. In response, my jittery nervous system calmed down and felt safer. I felt less depressed and more hopeful, but I was still far from feeling true peace or joy. Something was still broken. Finding a measure of safety and calm only amplified the call to keep looking inward.

FINDING PEACE IN THE WORK

One of the things I knew was deeply transformative for painful thoughts was The Work, the process developed by Byron Katie that I had learned about in my coach training. The process involves answering four questions about how you judge a situation and then turning the statements around to see them from different perspectives. The breakthrough is to depersonalize the past so it doesn't ruin the present experience of life. By the end, the negative emotional state has shifted permanently to a more positive state. The hurtful experience is often fully healed without needing the person who hurt you to do a thing. I've done the process many times since learning of it in 2013. Byron Katie's four simple questions seem to cut a path of peace through frozen mental patterns.

I felt frozen in blame and judgment thinking that was keeping me stuck. As I got more of my mental faculties back, I knew I had to release myself from holding on to past events. I did the process for the people I judged for not supporting the school enough, for not being respectful to Rosie, and for not protecting me from Vinnie's harassment. Through writing out the judgments, seeing how they made me feel, and who I would be if I didn't have those judgments, I came to see that my view was not locked in stone. I could change my thoughts to kinder ones. I forgave all of the people I judged to be toxic, one by one, by seeing that what they did was not personal. In doing so, I got them out of my head. This was good work because it cleared up a lot of emotional pain, but not enough to lift away the depression.

ANTIDEPRESSANTS

I finally faced the fact that despite the healing effects of counseling, meditation, and The Work, I was not getting better. Journal entries after I left work show me feeling alone, having bad days, and not coping with life, even with the positive things I tried to do. I desperately wanted my relationships with Tom and the girls to return to normal. My journal entries showed such dark, ugly thoughts about feeling unloved and disrespected that I knew didn't have a basis in reality. I was scared of this Shadow Sunita who was alien to the loving, peaceful person I wanted to be.

I had to admit that I was not making enough progress. It was now three weeks since I had stopped working. I wasn't sure how a disability claim works to determine pay. The insurance company, Best-Life Insurance Co, would get involved now to review my case, and it was a process I could not control. However, within my control was the decision of whether or not I should go on antidepressants. I went to see Dr. Joshi on March 19 to have that conversation. She gave me yet another questionnaire to test for depression and anxiety, and we could see my mental state had gotten worse, going from mild to moderate depression. I made the decision that antidepressants were the next step for me to get my life back. I would keep going with therapy and mindfulness, but it was time for medication. Dr. Joshi said I would need to see a psychiatrist to figure out the right dosage and medication, but that would take a month to get an appointment. In the meantime, she would prescribe a mild antidepressant.

LETTING GO

Walking out of Dr. Joshi's office with a prescription for antidepressants was my moment of surrender. I turned control over to the pills to fix me, and a weight lifted off of me. I went to pick up groceries at The Real Canadian Superstore, and I felt a lightness of spirit that I hadn't felt in a long time. Spring decor was out, and I stopped by the melamine plates in pretty patterns of cacti and hummingbirds. It felt fresh and new, and I wanted to feel like that. I bought a full set of the pink and green dishes to celebrate spring, so different from the white Corelle dinnerware at home. I hadn't even taken one pill yet, but I already felt better with the prescription in my purse.

After stopping at the pharmacy, I went home, put the pill bottle on the kitchen counter, and looked at it for a long moment. I was about to be a person with depression severe enough to require medication. It was like I was being inducted into a group, like becoming a citizen or member, and there was no going back. I let go of the fear of being a sick person on medication and swallowed a pill. Once I knew the medicine was inside of me, going to work on my brain chemistry, I surrendered control to it, and a feeling of detachment crept in.

March 20, 2018, Journal Entry: *Could the antidepressants be working so fast? I feel detached from reacting.* At the end of the day, I wrote, *I did a lot today. Many of the career coaching worksheets. Applying for jobs and following up. We all had a great dinner — no fighting. We used the new dishes. It was pretty and fun. I feel detached and calm.*

March 24, 2018, Journal Entry: *Still feeling really numbed. Like I'm observing myself.*

March 25, 2018, Journal Entry: *Exercising and meditating. Then chores — Sophia's Communion book started, tax forms and cleaning the basement. Keep busy and not think about sad things.*

I started to look for a new job at this time, knowing I'd never go back to JumboTek. I just knew that after all the times I had come back to JumboTek to find a better way to work, this was the end. It was too dangerous to play with my mental health. Fighting at work to have integrity with business clients was one thing. But it had become too difficult for me when it came to vulnerable people. Between how Rosie was treated and how the school was caught in the politics, I knew it wasn't right, and I'd responded in every way I could to protect them. But in that fight, I somehow lost my balance and mental health. The situation with Vinnie was too much for me to handle. JumboTek was not a psychologically safe place for me. I knew if I went back, it was like going back to an unhealthy, abusive relationship that felt good sometimes and bad at other times. I wanted to be healthy, and I couldn't do it in a place that promoted itself one way and acted in a different way.

As one of my friends says, "You can't *not* breathe the air." The air was too toxic now. The time away from work during my sick leave had reminded me of what it was like to be in peace, and I needed that.

My decision was clear but so was the fear that I might be without pay. Even though financially we could have lived without my income for a while, the need to have a job is very ingrained from my culture. I felt scared not having a job lined up. This time, I decided to be an independent contractor to stay psychologically safe at work. I hoped the contractor mindset would keep me away from politics and the power dysfunctions of tech companies. An ex-colleague helped me get my first interview.

March 27, 2018, Journal Entry: *Job interview at* _____. *It went well. It will be nice to work with* _____ *and get away from corporate politics. Saw* Black Panther *with Jessica. Evening was a bit strange.... I still feel detached, uncaring and not interested.*

March 28, 2018, Journal Entry: *Still so detached.*

FINDING PEACE IN SPEAKING THE TRUTH

At the end of March, an insurance caseworker from Best-Life called me to discuss my claim. She said I had to complete a personal statement to describe why I can't work. As well there was a form my doctor had to sign. Once all the paperwork was submitted, Best-Life would call me back with either an approval or denial of the claim. Not all claims are accepted, and I did not want that to happen to me.

I spent several days carefully documenting my responses to the three questions on the statement I had to complete:

1. Please describe your present illness or injury and how it prevents you from working.
2. Include a description of which duties of your job you are unable to perform because of your illness or injury.
3. As well, list the duties of your job you are able to perform.

For the first question, I listed the stressors I encountered, tying them back to several factors in the Standard. Because the Standard was written for an audience like the caseworker, I leveraged the wording of several of the factors for psychosocial safety to articulate how the job stress led to me feeling psychologically unsafe. I wanted my statement to be logical and valid from a safety perspective and to be taken seriously. It was also my chance to speak the truth in full.

For question 2, part of my answer was, "I feel unsafe to be at work on the same team with a colleague who I experienced harassment with last year." I also wrote, "My main duty to bring the J-Academy school model to Canada is unclear with respect to Indigenous Canada and the 'on-again'/'off-again' policies that seem to shift all the time — I do not feel until we have clarity between Canada and US senior executives in writing that I can work to deliver this school model in Canada because I cannot string people along when it comes to promises of better education and economic prosperity as discussed in TRC Call to Action #92 for corporate Canada."

For question 3, I simply wrote, "At this time I do not feel I am able to perform my work duties."

I thought about whether I should see a lawyer because it was clear from my statement I had a case. However, legal action would be much more draining than writing something in the privacy of my home. It would be nice to have financial compensation, even if it was a severance package. But I had no emotional capital to initiate such a discussion, replay my story for multiple people, and defend it. I was just digging my way out of the depression and didn't want to undertake a fight. I had to focus now on the antidepressants working and not add stress to my life in any way. I chose not to pursue legal action and stay only with the disability claim.

I emailed the personal statement to the caseworker, hoping she would believe me and support my claim. The act of writing the truth was therapeutic and freeing for me. I had been so emotional I hadn't trusted my emotions or perceptions. But seeing my experiences on paper and supported by the Standard, a best practice for mental health in the workplace, made me understand how much I had been injured.

I felt compassion for myself as I reread my statement. I hit the send button and put that truth out in the world. Next, I went to see Dr. Joshi for the other form to be filled out.

March 29, 2018, Journal Entry: *10 a.m. meeting with Dr. Joshi. She will sign the Best-Life short term disability papers. I came home and watched a movie. Lying on the sofa all afternoon. Went to pick up Jess after school in my pajamas. I do love seeing the girls after school.*

At this meeting, I told Dr. Joshi I was feeling better and not so unpredictable. She measured my blood pressure, which was now lower since I'd been away from work. She said to continue with the antidepressants until I met with the psychiatrist to confirm the dosage.

AN UNEXPECTED JOURNEY

I think documenting my experiences was cathartic. After submitting the personal statement for Best-Life, my energy seemed to rise.

April 1, 2018, Journal Entry: *Easter Sunday. The girls loved their Easter Scavenger Hunt. At church I thought of Lent and suffering. It feels like I'm coming out of the darkness and Easter Sunday today is a new beginning.*

I started to wonder if something other than the medicine was making me feel better. Was it a placebo effect happening? Did my getting better have to do with a doctor in a white coat giving me a prescription and nothing to do with the medicine? Before taking the path of antidepressants, a fairly long-term commitment, I needed to see if I was feeling better only because I had taken a pill and not because of what was in the pill.

I did something you are not supposed to do, and I would never recommend this to anyone. I decided to stop taking the antidepressants after just two weeks. Maybe the truth-telling through the claim process had changed me. But I knew something now for sure: I felt like a new person, and I wanted to live again. I was curious to go out into the world and meet people, a first since getting sick.

For some reason I felt inclined to search online for a meditation retreat. I knew from JumboTek and U of T that group meditation can add meaning and depth you don't get when you meditate alone. By sheer grace, I found a retreat in the tradition of Thich Nhat Hanh with a group from Toronto. It was in two days and within driving distance. The group was called True Peace Toronto, and that name just felt right. It was a silent retreat, which seemed scary, and registration was closed. But I still emailed the contact name, just in case. The following day I got an answer back saying there was a cancellation, and a spot was available. Without knowing anything about this meditation group or silent retreats, I said I would come. I wanted more of the peace I had gained while listening to Thich Nhat Hanh's audiobook.

I felt in my stomach that this was the next thing for me to do. My feet were as compelled to go to this retreat as they had been to touch the earth at Abrams Falls Trail in Cades Cove. I went to sleep unsure about the journey I would take, feeling deeply that the universe was orchestrating this to happen. Whatever came, I accepted not having control over the claim process or finding contract work.

I surrendered to not knowing and to allowing what came.

PART 5

Breakthrough

"The way out is in."
— Zen Master Thich Nhat Hanh

"It's not your job to like me, it's mine."
— Byron Katie

CHAPTER 21

Quiet

On the day of the retreat, I felt a mix of anxiety and excitement. I felt trepidation to be with a group of strangers in silence, but this retreat felt like something I should do. The weather seemed unsure of itself as well. April 6 should have been spring-like, but the land was still in the grips of an overcast and dreary winter. Tom hugged me goodbye as he left for work.

He said, "Be safe and call me the moment you get there." He pulled back from the hug, and his light blue eyes searched my dark brown ones for a sign that I was stable enough to take care of myself.

"These are all people from Toronto," I said. "I'm sure they're not a cult." This was probably the worst-case scenario in both our minds.

"Are you sure you'll be okay on your own with the kids?"

"Don't worry about a thing," Tom said. "We'll be fine. Take care of yourself and remember you have a family who loves you."

I could see he was worried about my physical safety and mental health. He knew that I'd been hard on myself for getting sick and for leaving my family with an Eeyore version of myself. I was glad to know that even if this retreat was a complete failure, I'd be coming back to a man who loved me enough to be patient with me.

His last words before setting out on his commute were about safety.

"If anything seems weird, just come home. Your Honda has snows on it and can drive through any weather."

He knew I was a nervous winter driver ever since the SUV rollover on the highway. Even though it was eighteen years ago, that memory snaps back in vivid detail whenever I'm in a car on a dicey driving day. I hadn't even realized this worry was on my mind, but he knew me. His concern for me and the support he gave me to leave our family and seek answers was a generous and loving gift.

The girls left for school. Sophia was annoyed and said she wouldn't miss me, Jessica wished me all the best with a hug. Sophia and I had a problematic teenage-parent relationship, and I was hurt by her words. I wanted a peaceful relationship with her, but I knew from Byron Katie and other teachers that I could not be at peace with anyone until I was at peace in my own thinking. I was much meaner to Mom as a teenager, and she responded with love and patience. I wanted to be able to give my daughters that kind of love.

In the empty house, the quiet felt soothing. As I tidied and finished the laundry, I wondered *What version of me will return to this house?* Although the crushing sadness had lifted somewhat after I tried the antidepressants and wrote the statement to the insurance company, I still wasn't fully myself.

After taking care of things for my family, I turned to pack for my trip, taking warm clothes for the weather and loose-fitting clothing for sitting meditation. I threw in a pair of pink house slippers, as shoes were not allowed in the retreat centre. I looked to my night table where I kept things I depended on. I grabbed my journal and joyful purple pen. I went to my meditation area and packed my cushion and polished stones, all of which I'd acquired during the U of T Applied Mindfulness Meditation program. During one of the classes, we watched a YouTube video of a Buddhist monk meditating on different qualities using the colour of the stone to stay present. After that class, I bought a few of my own to keep near me. The pink stone was to meditate on being fresh as a flower, the brown one as solid as a mountain, the blue one as fluid as water, and the white one as clear as air. Paying attention to their colour variations, coolness, smoothness, and shape help my mind settle and believe there is that element of goodness within me. I also took the get-well card Rosie had painted. Rosie had captured the cut blooms with the strokes of her palette knife and created a timeless bouquet for me. It reminded me of her love and kindness.

The retreat had guidelines apart from being in silence. The website had said reading wasn't allowed nor cell phones, except for emergency use. The food would be vegan with set mealtimes. I once heard someone say they resisted mindfulness because their mind was like a scary neighbourhood you don't walk alone in at 3:00 a.m. This resonated because it felt both scary and boring to be with my own thoughts for extended periods of time. I couldn't imagine not snacking in-between meals and not alleviating boredom with reading or browsing my phone. I would try my best to be without distractions, but still, I packed the beachy romance novel on my bedside table. A milk chocolate bar, a bag of almonds, and a couple chocolate chip granola bars from the kids' lunch stash also went into my bag. And that was it. I was ready to go. With my bags in the car, I embarked on the two-hour drive north to Midland, where I'd meet the group at Sugar Ridge Retreat Centre.

TRUSTING THE PROCESS

In the quiet of the car, I began to have doubts about putting myself in the hands of another organization. After leaving one toxic organization, it was a leap of faith to turn around and trust another one. I hoped their methods were not about setting up a hierarchy of yielding to someone else's higher position. I was done with that. This group, True Peace, didn't feel like the work organization I had left behind. There were no "bigwigs" or "important people" to make happy. Much of the drive was spent pushing down my anxieties and trying to replace them with positive thoughts. I needed this to be a process I could trust.

From what I had learned in the U of T program, Buddhism doesn't say that access to the Divine is controlled by a few. The Buddha wanted people to engage in a dynamic relationship with the true nature of reality without needing an intermediary expert. If I could paraphrase my understanding, it would be that the Buddha said, "I found a path out of suffering, and it's repeatable, but see for yourself. Take it as a starting point and make it work for you as an individual."

This felt comforting because, over the years, I had adapted the detailed processes of project management and seen how these methods led to successful projects. I know that following an established and proven process pays off many times over. I trusted that the same effect happened in the spiritual realm because Buddhism is a methodology, just like project management. Project management is based on communication as well as time and cost management principles that can be applied to meet any project goal. Instead of a work-oriented goal, though, I would be following the retreat structure to get to my end state of a healthy and vibrant mind that the antidepressants couldn't quite deliver.

But up to that point, I had learned about a secular and sanitized version of Buddhism designed to be acceptable to Western society. I was curious about its original, undiluted form, and wanted to know more about the traditional way it was meant to be learned. I wanted truth and integrity from all things, including meditation methods. This retreat seemed like it would give me access to the original way of teaching mindfulness meditation, something my Western teachers had kept behind the curtains. I trusted this was a tried-and-true, millennia-old process, and I wanted to experience it full-strength. If I came back and still required the antidepressants, I would say yes to them. However, I wanted to try this path to peace and well-being first.

DAY 1 - FRIDAY

Soon the city density fell away, and the landscape was replaced by more trees, large, dormant fields, and the odd cluster of homes. As the scenery became more open and natural, I started to feel freer. My responsibilities for laundry, grocery shopping, tidying the house were dropping away like the crowded neighbourhoods. It was a relief to leave behind the mental load of social interactions with family and friends.

The centre was at the end of a long driveway lined by wooded areas. A circular building with a bright red roof came into view, and with it, the calm I felt on the drive gave way to the anxiety of spending five days with a group of strangers in a tradition that I didn't know. I parked and texted Tom that I had arrived safely, keeping any hint of my trepidation out of the message. I entered the building and greeted an older woman in her sixties who smiled warmly.

"Hi, I'm Sunita," I said. "I'm the one who registered late."

"Oh, welcome! I'm Marg," she said. "I'm so happy we could fit you in, and that it all worked out."

She seemed genuinely delighted to have me there, and I breathed a sigh of relief.

She explained that I'd be sharing Cabin #5 with three other women. My name was written as "Sinit" on the paper she gave me, but I didn't correct it. People misspell my name all the time and it doesn't bother me but I didn't want her to feel bad. The paper also showed I was assigned to clean up after mealtime, and that the last assignment was a dharma sharing group. I asked if there was a key for the cabin, and she said the cabins were not locked during the retreat, which I thought was strange.

"The parking area at the building is only short-term," she said. "If you could please move your car to the parking lot off the main driveway, that would be great."

After moving the car, I found Cabin #5 down a path from the parking lot. The cabins were arranged like satellites tucked into the forest surrounding the main building. Mine was tiny with a bright red roof. It had a glassed-in porch area through which I could see two beds. The porch door was unlocked, and then another door led to an inner chamber with two more beds, a small dresser, table, and chair. The porch walls were painted in a sunshine yellow, and I knew I wanted to sleep out there rather than in the darker interior cabin. I would be with strangers behind an unlocked door in the woods. It flashed across my mind that Mom would be scared for me, but I didn't want to fear the future. I wanted to trust in life.

It felt like I would be sleeping in nature, the bare trees covered in their robes of white snow standing like sentinels in the quiet forest.

I put Rosie's painting, the bag of meditation stones, and my book on the window ledge, and tucked my duffel bag under the bed. I looked around my new home, letting the sparseness of it penetrate my mind, and felt my body relax. My cabin in the woods. I could feel the magic already.

CHAPTER 22

A Soft Landing

It was time to meet new people, which made me feel anxious. *What if they don't like me?* is a thought I usually have. I headed back to the main building, where I found a spot for my boots on an old towel. The boot trays were filled with winter footwear, and I could hear a mix of voices as I put on the pink house slippers and went in.

I could see right away that most of the attendees were women, and they ranged in age from their thirties to their seventies. Most were white people, but there were some visible minorities. It felt like the mix you'd find in a yoga class in my suburban area of Toronto, right down to the men being in the minority.

My eyes were drawn to the double-sided fieldstone fireplace dividing the dining and lounge areas. The lounge was cozy with chairs and doubled as a boutique shop filled with beaded and natural stone jewelry, Buddha statues of all sizes, meditation clothing, healthy lifestyle books, and other knickknacks. The dining area was bright and airy, with banks of windows that somehow made the overcast day seem cheery. Well-tended plants dotted the window ledges, and yellow daffodils topped long oak tables set in rows in the dining hall.

I went over and joined a group of people sitting in the lounge making name tags.

"Hi, I'm Denise," an older Black woman said in a warm Jamaican accent. "I haven't seen you at our practices. Are you joining us for the first time?" Some of the others, a Latino couple and two white women with grey hair, looked up curiously.

I explained that I had come last minute and had never been to a retreat before.

The Latino man said. "Glad to have you. I'm Miguel, and this is my partner, Mia." I shook their hands, feeling the genuine warmth of welcome.

After we chatted a bit more, Mia mentioned that everyone in the group came from different religious backgrounds and levels of mindfulness. "There are lots of beginners here, so don't feel intimidated," she said. Her reassurance made me feel like she could read my mind.

A middle-aged scholarly-looking man sitting off to the side said, "I'm Peter. I come every year because it really brings up the stuff I need to deal with." His openness and vulnerability to share that kind of information with a stranger surprised me. Toronto is a friendly place, but people, especially men, still take more time than this to warm up.

Peter's comment gave me pause. I wondered what stuff would come up for me. I could sense the group was relaxed and easy-going but serious about the retreat process. I felt at ease as we talked more and I learned that most of the people were business professionals like me. They reminded me of the mindfulness and coaching communities at work, but these people were somehow further along in their training, and more intimate.

It gave me comfort that I was in a community of like-minded people. No one looked at me like some exotic person or commented on how jealous they were of my tanned skin colour, which can happen when I leave Toronto for more rural parts of Canada.

I used the markers on the table to create my name tag, spelling my name properly this time and adding red and purple flowers. I wasn't sure what the little piece of paper Marg gave me during registration meant, so I asked the people around me what a dharma sharing group and working meditation was about.

"We share in the work here, which keeps the costs down," Mia said. "Like cleaning the bathrooms or mopping the floors." I hated cleaning bathrooms and was happy to see I was assigned after dinner dishes.

Miguel said, "The best part is the dharma sharing. You'll be in a small group where you can meet and talk about your experiences while in meditation."

"Actually, you're in the dharma sharing group I lead," Mia said. "We meet here in the lounge."

"We can talk during the retreat?" I asked.

Denise answered me this time. "Not conversationally, but to help us process our experiences. It's an important component to understanding the dharma, which means the nature of reality."

It clicked into my mind that the U of T program had dharma sharing when we practiced meditation and broke into groups of two or three to discuss our experiences and findings. The small group discussions had always impacted me more deeply than the class itself. When others, even strangers, gave their attention and compassion, it made me feel seen and worthwhile. In the space of that generative love, insights or painful experiences were processed with more meaning. The teachings were imprinted in a profoundly personal way.

The group explained that "Noble Silence" started after dinner on Day 1 and ended before lunch on Day 5, to give people a chance to say hello and then goodbye. In between, we would not speak unless it was about the dharma, such as in the dharma talks, dharma sharing, dharma Q & A, or individual consultations with more trained Buddhist members. They pointed me to the agenda posted by the fireplace.

After thanking them for the orientation, I perused the agenda. It was very detailed and even more scripted than I had imagined. I took a photo for reference, and no one gave me any dirty looks for having my cell phone out. I noticed a box of earplugs and the strips you wear on your nose to stop snoring. One of my fears about this retreat had to do with snoring and being a terrible roommate to the person unlucky enough to be stuck with me. Although Tom didn't mind what he called a "light purr," I felt ashamed of my snoring. It was evident this group was compassionate enough to recognize the humanity of this issue and put it on the table, literally. I grabbed a few snore strips, thankful that imperfection was okay here. My fears that the group would be organized like a hierarchy faded as I saw how kind and accepting they were.

FOREST FRIENDS

I had a bit of time before dinner and went for a walk. On my way out, I noticed gorgeously carved wooden doors that seemed to be made of teak. I was drawn to them, and took a peek inside. The meditation hall was a circular room with high ceilings, and the walls were punctuated with rectangles of sunlight that softly bounced off the cork flooring. People had dropped off their meditation cushions, which reminded me that mine was still in the car. I made a mental note to grab it after my walk and went back to the foyer to exchange my slippers for boots.

I walked in solitude on a path into the forest, but it felt friendly. I *felt* the dark bark of the trees against the white snow as if I had run my hands over it. The rocks covered in moss seemed to also *communicate* with me. It reminded me of the tree stump on the long-ago hike in Oregon that seemed to be alive with joy in the presence of the leaves. Without the busyness of everyday life, I felt an abundance of fullness in the world. I had dropped *doing* things, but found that without doing I was left with the activity of *being*, and that was not empty at all.

After getting my cushion from the car, I put it in the meditation room and headed to the dining room, where people were talking and laughing. I found a spot and said hello to a new group of people. Volunteers brought delicious-smelling food from the kitchen serving counter and set it out for family sharing as everyone rose and the room became silent. A woman in the group stood next to a large knee-height brown metal bowl with engravings. As she struck it, a loud, rich sound reverberated through the room. After the last vibration faded, we kept standing, all of us in utter stillness, except for the muted sounds of the kitchen staff. Then came my first exposure to the reading of the Five Contemplations before Eating as proscribed by Plum Village, a Buddhist monastery in southern France. When the last sound faded away, a man started reading the words out loud:

This food is a gift of the earth, the sky, numerous living beings, and much hard and loving work.

May we eat with mindfulness and gratitude so as to be worthy to receive this food.

May we recognize and transform unwholesome mental formations, especially our greed and learn to eat with moderation.

May we keep our compassion alive by eating in such a way that reduces the suffering of living beings, stops contributing to climate change, and heals and preserves our precious planet.

We ... nourish our ideal of serving all living beings.

I'd never brought so much conscious intent to the act of eating before hearing these contemplations and trying to put them into practice at the retreat. Apart from an exercise in the U of T program that involved mindfully eating a raisin, I usually ate quickly, often while talking, reading, watching TV, or being on my phone. I fell into the slow pace of the others and found a rhythm of bringing the fork to my mouth, setting it back down before starting to chew.

The meal surprised me with how tasty it was for being a vegan Mexican casserole. Sometimes I made eye contact and smiled, but it didn't feel strained. I had been in many gatherings where people shared food in companionship, but the absence of small talk left room to pay full attention to the food. As I ate, I thought about the photosynthesis process, the people who had grown the food, and my good fortune to have this food when so many others did not have enough. With each forkful I saw a chain of events stretched through time, and I was humbled to be the end of that chain. Eating lasted about twenty minutes, but joyfulness and gratitude grew in that time like never before during a meal.

As the meal ended and we started talking again, I asked some questions that were still on my mind.

"What is a Sangha?" I asked. Sangha was part of the group name, and I noticed it was also mentioned in the fifth contemplation of mindful eating.

"Sangha is a group of people who practice the dharma and support each other," a young woman said. She was quiet and looked tired. I guessed that she'd had a long work week and been worn out by the drive out to Midland. "True Peace is mostly lay people, but some have gone to Plum Village and are training to become ordained."

I liked the idea of Sangha. As a project manager, I know the power of a group of people working towards the same goal because I have seen the capability a team can have over an individual working alone. *Dharma* was a term I couldn't quite grasp yet, but Sangha was a power I was aware of.

I was moderate with dinner but ate too much of the freshly baked chocolate brownie with raspberries. Next time, I noted, I should take even less food. I started to gather up the plates for my assigned chore, and headed to the kitchen. I noticed two dogs at the back door of the dining hall. One was a small short long-haired dog that looked like a grey mop grazing the floor. The other looked like a black and white sheep dog, and I noticed its long teeth as it looked up at me carrying the dishes with leftover food on them. As a child, I had been chased by a dog as I walked home from school, and I had run into the woods to escape. The whole experience had been terrifying: I was alone with the loud barking, and there was no one to help me. The dog knocked me down, and I only escaped by throwing some leftover lunch food off to the side and running away while it ate. Throughout my life, since that incident, the mere sight of a dog could bring me back to that dormant terror. Over the years, our dog-loving friends could not understand why I didn't fall for their dogs and remained aloof to their dogs' many attempts to befriend me and gain my approval. These two dogs didn't seem aggressive, but I felt the old fear rise. I breathed through the panicky feelings, reminding myself that this was a different situation. But I still carried the plates with scraps of food high up as I stepped around both animals to get into the kitchen.

It was a bit of mayhem in there with the staff and retreat people assigned to dinner cleanup all jamming into the small space. The last thing I expected was to run into one of my university classmates. I could hardly believe this coincidence. Joe and I took Engineering Physics together, which focused entirely on the physical world, yet we meet up again at a retreat centre about the conscious world. It was a jarring reunion because he was busy with kitchen work, and we hadn't seen each other in twenty years. I found out he lived in Midland and worked at the retreat centre. How odd for us to meet up like this. Still, we had bonded over many late study nights, and it was like no time had passed. We hugged hello in the busy kitchen, and Joe promised to catch up after Noble Silence ended. Joe must have noticed that I was leery of the dogs, or maybe he knew of my fear from our university days, because he made a point of saying that both dogs were friendly. The little mop dog was Ollie, and the bigger black and white one was Eddie. Everyone says their dogs are harmless, so that didn't dispel my fear. I still gave both dogs a wide berth as I left the kitchen.

It was soon time to go to the meditation hall for the welcome and orientation session. After that, we got blankets to lie on the ground with, the lights were dimmed, and we were taken through a guided relaxation meditation. I went into a slow process of standing down my nervousness and anxiety as I let the energy of the people and the forest setting seep into me. The coincidence of knowing at least one person here felt like a sign that I was in the right place. The large bell was struck to signal the end of the meditation and the beginning of Noble Silence. We all silently got up from the relaxation pose, put away our blankets, and made our way to the bathrooms to get ready for the night.

Back at the cabin, I was happy to see that Mia had taken the bed with me on the porch, and that Denise and her friend were in the main cabin. I snuck a quick text message to let Tom know that I had met up with Joe, a trusted friend, and that I wasn't with a group of ax murderers or a cult. It was safe here.

Although this day had been filled with silence while I was packing at home alone, driving, and walking in the forest before dinner, Noble Silence had a different quality of quiet. The word *noble* originates from the Latin *nōscere,* meaning to know, to recognize. Lying in bed, I started to know what life was like when conversation was not required. This first evening created a soft landing for this retreat process to begin. I took pleasure at looking into the forest so close to my window.

April 6, 2018, Journal Entry: *This cabin is home. I hear the bells. Home I am. I am home. The wind is picking up. It shakes the tree branches, and soft clumps of snow fall down. I'm protected here in my little cabin. Did the pioneer settlers feel this moment too? I feel it's a moment, or feeling, shared by many of those who settled the land, lived off it, and with it. Rosie's painting is with me. And my stones. Solid as a mountain. Fluid as water. Open as air. Fresh as a flower. The wind is waving the entire tree now. A great big hello. Hello back.* 😄 *I let go of past hurts. They can blow out of my heart, shaken loose by my intention to be kind, and fall away like soft clumps. I let go of worrying about the future. I may bend like the tree, but I will not break. Everything will be in balance. The future will take care of itself.*

The universe had become a friendly, warm place in just a few hours. I put the snore strip on my nose and closed my eyes. I was tucked under a fluffy duvet, tucked into a tiny cabin, tucked into the snowy forest, tucked under a starry black sky. The transformation had started ever so softly.

CHAPTER 23

The Dharma Finds Me

DAY 2 — SATURDAY

This day began in darkness. Before the 5:30 a.m. bell, I awoke keenly aware that I was in a different orientation to the earth than my usual place. Sleeping in Yellowstone National Park and many of the national parks in the United States has given me a sense of being on the land that I never get in the city. Here too, just two hours north of my suburban home, I felt the energy that settles in wherever humans are less abundant.

After two childbirths, holding my pee for a long time in the morning is no longer an option. A mad hurry to slip from my sleepwear to my clothes, don a coat and boots in the dark, and then find my way through the cold winter air to the main building was not how I envisioned a peaceful retreat starting.

In the bathroom stall, someone had posted a small reminder to be mindful, even when using the toilet: "Defiled or immaculate, increasing or decreasing — these concepts exist only in our mind. The reality of interbeing is unsurpassed." I didn't know what *interbeing* was and how peeing was related to it, but it seemed that the verse meant reverence for life and appreciating all aspects, even the unglamorous ones.

The other verse posted by the sink made more sense to me: "Water flows over these hands. May I use them skillfully to preserve our precious planet." These cards had me pause during activities I usually do on autopilot. This day was only a few minutes old, and I was already arriving at my destination — the present moment — just by using the toilet and washing my hands.

As people entered the meditation hall, we again sat in a circle. The vibrations from the bell flowed through me as it called us into meditation. Someone started singing slowly to welcome the day, and the pace of the bell increased as the singing continued, joyfully greeting the day. The song was "The Morning Chant" from Plum Village, and it was a beautiful way to start our day. The lyrics were about setting an intention to bring our minds into meditation. In the last line, the language changes from English to a Sanskrit refrain that the group chants in response: *"Namo Shakyamunaye Buddhaya."*

I did a quick check-in with my mind, asking *Is this too religious? Too weird?* The answer came back just as quickly. *No,* my inner self said. *This seems okay.*

The words were sung slowly, meditatively, and with love. The lack of hurrying was enough of a departure from daily life, and I stumbled along with the unfamiliar syllables. Even though I was clumsy with the sounds, I immediately felt a sense of something beautiful and interconnected with our voices. We repeated the refrain twice more at an unhurried pace, taking time with each syllable.

Then it was time to sit in silence and stillness, each person looking within. The energy from the singing and the bell seemed to clear my mind, and I watched my thoughts with more curiosity and expansiveness. It's like when I don't realize my glasses are dirty, then I'm amazed at how clear everything is after cleaning them. I felt like that during this first morning sitting meditation when I looked inward.

We moved from sitting meditation to walking meditation. I felt the familiar joy of coordinating breath to footfall that helped me so much during that first sick leave. There were moments when I caught a glimpse of what no thought feels like as I focused on flecks in the cork flooring and adjusted my core balance to walk so slowly. In this space, I noticed the sunlight change as I approached and passed by a window. My proprioceptive awareness — my sense of the position and movement of my own body — extended to all of the bodies around me. I felt the ground and saw how I was connected to the Earth and the larger universe. It was a felt sense of being part of a whole. There were moments of joy where it sank in just how much of a miracle it is to walk and breathe. There were moments of gratitude that I could walk and feel safe when there are many women in the world, even in Canada, who don't have this privilege. For all of the women who don't have the choice to walk where they want, I walked for them. Just like that, the meditation became a freedom walk.

My mind calmed through this hyper-awareness of the present moment. Forty minutes went by much faster than I thought it would because it was split between sitting and walking meditation, which allowed different vantage points to watch the mind.

At 7:30 a.m., we moved to the third meditation practice of the day: eating meditation. The bell was brought out of the meditation hall and signaled us to listen to the five contemplations of mindful eating. I was surprised that there were non-vegan options like a bowl of boiled eggs and coffee cream. Breakfast had always been my most hurried meal, usually split between eating, making lunches, unloading the dishwasher, and helping the kids get ready for school. I thought about Tom being in a frazzle at home, trying to get the girls out of the house for their Saturday activities without my help. For a moment I felt worried, but had to let it go. There was nothing to be done, and I couldn't be sure he was struggling. I tried to let go of worrying about something I couldn't be sure of and couldn't change. Maybe the girls were being helpful, and all was well. I just didn't know. At this second meal of the retreat, I was again amazed at how pleasant it was to watch my mind from the vantage point of mindful eating of coffee and toast.

The slow pace of everything, from the deep relaxation the night before to the chanting and mindful eating, had a calming effect on my nervous system. It felt like I was detoxing from stress because there was nothing pressing that had to get done, and no one expected me to show up a certain way. The absence of speech, decisions, and distractions relaxed me in a way that reading and talk therapy hadn't. I had initially been worried about the lack of interruptions due to Noble Silence. I was surprised that I wasn't bored, and instead felt nourished.

Working meditation followed, and I put the dishes in the industrial dishwasher in continued silence. In just a couple of hours, I had experienced four types of meditation — sitting, walking, eating, and working. It was not at all how I had pictured a silent retreat. I thought I'd have to sit in one place for eight or fourteen hours a day. I expected to be physically sore and mentally uncomfortable at times. In my Mom's annual Hindu prayers, it was boring and painful to sit for four hours on the floor of our basement or living room while the pandit, who came to the house, moved from one prayer to the next. But this morning's activities seemed to be all about the enjoyment of everyday activities. Even though I was sitting in silence with new acquaintances, there was joy in the social connection that permeated the activities.

It felt like the dharma, the nature of reality, was finding me. I saw more deeply how things were impermanent. Feelings last only a few seconds, thoughts appear and disappear, sensation comes and goes, and even the breath rises and falls. Nothing stays the same. During meditation while I was depressed, I had noticed that watching my emotions resulted in feeling less sad. Even a heavy sadness could not be permanent.

The next activity on Day 2 was a dharma talk, and it reminded me of how a story from the Bible is discussed in a church service. Sato was a petite Asian woman with quiet energy and a relaxed but wise way of speaking. She wore a loose-fitting shirt, almost like the top worn in karate, and when she spoke it felt more like a TED Talk than a scripture download or lecture. We watched a dharma talk video by Thich Nhat Hanh, or Thầy as people in the Sangha refer to him fondly. *Thầy* (pronounced *tie*) means teacher.

April 7, 2018, Journal Entry: *"Keep your appointment with life" — Thầy. The garden ... water and sunshine cannot grow a plant without the seed being there. What seeds are in you, and when they are watered, do you look at the water or the seed? Anger is the water. But can only blossom in you if you have a seed. Find the seed. View it with compassion and transform it to love. A little girl asked Thầy, "What is the purpose of life?" Answer: "To enjoy life." To take enjoyment from what life offers. Inter-beingness. We are transmitting and receiving energy at all times... We are not insignificant. We are a vital part of the collective. We can affect the ocean of fear around us.*

The dharma teaching to come back to the present moment, as it is the place to connect to all of life, left me feeling expansive and without boundaries. It's such a simple but profound way to look at being alive.

A dharma talk video by Joanne Friday showed me that mindfulness and concentration were gateway skills to compassion. Joanne Friday was supposed to lead this retreat, but she was ill, and instead Sato had stepped in. From the smiles on everyone's faces as her video talk began, I could tell that Joanne was a beloved teacher. She called being angry a dharma door, meaning it was an opportunity to let the dharma in by bringing up seeds of compassion to tend to the anger. Joanne Friday looked like a fairy godmother, with her petite build, white hair, and gentle manner. She shared four questions that helped her respond with compassion to dharma doors.

1. Am I sure?
2. What am I afraid of?
3. What am I attached to?
4. Is this of any benefit (to me or others)?

I had been faced with no shortage of dharma doors with the corporate dysfunctions of the last year, including threats to my integrity and personal safety and to those of others whom I cared about. Like the four questions Byron Katie poses in her inquiry process called The Work, Joanne's questions seemed designed to diffuse judgment, attachment and negativity.

The concept of interbeing was discussed too. This word was coined by Thich Nhat Hanh, and the monks he ordained were part of an Order of Interbeing.

As Sister Chân Không explains in an interview on the Plum Village website, "Interbeing is like the flower that cannot be by herself without the sunshine, without the rain, without the caring of the gardener, and without so many conditions. So, normally we must set up interbeing — or co-being. We co-exist. We cannot exist by ourselves. There is nothing in this world that or who exists by itself alone."

I thought about the verse in the bathroom stall that "interbeing is unsurpassed." Even one of the first activities of the day, going to the bathroom, can be an opportunity to awaken to the true nature of reality.

The ideas I was exposed to during my first full day at the retreat were not new to me. I had already had some exposure to sitting with unpleasant emotions, feeling joy in meditation, responding with compassion, and nurturing a spiritual connection. What was new was that I was saturated in the present moment with these ideas, and my concentration wasn't diluted by other activities. It was a potent way for the ideas to settle into my skin, bones, and heart.

After the dharma talk, we went for a group walk outdoors. It was a crisp, sunny winter day. We formed a circle in the parking lot and widened it as people joined in. I heard some of the Sangha members excitedly calling out favourite songs to sing about clouds, birds, and freedom. I was surprised to learn we'd be singing on this walk, but it seemed that these songs illuminated the dharma as much as the dharma video talks did. Singing hymns at Hindu prayers and Christmas carols in church has always made me feel connected, happy and emotional, and the same happened here. These songs were uplifting, and one that I especially loved was "Breathing In, Breathing Out," which meditated on our similarities to natural elements like water, the earth, a flower and the dew. The lyrics ended with "I am free." I did feel free singing it with the others.

We sang many other short songs like this in the circle holding hands. Joy bubbled up as the others' voices, and the words of the songs, gave me a sense of interbeing. We broke into little groups to embark on a slow walk, pausing at trees or rocks to pay attention. We had big stretchy smiles as we wordlessly shared the same feelings. We didn't control our steps or breathing. We were a thread of joy weaving trees, rocks, birds, people, and all of reality into one. There was no separation between us.

It was good that we moved back and forth between activities that took concentration, like formal meditation and the dharma talks, and activities like singing and walking outside. It gave my mind time to rest and digest. The big, billowy concepts of interbeing and impermanence came alive in being with others in song and nature. So far, the retreat day was masterful in reinforcing an unsayable concept like dharma through a sequence of well-orchestrated activities.

DHARMA INTERVIEW TIME

During a lunch round of eating and working meditation, I thought about the private consultation with Sato that was next on my agenda. I had signed up for the 1:30 p.m. timeslot on Day 2, not knowing what to expect but also not wanting to leave any experience untried. The consultation was still considered Noble Silence because it was a time to discuss what the silence brought up for me. But as I entered the room I couldn't think of anything to say.

I was jolted to see that the room was the business office for the retreat centre, occupied by three desks, a printer, computers, and other business items. It had been weeks since I had stepped foot in a business workspace, but my body didn't tense up. I had come to associate safety with Sato, who looked very out of place in this business setting, with her loose flowy clothing, no makeup and hair tied back. Sato invited me to sit on a chair and put me at ease with her peaceful manner.

I took a deep breath and sat down in the field of her energy.

CHAPTER 24

Noble Silence Speaks

It wasn't just that Sato was peaceful. It was like I was in a force field of energy pulling me towards her. I had been with her many times in the meditation circle and dining hall, but being alone with her was different. I felt emotional even though I hadn't said a word. I think what I felt was love, but not the personal kind I feel with my parents, Tom, or the kids. It was indiscriminate love. The kind I felt during the surreal and out-of-body experiences I had of pouring love on Japan in my dream, of melting after the hot yoga class, of running at Cades Cove and of being with my ancestors in my brother's hospital room.

As I grounded myself and followed my breath, being in this energy felt like I was coming back home. I knew I had an exceptional opportunity, so I brought my full attention to this moment. I connected to my body in the chair and feet on the floor, followed my breath a few times, and felt that I could have sat there the entire time and stayed silent. I scanned my feelings and watched my thoughts. Unlike the talk-based therapy I had after the depression diagnosis, this appointment had the presence of stillness or of the Observer, as I called it.

Likely only a minute or two went by, but it felt much longer. I came to see that the silence was not an empty void, and I wanted to share what was in my heart with Sato. I don't recall what I said, but I'm sure I would have described how lacking in integrity my job felt and how powerless I felt to watch harm being done by a workplace that was supposed to be good. I explained why I came to the retreat looking for my path back to myself.

Sato listened with a quality of attention I've never felt before from another person. She didn't give me her viewpoint or thoughts. Then she asked me one question that hit me with such force.

"Sunita, why do you need to fight so hard for the underdog?"

I didn't know what to say to this question. I'd never seen myself as someone who fought for people. My mind was stumped, but my body responded. The tears started coming as if I was a child crying, and an image, unbidden from a childhood I barely remember, surfaced.

A child's voice from within said something completely unexpected: "I'm scared. Nani and Nana are fighting. He's hitting her."

I was shocked by these words, but I made an immediate decision to try to connect with my inner Voice. As I did so a flood of emotion opened in me. A scene formed in my mind. I imagined my grandmother, Nani, was in front of me, blocking me so I wouldn't be hurt. I was perhaps four or five, and the adult me who was witnessing this memory felt protective of this little girl who was so scared because someone she loved was being hurt. I could see how much the experience was overwhelming her, and I wanted to reach back through time and tell her it was okay. It was clear that she could not deal with this pain she was witnessing between her grandparents, the harm to her grandmother, the injustice and violence of it all. In an instant, the needs of that little child and the needs of my adult self in the workplace came to be the same thing.

Safety.

The little girl was the part of me that was scared when work became unpredictable and when people in power did and said things that threatened others' psychological safety. In the girl's world, unpredictable behaviour and power-over relationships were dangerous. Somehow my mind had kept that child's sense of danger alive in how I processed adult experiences.

It was like the pieces of a puzzle were dropping into place as I connected what drove my values and volition as an adult. Sato was also a piece of the puzzle to fit these connections together. The river of compassion she generated was a timeless invitation for the truth to surface. I started telling Sato how it was coming up for me that pieces of my past were tied to pieces of my present. This was a soul-level conversation possible only within the boundaries of Noble Silence. Flashes of understanding came in this undemanding space. As the words tumbled out, a sacred reunion was taking place between me and my inner child consciousness that had been frozen in fear. With the warmth of compassionate listening and mindfulness of the Observer, the fear began to thaw, and the burden of "never not be afraid" loosened its grip.

Another piece of the puzzle was Rosie. Our mutual toxic co-worker, Vinnie, had disparaged her intelligence, and she saw this as a threat to her job, her worth at work, and relationships she held dear. She lived in constant fear of losing the job she cherished and was unsafe psychologically in the workplace. I had set myself up as her champion and vowed to help her — something I wasn't able to do for my grandmother.

Still another piece of the puzzle was realizing that I lived in a country that treated Indigenous people unjustly with regard to legal, childcare, and other basic human rights such as clean water. First Nations, Metis, and Inuit peoples were supposed to be protected by the treaty promises, yet they were not. The stories I read in the TRC publication *The Survivors Speak* were accounts of unimaginable sexual, physical, and mental abuse. Yet these stories were not just accounts, they touched on abuse of power, something that was personal to me.

I told Sato that the workplace and the country I identified with had become unsafe in the last few months. On top of this, the man who made work feel unsafe psychologically was a mirror of a childhood experience where men who had power could hurt women. But really, what I could not stomach was being put in the position of being dishonest or playing games with the school I had promised to help.

In all these varied experiences, the common theme was I wanted to protect others like my grandmother had tried to protect me in the memory. I tried to fix unjust situations in the world because I had been powerless to do so as a child. As this final realization broke through the surface, it felt cathartic to understand what hurt me, and tears poured out. However, it wasn't pure misery that was driving me; some of those tears were loving ones for the scared part of me I had forgotten.

Sato laid a hand on my arm and just supported me as I reunited with a consciousness that wanted to be seen and heard as much as any real child wanted those things. Sitting there with her, I felt whole and peaceful. After this outpouring, Sato gave me her thoughts.

She said my cup was too empty. I was giving so much compassion for others, and there wasn't enough left in my cup to take care of my own needs. She said only when my cup was full enough with good feelings could I tend to others' needs. I think she was saying that I didn't have good feelings inside of me and that as long as that was the case, trying to love others wasn't going to work properly. I needed to make my interior wholesome, and once I tended to that, I would be full enough to give positive energy to others. I was trying to show love when I didn't have enough self-love. My cup needed to be full of love for the frightened parts of me before I could love others fully. I had heard this parable before of not being able to pour from an empty cup, but now it was like the words had the power to shift my thinking. Sato's quiet advice blasted the belief that I had to be on alert to stop bad things from happening in the world.

I sat for a few more minutes, following my breath and feeling out the truth in her words as I grounded into my body. It was hard to believe that the fifteen-minute session still had time left, considering how much broader my understanding was. It felt like this was a truth of all truths, one that had the force to shift me from confusion to profound peace. I thanked Sato and left with much to contemplate.

REUNION

When I stepped into the hallway, I saw people hurrying into the meditation hall for yoga practice. I wanted to be alone to process this memory and understand this idea of a younger Sunita with needs I wasn't meeting. I decided to go back to the cabin. As I crossed paths with people, it was a relief not to speak and only give a wordless greeting. The act of putting hands together and bowing to another person conveys more of a humanistic greeting than any words can. I was grateful for this retreat in how it connected me to others and to nature in the profoundly satisfying and wordless way of interbeing.

No one else was in the cabin, and I was grateful for the solitude. I cocooned myself in the duvet and picked up my purple pen and journal. I needed to write as quickly as possible, to capture the memory fragments and realizations of the last few minutes.

April 7, 2018, Journal Entry: *1:30 p.m. Consultation. Before doing good, become whole. Fill my cup with good feelings before I empty it for others.*

I thought back to what a young me in Guyana could have seen that scared her. I visualized a photograph of me as a young child jumping on a pile of hay. It is one of those old photographs with white borders that my parents brought from Guyana when they left with only a couple of barrels of possessions. I was wearing a red halter top and black shorts. I had one hand raised as if I was punching the air in happiness, and it looked like I was laughing. I held that child in my mind's eye and thought about her.

It came back to me that when I lived at Nani's house, I was called Little Sunita because Mom's teenage cousin was also named Sunita. I think they called her Big Sunita when I was around.

April 7, 2018, Journal Entry: *Little Sunita, I'm protecting her. (my ego?) is protecting her still.*

Why am I such a fighter for the underdog? What makes me want to stand up for them?

Rosie?

Rachel?

Indigenous peoples?

Stacey? The students?

Why do I feel I'm the one to speak up?

What do I need to heal with Little Sunita?

I called across space and time to ask what happened to make me the way I am now — wanting to take on issues about women and people treated unjustly by patriarchal forces like corporate power and colonial systems.

The poet Rumi says, "Out beyond ideas of wrongdoing and right doing, there is a field. I'll meet you there. When the soul lies down in that grass, the world is too full to talk about. Ideas, language, even the phrase 'each other' doesn't make any sense."

This is the closest I can come to describing how I *met* Little Sunita in my journal. I asked *her* — me, really — to meet me, lie down in the grass, and have a conversation. In this space, a letter came out. It was like it was dictated by some force beyond my conscious mind, and the purple pen moved of its own accord. I was a transcriber who just wrote as the words came in a stream of consciousness.

LETTER TO LITTLE SUNITA

April 7, 2018, Journal Entry:

Dear Little Sunita,

I think you must have been scared and helpless as a little girl staying with Nani and Nana. I imagine it could have gotten very violent, and you saw some terrible things. Maybe you heard yelling. And shouting and screaming.

Maybe you wanted to protect Nani from being beaten and hit? Maybe you had to make yourself be quiet and small and let it happen, powerless as a small child. Maybe Nani even hid you or shielded you with her body to protect you from getting hit by accident — or on purpose? Were you naughty and caused Nana to get mad? Did Nani take the brunt of the anger and violence for you?

What happened? What did you see? What do you feel helpless and sad about?

What happens when we see people getting hurt or treated unfairly now? How does it make you feel?

I am now 45. I am safe and unharmed. Nani is safe now for many years. I can protect her now from bad, mean, angry men. In fact, I have done that. I'm strong and smart. I can stand up now. I have a voice. I can and will use that voice when others cannot.

I want you to know you are safe. You are loved.

Whatever happened, it was not your fault or responsibility. You were a child, meant to be ... protected.

I promise to protect you now, and you can be wild and loud and free. No more making yourself small to disappear and not be noticed or fear drawing attention to yourself.

You don't have to hide.

No one will get angry.

No one will hit you.

No one will hurt you.

Whatever happened in the first 7 years of our life is in the past. This is the present and it is glorious.

I can't tell you how amazing our life turned out.

Two beautiful little girls are here now. Strong and I encourage them to be who they are and never hide themselves — for anyone. I'm in a cabin now in the woods. This cabin reminds me of our little playhouse. It has a front room and a back room. When I look outside I see trees and almost can imagine I'm free and carefree as when we were 5 or 6 years old playing in the playhouse.

I remember making mud pies, I think in old bottle caps.

And I remember a shiny green succulent leaf and when we broke it in half, milk came out. I remember the Coca Cola machine and getting the bottle caps out. I remember the smell of the school bus.

I have such few memories of you Little Sunita.

If they were traumatic, scary, and too much for your tender child heart, then you did what you had to do to survive and stay safe.

You must have rationalized things and made sense of things as you knew best. I imagine you had a logical plan, maybe even a little analytical and methodical.

I only have compassion for you Little Sunita. You were and are a brave girl. You love your Nani and it would be terrible for you to see her get hurt and attacked. That bad man cannot hurt you. He did not know better. I am the adult now and I know better.

Buddhism is about compassion and the wisdom to apply it to suffering.

You suffered. We do not need to suffer now.

With compassion and love we can let that go and trust that we are safe, we are held in loving-kindness, our life is now filled with ease and joy.

Love, your forever friend,
Big Sunita

LETTER TO BIG SUNITA

After I finished signing this letter, sitting on my bed in my cabin at the edge of the woods, I read it aloud to find out what I had written. It had flowed so quickly that all my attention was on writing to not miss a word. As I read the sentences, it felt like power and truth were on the page. I understood why I tended to play small because drawing attention to myself was dangerous. That strategy was still a current part of my responses to life and needed to be changed to fully grow into my best self.

I knew the starting place for this kind of change had to be compassion and love. The retreat had flooded me with the wisdom that the first response to anything is compassion. I opened the small sack of polished stones that I had brought with me. The pink stone I used to meditate on the concept of being "fresh as a flower" was translucent with streaks of dark rose. I held it as if holding a scared part of me: Little Sunita.

After some time in stillness, Little Sunita had a message for me. I picked out a pink pen from my pencil case, and with my left hand I wrote back and drew a picture of us holding hands.

April 7, 2018, Journal Entry: *Dear Big Sunita, I am free. Love, Little Sunita age 4*

I put my pen down and sank into the bed and into the silence, holding the pink stone with as much love as I could pour into it. It was time to be quiet and do the work only I could do.

Love myself.

CHAPTER 25

A New Worldview

That dharma session with Sato and then the letter writing with Little Sunita was the beginning of a new road for me. I felt I had travelled to a place old and forgotten. A place where my sense of peace was taken away. My path back to peace did not start in 2018 but sometime in my early childhood. My role now was to tend to this child who had had her peace taken and pour love into her. My job was to show her that *today* is safe despite what happened in the past. Little Sunita was still in me, as much as my memories are, and now it was my job, no longer that of my parents or grandparents, to restore her sense of security. It was time to reunite her needs with mine and meet them with the adult capacities I now had for autonomy and love.

I don't know why this took forty years to happen, but it did. I was grateful that the afternoon on Day 2 was very open without another event until 5 p.m. I snuggled into the bed, holding the pink stone, and let my mind wander without trying to dissect analytically what had just happened. I didn't want any mental talk. I just wanted to find that kind of comfort I used to feel when I sat with Nani on the sofa in friendly silence while she patted my hand. This was a life-changing afternoon because I felt as if I'd become more whole and more complete. I needed those few hours of stillness curled up under the covers to be with my new state of consciousness.

When it was a quarter to five, I gathered my thoughts and headed back to the main building.

I found the silence and repetitive activities of breathing, eating, and cleaning up dishes were timed perfectly because they let me process the afternoon's realizations slowly and mindfully without feeling overwhelmed. By evening there were just two more parts to this miraculous day. Touching the Earth and deep relaxation.

TOUCHING THE EARTH

Touching the Earth meditation is a metaphysical practice that allows energy to flow from the Earth and ancestors. Its purpose is to cultivate compassion, forgiveness, and interbeing. From a procedural perspective, the practice involves bending down until your forehead rests on the ground and repeating phrases such as, "In gratitude, I bow to all generations of ancestors in my blood family."

With the readiness of someone who had just met her childhood self, I was able to access everything that Touching the Earth meditation had to offer. The pain, fear, and distrust of life flowed from me, and in return, I felt trust, safety, and joy flow back from the Earth and my ancestors through my forehead. When I left this practice, it felt as if I had not just *let go* of bad stuff, but that it was willingly received, transformed, and returned as love. It was as if I was no longer a distinct and separate person. I had the experience that I was in continuity and flow with the land and with the spiritual realm of my ancestors and loved ones who were alive and far away. I wasn't skeptical because it was as real as breathing fresh air after being in a stuffy room. My entire being knew a transmission of energy had happened, even if my scientific mind could not prove it. I entered this practice unsettled from the feelings that had surfaced and emerged lighter of spirit as if the Earth had accepted any bad energy that was stirred up.

Deep relaxation followed as we settled into lying-down positions around the room for a group relaxation meditation. I thought of the phrase "soft animal" from the poem "Wild Geese" by Mary Oliver. After the soul-rocking letters I had written and the profoundly spiritual experience of touching the Earth, it was soothing to lie on my mat with others close by and let the Earth cradle the soft animal in me.

Having gone through so much in one day, I could have fallen into bed exhausted or stayed up all night thinking. But neither of those things happened. I went to bed feeling well-rested, even before I fell asleep. I had spent the day travelling to a deep part of myself and had confronted some long-buried pain. Yet I was so light of being after the letter-writing and releasing old energy through Touching the Earth and deep relaxation that I fell asleep like a child does — soundly and in peace.

DAY 3 — SUNDAY

This next day started like the one before it, and brought new opportunities to further hard-wire the dharma teachings through breathing, walking, eating, and working in the kitchen. I regained a childlike enjoyment of the snow falling, the smells and taste of the food, and the freedom to be in nature. Through these activities, it was sinking in that *if* dharma is *the* life force, then the most urgent thing to do was enjoy *the life force*.

It was also sinking in that this life force is friendly and helpful and not aloof or punishing. This life force wanted to have a relationship with me that was fun, playful, joyful, and trusting. *It* didn't want me to be serious or restrained in my life. *It* didn't want me to be careful lest someone get angry. *It* didn't want me to be cautious just to keep the peace. *It* wanted me to be carefree.

As I went on a solitary walk, Ollie, the little dog that looked like a slightly dirty mop, started walking with me. I was stunned by the lack of fear rising up and realized I was connected with my inner child. Little Sunita felt safe being in the woods with this dog. She didn't have the fear that I had acquired later in life. I knew Ollie belonged to the retreat centre but didn't realize he just roamed the grounds freely off-leash. I didn't think he should follow me off the property and be on the main road, but I didn't know how to send him home. So I decided to let Little Sunita have fun and enjoy Ollie and not let bad memories take away the delight of walking with a dog.

April 8, 2018, Journal Entry: *I went for a brisk walk after breakfast. The little dog came with me. We went for a run — a race. He won. Ha. I can see the friendship, energy and compassionate joy we receive from animals.*

Perhaps the fear had eased during the connection to my inner child and then flowed away during the Touching the Earth meditation. In the wake of the previous day's activities, I saw walking with Ollie in the woods as a safe and fun experience. The power of the compassion and joy generated by the retreat practices filled my cup and poured over in a way that allowed me to see through decades-old fearful beliefs.

April 8, 2018, Journal Entry: *I did loving-kindness for Little Sunita. May she be safe. Happy & Joyful.*

The Day 3 dharma talks came next and covered many concepts, including "right speech" and "right action," which meant choosing to respond with kind words and deeds even if that means staying silent or not doing anything in the heat of the moment. We practiced breathing exercises to build the energies of mindfulness, concentration, and insight. The talks covered five aggregates: form (body), feelings (emotions), perception, mental formations, and consciousness. The feelings aggregate was broken down for us into four types: pleasant, unpleasant, neutral, and mixed. This breakdown reminded me of learning theory in piano lessons as a first step. I hadn't encountered anyone teaching me a human being's composition like this before, and I found it enlightening.

I learned about the Five Remembrances, a teaching that says while we cannot escape certain realities, the fear energy of these realities can be lessened through mindfulness. We cannot escape (1) sickness, (2) growing old, (3) death, (4) change and losing our loved ones, or (5) the impact of our thoughts, our words, and our actions — these continue past our worldly life.

The gist of the dharma talk was that by meditating on these core teachings we can help lessen suffering and pivot to a more joyful experience. After listening passively, we took the practice outside to experience it through walking meditation. I had the insight of no-self where *I* was the fire of the sunshine melting the snow, *I* was the muddy puddles on the earth, *I* was the wind blowing by, and *I* was the water. I saw peace and miracles everywhere. It felt so right when Mia came up and linked her arm in mine, and we walked like childhood friends.

April 8, 2018, Journal Entry: *I think this is when my inner child came out. I started seeing things differently. This morning Sato said the way to heal your inner child is to water seeds of joy. On this walk I realized I never enjoyed snow with my inner child. We were delighted in snow. And then thought of all the forts we could make in the woods. And what an awesome game of hide and seek we could have! And mud pies and snow balls. 😄 Mia put her arm through mine and I said to my inner child, "See, we can make friends. It's easy. The world is full of kind, friendly people. You're safe."*

DHARMA SHARING

The first dharma sharing session came up on the afternoon of Day 3. This was a time to talk about our inner experiences so far. We gathered in the lounge, sitting on the sofa and chairs and even on the floor to create a sharing circle. It was still considered Noble Silence because our speech focused on our inner journey. When my turn came, I opened my journal to the letter I wrote to Little Sunita and read that aloud once more, but this time to other people. Speaking the words to other souls who listened in mindfulness, concentration and compassion made me feel the truth of these words even more. Something magical happens when the truth comes out, and you speak it aloud. The hiding energy — the energy you have spent hiding — becomes love energy. Tears started flowing with my released emotions, and others cried for Little Sunita too. Mia was doing the noisy, messy cry that comes with raw emotion, making me cry harder. I paused to make eye contact and let the love from the group flow through to my inner child self, to show Little Sunita the world is indeed a safe, loving place.

That brief time in the cozy lounge felt sacred and healing. It was so profound that I couldn't even journal it. I made a short entry: April 8, 2018, Journal Entry: *I showed my letter in the discussion circle. I cried so much.*

Later on Day 3, I passed by the message board that was used to send written notes and saw one for me. The message was from Mia, the same person who linked her arm in mine on the morning outdoor walk, led our dharma sharing group, and shared the porch sleeping area with me. She wrote me this message on a yellow sticky note:

Sunita,

Sunita has so much to reassure Little Sunita & Little Sunita has so much to remind Sunita. I was so happy to walk with the two of you!
SHE IS ADORABLE!

I smiled at Mia's note. I had heard her leave early in the morning, and I think it was because of my snoring. I felt guilty that the snore strip didn't work, and that maybe she couldn't sleep because of me. Usually, I would feel terrible about something like this and ruminate harshly against myself. But, in this state of being loving to myself, I recognized that Mia held no anger towards me, so why should I be angry at myself for something I couldn't control? I chose to be less self-denigrating and more loving towards myself in my inner dialog.

Day 3's evening session was less formal, and included a question-and-answer period. This was still a valid Noble Silence activity because we spoke to the inner journey we were all on. I saw relevance and wisdom in the questions and noticed how similar my inner journey was to that of everyone else. Because I was so at peace, this information landed on a much more open mind and stuck a little better than it would have otherwise. One answer I found helpful was how to bring up the energy of mindfulness when I'm angry. The answer was to visualize that breathing in takes the oxygen out of the burning emotion of anger. We could tamp down the burn of anger by breathing its fuel away. My ears perked up when someone asked about perfectionism and being a workaholic. This seemed one for me to pay attention to. The response was to look at our roots. In our family, as a child, if we took on adult responsibilities and sought praise or needed to take on adult responsibilities to survive, approval needs can take root. Later those needs appear as perfection or rigidity. Could I have this root, I wondered? *Yes,* was whispered back.

DAY 4 — MONDAY

Day 4's dharma talk covered "monkey mind" and how to train the mind gently to return to the present moment as it constantly wanders away. We discussed the technique of labelling thoughts to help see them better. Taming monkey mind is like a mother who gently calls her child back if they wander too far away. Mindfulness is not a command-and-control approach, like that found so often in academic and corporate life. I was so trained to "get it right" and "follow procedure" that I would feel like a failure for getting distracted after a few breaths. Unlearning judging and punishing ways happened organically as I followed my breath, got distracted, and started over with kindness in my heart. Breathing meditation became compassion meditation in this way. I could see that daily practice would hardwire a compassion-first response that could help me deal with unhappy events in the rest of the day. The mindfulness work I did on the cushion could thus be carried into the world.

To expand on how temporary and varied thoughts are, we were given a handout with fifty-one mental formations. I love any kind of list, especially ones categorized into buckets. I was glad to see the list of wholesome mental formations outnumbered the unwholesome ones. It dawned on me that the mind can form anything, good or bad, and that none of it is permanent. I had the equal capacity to bring joy (also written as 喜/hỷ/ mudita) to my mind as I did hatred (also written as 瞋/sân/ pratigha) or anger (also written as 忿/phẫn/krodha). Seeing the multitude of mental states on a sheet of paper, like a menu, was liberating because it reinforced that I wasn't equal to, or bound by, the mental formations that filled my mind. I was the Observer who could notice them, label them, and consciously choose to let go of them.

A lot had happened in the forty-eight hours since the session with Sato. I had connected to my inner child and learned that I needed safety and self-love more than I knew in order to counter past experiences of being afraid and hurt as a child. Perhaps even forgotten experiences in Guyana, such as being lost on the road home from school or the childhood accidents and injuries, had left an element of trauma that now needed to be healed. Touching the Earth and connecting to my ancestors was really unexpected yet gave me a sense of myself beyond my lifespan. Seeing others treated unjustly had always triggered me to feel sad and upset but maybe it had something to do with past generational trauma that I carried unconsciously. I naturally responded with empathy if I witnessed a person being wronged but didn't know why it felt destabilizing or that it was a call to pay attention inside as well. The solution I had been given, which was really a call to action, was to respond to my inner mental and feeling states with love and compassion.

Dharma sharing and dharma talks had all helped me find my bearings with this new worldview by giving me a glimpse of reality as it really is versus what I could intellectually know from science. I decided that I wanted to be alone with these thoughts.

Rather than take part in the Day 4 dharma sharing circle, I went for a walk to process this new idea of ancestors continuing in me.

CHAPTER 26

Awake in the World

I headed out to the country roads, turning over in my mind the ancestor connection I had felt during the Touching the Earth meditation. Ollie wasn't around, but I didn't feel like I walked alone. It felt like the inner children of my bloodline walked with me that day. I realized my parents and grandparents must have experienced fear early in childhood just like I did, likely even more so. I felt like I could comfort these children in the present moment even though they all would have existed at different times. I breathed in for my father, my mother, and my grandparents. It felt like the in-breath and out-breath sent healing energy on a timeless plane. I reasoned that my parents' and grandparents' DNA was in my cells, so my breath did reach them, in a way.

I picked up pink, red, orange, grey, and white rocks off the gravel road to represent the inner-child consciousness of my parents, grandparents, Tom, Jessica, and Sophia. I didn't think about it too hard. I just sort of felt out which rocks represented each person's inner child. It felt like I held them in my heart as I held the rocks in my pocket. My heart grew to welcome them, and to give them love and compassion. I imagined the inner children of my loved ones had experienced scary things like I had and had buried that pain. I felt immense compassion for all these inner children and sent them love to help heal whatever hurts they might carry.

As I walked, an unseen dog started barking viciously from behind someone's fence. The childhood terror rose up, but this time I saw it as a mental formation, and it had no power. I wasn't being attacked by a real dog. I was only being attacked by a *memory* of a dog from a long time ago. I smiled at this mental formation and transformed it from fear to faith that the dog could not escape the fenced backyard. In response to this mental change, I felt my heart rate decrease and my breathing slow. I realized the same old reaction of being scared would only scare these inner children, all of whom were now dwelling in my heart. Like all children, these inner children know when adults are stressed and they trust body language over the spoken word. I couldn't just tell them they were safe; I had to show them through my body's responses.

April 9, 2018, Journal Entry: *A dog barked at me as I carried the rocks. I got scared but recognized I can protect myself against the dog. This showed my inner children that I am capable of protecting "ourselves."*

Later in this walk, I came to a picturesque red barn with cows milling around. I stood to look at them, and they all walked across the field to look back at me. I hadn't realized cows were so curious. The inner children and I had the simple pleasure of standing together with cows on a grey April morning in Southern Ontario. Picking up rocks, naming them my ancestors, and giving them safe passage past a barking dog and curious cows felt like my own private coming-out-of-fear ceremony.

TEA CEREMONY

If Days 2 and 3 were entering the dark night of the soul, Day 4 was coming out on the other side with a special tea ceremony celebration in the evening. The experienced retreaters were excited about this, and their energy made me excited too. The meditation hall was prepared in secret after dinner for the surprise.

The tea ceremony started with candles, flowers, origami birds, and paper leaves decorating the floor. We each took turns bringing some kind of art to the room — a reading, music, singing. Anything from the heart. As each person shared, it was like a wave of joy began flowing around the circle, growing ever bigger. We laughed and enjoyed each other's offerings. I read a poem, coincidentally called "Finding Peace," by Vicki L. Flaherty. I found it folded in the back of my journal and knew it was the perfect art to share with the retreat people about how I was feeling. All the verses described the power of mindfulness, but this one called out to me as I read it aloud to the group.

> Cleanse your mind…
> Let go of each thought as it arises.
> Let the fear float freely up and away.
> Welcome grace, hope and joy to fill the open space.

Looking up, I saw big smiles and nodding heads at the wisdom of the words. It was soul food followed by real food, staples of my British colonial childhood — biscuits and hot tea.

We were each gifted a print of calligraphy by Thich Nhat Hanh. The words *go as a river, go as a sangha* were written beautifully within a circle. The joy of the tea ceremony sharing art, food, and laughter seemed to be precisely what life should be about — embodied joy.

Again, the deep relaxation at the end of this day helped settle the joyful energy and let my body come to rest in a deep state of peace.

DAY 5 — TUESDAY

The morning after the tea ceremony dawned differently than when I had arrived just four days earlier. After being covered in ice and snow, the landscape had started to awaken. Now there were bare patches of grass ready to grow green again, and the tree branches had shed their robes of white. Spring was gently awakening the landscape.

I understood now what Peter, the scholarly-looking man I met on Day 1, had meant when he said the retreat brings up the stuff he needs to deal with. In childhood, my sense of safety had been swept away. In this retreat, I had found a way to connect to my inner child and even the inner children of my ancestors, husband, and daughters. I saw we were all trying to fill common needs of feeling safe and loved.

Like the landscape in springtime, I had been transformed by letting the warm energy of joy thaw the frozen fear. I was no longer leading my life in a way as to be so quiet and small that no one would get angry at me or hurt me, or chase me through the woods. I had adopted those strategies to protect myself long ago. Now, I had the tools of applied mindfulness and compassion to dissolve those limiting beliefs little by little. I was learning that compassion meant being kinder in my inner dialog because an inner child's consciousness existed there too, and it needed to feel safe and loved.

ISLAND OF REFUGE & GUARDING THE GATE

The last dharma talk was about taking what we had learned and integrating it into our life outside the ideal circumstances of the retreat. The retreat was orchestrated to allow for little to no distraction. I had time to enjoy a meal I didn't prepare, I spent hours walking in nature, and I was with people on a similar path. There was no one to fight with or take care of, so I had ample time to reflect. These were the ideal conditions for insights, creativity, and healing. Noble Silence helped me *hear* the whisper of my inner Voice, which wanted to guide me. I wondered how I would manage when I returned to everyday life filled with the stress of working, managing a family, and the constant news of war, famine, natural disasters, and human rights violations that filled the world.

The first advice was to become an "island of refuge." When anger arises or other negative mental states form, I can recognize them and then go for a mindful walk or breathe to calm those feelings. If I'm feeling tired and depleted, I can practice deep relaxation. I can make my body an island of refuge through these simple breathing practices, walking and relaxing the body section by section. The inner child in me would delight in the safety of this kind of response rather than being scared when I got angry. Everyday things like washing hands, using the toilet, or washing the dishes are ways to fill my cup with goodness by generating wholesome mental formations. If I felt lost or alone, I could seek connection and strength from my ancestors and the land through Touching the Earth meditation. I didn't have a dharma sharing group or dharma teacher to consult with, but I could practice dharma sharing, if only in my journal. I also had friends and family to lean on. I could remember to pause when dharma doors popped into my life and become mindful. I could set intentions to speak more compassionately and listen more deeply, in order to generate connection to others.

The second piece of advice was on "guarding the gate," or being conscious of what not to allow into our bodies and minds, such as unwholesome food, social media, work, or people. What sense impressions am I not guarding the gate against? Do I let media images that say I'm not skinny enough give me an unhealthy body image? Do I feel like I'm not doing enough because of what I see others accomplish on social media? Instead of finding time, am I filling time up by watching too much Netflix or picking up my phone hundreds of times a day? Am I numbing out from stress by consuming too much sugar and alcohol?

During the Day 5 dharma talk, we discussed why we let these things in, and it came back to perfectionism and the desire to be more in control. This was still a hotspot for me, despite all the inner work I had done during the years to let go of approval needs. I wondered if my lack of balance originated from *my thoughts* about the need for control and validation rather than the external demands of work and family. Not feeling safe or valuable was perhaps like weeds in a garden: They never go away and require constant tending. The tools of mindfulness, concentration, and insight were tentative new skills, but I had seen how they allowed past events to come up and be transformed. Perhaps with daily use of these tools, I would weed out beliefs that prevented me from seeing I was valuable and good enough just as I was. Perhaps I would see that I was safe to enjoy life fully without trying to control it. Maybe I would get to the place where I lived life with an attitude of love and trust, even for myself.

I TOUCHED A DOG, AND I LIKED IT

During our final outdoor walk, we stood in companionable silence for several minutes, just looking, breathing, and connecting. It was like a symphony was building in every cell of my body. I was awake to not just being alive, but being alive *because* of water in the stream, gifts from the trees, energy from the sunlight, and being seen by my fellow retreaters. The concept that we exist in relationship to each other was a deeply felt experience for me on this walk. I couldn't find any separation between me and the land, the animals and me, or the other people and me.

At lunch, after the bell rang for the final reading of the Five Contemplations before Eating, Noble Silence ended. Talking and laughing filled the sunny dining room. I learned the group practiced twice a week in downtown Toronto. I hoped to be able to join them again over the summer. I was happy that I would have the chance to see Sato, Mia and the others again.

As I put away the dishes, my old classmate Joe and I sat down for a cup of tea. We caught up quickly on our families and careers since our university days, exchanging emails to talk more later. I told him about my walk with Ollie and how much I enjoyed the food. I bought the retreat cookbook and Joe said that I shouldn't be afraid to experiment with the recipes.

It was time to get my things and leave. I saw Eddie, the black and white dog, lying by the back door, one paw outstretched. Ollie was nowhere to be found and likely roaming the woods. Eddie was just being a dog, content in having a sunny place to lay his head. For the first time in my adult life, I did not feel any aversion or notice myself thinking that "dogs are dirty." I also did not have any fear that his teeth were sharp, or that he could bite me. In the absence of these two powerful emotions, I saw that the mental formations for dogs that I had built in my mind had transformed radically. Fear and scorn for dogs were foundational stories I had carried for decades. It felt free and peaceful to have those heavy mental constructs renovated in my mind into a lighter, airier mental construct for dogs. I realized in an instant that dogs — all animals — are beautiful. How could fear exist when I was interbeing with Eddie? I felt drawn to Eddie and patted his belly. *Hi, friend,* my soul seemed to say.

I held Eddie's paw and took a picture of this union. My family would not believe I had willingly touched a dog and felt joy unless they were presented with evidence! This inner change was proof that I was returning home as a different person. I had not created some temporary and illusory sense of peace while on retreat. I was leaving with less fear and more peace than when I had arrived five days earlier. I was more awake to the gifts of life. I had found joy again in living.

PART 6

Breaking Open

"To walk in the world is to find oneself in a body without papers, not a citizen of anything but breath."

—Kazim Ali, *Silver Road: Essays, Maps & Calligraphies*

CHAPTER 27

Coming Home

On the drive home, the stress started creeping in about the pending decision from the insurance company on my disability claim. I also felt my fear about entering the scary world of contracting after eighteen years of staying in one place. Once I made this move, I would need to hustle to find work every year or two. But I had gained insight into fear, approval, and control, and I also had a toolbox of compassion and loving-kindness meditations to help me (listed in Appendix B). I had two calls to action to take back to my everyday life to help me not lose my newfound sense of peace and hope:

1.) Create an island of refuge with a daily practice of the tools I had started to hardwire into my body and brain to fill my cup with joy.

2.) Guard the gates of my mind to limit hurtful things I say and do to others, especially to myself. Don't use food, alcohol, social media, TV, or other sensory inputs to avoid feeling hurt and stressed.

On the front passenger seat, so it wouldn't get wrinkled, was the calligraphy print by Thich Nhat Hanh, reminding me that I was returning home fluid like a river and connected to a Sangha — a community. I resolved that I may not know how to be a less controlling person now, but that I did know how to be in the present moment, be open to the Observer part of myself, and trust that it would show me the way. I knew that joy experienced in daily activities like drinking tea, washing hands, walking on the Earth, or singing from the Sangha songbook would help me be resilient when faced with other people's negativity. I vowed to protect the inner child's consciousness because it was my key to psychological safety. My mission was to love myself, water my own seeds of joy, and let that be the starting point for work and family goals to be peaceful, healthy, and happy. Despite my worries, I was excited to return to my life with this awakened sense of interbeing and a toolbox of practices to find joy in life, fill my cup, and then pour love back into the world, including myself.

I arrived home to an empty house. Tom was at work, and the girls were at school. Apart from a few texts to let Tom know I was okay, I hadn't communicated with my family. The house *felt* different. In my home of the last five days, I had come to see so much beauty in the simplicity of the retreat dining room, bathroom, and cabin. As I walked through my home, it felt alive with my attention, and a feeling of gratitude rose up. This home had sheltered us and provided a safe place for our family. It had welcomed each child as Tom carried the newborn baby across the threshold, and I followed, still weak from childbirth. Both girls came home the day they were born, thanks to the midwife-led births our hospital had accommodated. Jessica had overheated on the warm fall day in the hat I had given her, and developed a heat rash. Two years and two weeks later, Sophia was carried over the threshold happily asleep. By the time she was born, I had learned not to dress a baby too warmly. We had so many gatherings, from birthday parties to family dinners, as we told each other about our days' best and worst parts. I wanted to bring joy to the house that had held us safe all these years, and I resolved to do spring cleaning while I wasn't working. Usually, I would think the spring cleaning was for the humans, but with the sense of interbeing I was feeling, it felt like a way to make the house happy too.

As I put my dirty clothes in the laundry hamper, I felt pulled to tidy and organize the house. It was overflowing with years of accumulated stuff. At the retreat, I was happy with just a few possessions. I didn't want to have unneeded things in my life, whether it was a material object or a belief.

I prepared a snack for the kids and noticed that the maple kitchen cupboards looked dull. They seemed to *ask* me for a loving wash-up. I added Murphy Oil Soap to the grocery list on the fridge and thought of how meditative it would be to wipe down all the wood in the house. After five days of vegan, organic food, my body also wanted to feel as healthy as it had on the retreat. I scanned through the Retreat Eats cookbook and added vegan sausage, kale, blueberries, quinoa, sesame seeds, kimchi, and almond yogurt to the grocery list. Tom and I cooked straightforward meals of fajitas, pasta, burgers, and stir-fries with a very narrow range of vegetables for the picky eaters. I'm not sure what the family would say about this new direction in food.

Then the kids and Tom came home, and we were a family again. I couldn't really explain a lot of the silent retreat to them. They laughed when I told them of getting dressed in my coat and boots and walking like a penguin to the bathroom. They did not share my enthusiasm for vegan food, but they skeptically agreed to try it. I didn't tell my Earth family that I had some additional family members in my heart now. I didn't tell them about my inner child or the rocks I had collected on my walk to represent the inner children of four generations of family, including them. I knew I couldn't adequately put into words this soul-level experience.

They were most amazed to hear that I liked the retreat centre dogs. Only my photos of holding Eddie's paw and walking with Ollie in the snow convinced them I had changed. I think all of my invisible inner children, still very present in my heart, cheered when Jessica and Sophia asked if we could get a dog. Tom was shocked at my abrupt change in orientation to dogs, but like the kids, he wanted to act before I changed my mind. The research began, and by the weekend we had an appointment to visit two Labradoodle puppies. Sophia held the little brown one with a white patch on his chest and immediately fell in love. Labradoodles are gentle and non-aggressive, a perfect dog for the scared girl in me.

A week after getting home, I still felt connected to Little Sunita.

April 17, 2018, Journal Entry: *So I have met someone special. My inner child. We had time together at the True Peace Retreat. I wrote her a letter. She needs me to listen and connect with her. I do that now.*

I have been breathing and keeping my appointment with life since the retreat. I walk in peace. I see with new eyes — no longer needing things from others. No self. Interbeingness.

I believe Little Sunita is getting a dog! So, seeds of joy will be planted in companionship and walks in the forest and sitting and playing.

I just reread my notes. I continue to fill my cup and become whole.

We decided to name our new family member *Harvey the Doodle.* I saw this precious being as a teacher who would help me overcome fear and relearn how to be playful. Harvey was tangible evidence that I was different after the retreat — I had a more joyful outlook on life, my fear had dissolved, and I felt healthy. It felt like my nervous system had been reset after years of being under too much pressure with career, homemaking, and parenthood goals.

THE RETREAT RESET

The retreat hauled me out of my busy daily routine, where I had barely any time to reflect on what it is to be alive in this world, and dropped me into Noble Silence. We filled the awake time with activities like walking, eating, and washing up after meals, which immersed me in present moment awareness for long periods. I had no idea so much joy could be generated just by being present. I had read of this but never experienced it so thoroughly.

As humans, we're wired for social connection, and we have a nervous system that craves pleasure and safety. The retreat worked at this level to show me that I was safe and that life was joyful. It did so in a way that no amount of exposure to secondary sources of safety and joy — in the form of books, podcasts, videos, or courses — could ever have done. It might have been the first time since childhood that I took this much time to feel pleasure in the simple acts of being alive.

The sheer extent of continuous time in the retreat was a reset because it wasn't like going to a yoga class or meditating for twenty minutes and jumping back into a scheduled life. These charts illustrate how different my day was in the five-day retreat versus a typical workday in the ten years from 2007 to 2017.

Figure 1: Time in Hours Spent on a Typical Workday vs. a Retreat Day

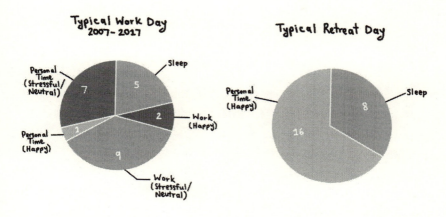

It's a drastic difference because during these years of working full-time with two kids, I had little sleep on a typical day. Also, most of my work or personal time was stressful or neutral because I felt short on time or was speaking up against negative workplace practices. To top it all off, most of 2007–2017 was spent feeling like I didn't do enough.

On the other hand, a retreat day had activities designed to evoke joy and interbeing. Absent was the feeling that there wasn't enough time, or that I didn't accomplish what I set out to do. A true treasure of the retreat was the deep social connection of being accepted by the group and sharing collective wisdom.

During the retreat, my body downshifted into the parasympathetic nervous system for long stretches of awake time. My stress hormones like cortisol, adrenaline, and corticosteroids had no job to do for the first time. They went on their own retreat and left me with a clean mental state with which to absorb life. I received a treasured gift during this suspension of *doing* and this immersion in *being*. The Noble Silence took me to where I needed healing. That resolution brought inner peace and lifted the depression. While my instinct to stop the antidepressants might have been right, I knew it was wrong to do so without medical advice. I felt a bit nervous about confessing my actions to Dr. Joshi but knew it was time to have her thoughts on my decision not to take medicine.

CHAPTER 28

Cleared for Work

I sat on the crinkly white paper covering the exam table, looking at the toy train decals on my doctor's office wall. Only a month ago, I was looking at these same walls getting a prescription for antidepressants. Now I felt so together and at home with myself.

Dr. Joshi checked my blood pressure before we talked, and it was well within the normal range (112/74 mm Hg). I told her about the retreat and how I met with Sato, journaled with my inner child, and found a connection between the workplace stress and the childhood stress I had locked away.

I shared my *aha* moment that being on guard for months due to my male co-worker's unpredictable and threatening behavior stressed me because I was on guard as a child in case authority figures became unpredictable and aggressive. The other *aha* moment was that being a helpless bystander for Rosie in the power-over and patriarchal workplace triggered me to protect women after being a bystander to my grandmother's abuse. Women in my family had to hide things so as not to get in trouble with their husbands, and I hated that domestic abuse was swept under the rug. This secrecy and lack of transparency felt wrong, and like a sign of systemic problems within the family. The women were being manipulated, and the men were abusing their power. I explained to Dr. Joshi that when I thought my work was playing games with our Indigenous partners, it caused a deep conflict that broke my mental health. My workplace touched on too many nerves at once, and I had to go inside to listen to the original hurts before I could regain my physical and mental health.

As a child, I had been powerless to make things fair, but as an adult, I felt called upon to stand up for others' rights. I had more insight now about why I needed to be in control to feel safe. These realizations helped me understand why I felt emotional stress at unfair, power-over workplace practices and why I felt stress when things changed beyond my control at work. I took events too much to heart when circumstances violated my sense of fairness and autonomy. And it was my heart that broke. I now understood why I couldn't reason my way out of the depression. It wasn't my rational mind that was threatened, so it wasn't my rational mind that could fix it. The fear centre of my mind, formed in childhood, needed to be fixed. The retreat practices helped reset my sense of safety and connection in the world. I felt better than I had in years after the sleep, healthy food, inner spiritual connections, and community life I had been immersed in. As a capable adult, I repaired my sense of safety, and the workplace situations did not have the same hold over me.

I didn't know if Dr. Joshi, grounded in medical science, would be skeptical about my reasonings, which seemed to be conjecture from my subconscious rather than a reliable memory. But she said that in my case the retreat was like CBT, cognitive behavioral therapy. CBT has been proven medically to alleviate symptoms of depression. She gave me another assessment for depression and anxiety, and my responses showed I wasn't depressed. Dr. Joshi validated that I didn't need the antidepressants any longer. She didn't seem upset that I had stopped them on my own, or if she was, I didn't sense it. I left her office feeling free of the illness that had been so instrumental in putting me on a path to inner knowledge.

If the retreat was cognitive therapy that could turn my mental formation of *dogs will harm me and might bite* into *dogs are fun to play with,* then perhaps I could reframe my emotional responses to, and at, work. Could I see past the toxic people and heavy-handed practices to realize that I was not threatened but that I was indeed strong enough to respond with compassion? I had high hopes that my work life could feel good again, and that I would find joy in the work itself. The next thing to find out was what the insurance company thought about my claim.

THE DISABILITY INSURANCE VERDICT

The question of whether my disability claim would be approved worried me still. Not having income was an ancestral fear in me, and I couldn't just think it away. I did my best to attend to the worst-case fear that my claim would be denied, which meant I would not be paid for the past weeks of being ill. Mindful walking, sitting, and eating meditation helped calm my anxiety about my financial situation.

The day after I spoke to Dr. Joshi, the insurance agent called and told me my claim had been approved, which meant I would be paid in full for the two months since my last sick note had expired. In addition to agreeing I was ill, they deemed that I should remain off work for two additional months. I was relieved to know I would be paid in full for this time off. But it did not feel right to continue to take money for being on a disability leave when I was no longer sick. I told the agent I was no longer on antidepressants because I had gone through a CBT-like therapy process. I asked her what it meant to my disability pay if I wasn't sick anymore, and I also disclosed that I would not be going back to JumboTek. My health was too precious and tentative at this stage, and the toxic work environment was too dangerous.

She responded with compassion and kindness. She said my disability pay was approved, so I would be paid right to the end date they had determined unless I returned to work or chose to resign. She said I'd still need to see the psychologist as part of the terms of the disability pay, even if I no longer felt depressed. At the end of our call, she said she was sorry for what I had gone through, and I felt her compassion. She said that in my position, she wouldn't want to return to a work environment like the one I had described in my statement.

I wrote in my journal, *They believe me.*

The Best-Life's decision meant a lot to me because someone who worked in disability claims for their living believed I became ill due to the psychological safety issues at work. I believe my claim had credibility because I documented my illness by referencing several of the thirteen psychological safety factors in the Standard, published by CSA Group. This publication was a blessing that I found at the right time to give me the language to submit my claim.

THE MAGIC OF TIDYING

Spring came, flooding the world with warmth, green leaves, and golden sunshine. I wanted to be mindful during this time off, even in the housework. From the time I had returned home from the retreat, I had been itching to organize my nest, and now I had my opportunity. I wiped the stairs and cupboards with Murphy Oil Soap and washed all the windows. I could generate joy by feeling the warm water as I wrung out the rag and inhaled the fresh scent of the soap. I read Marie Kondo's book, *The Life-Changing Magic of Tidying Up*. It was meditative to mindfully hold my possessions and *feel out* if they brought me joy in the present. Memories came flooding back with each inquiry, and I was able to let go of the item with gratitude if it no longer served me. I still had the suit I wore to accept my Women of Colour in STEM award. The style was outdated after ten years, but I recalled how excited and proud I was wearing it during the awards banquet in Atlanta. I let it go with gratitude for the generosity of my manager and company in sending me on that trip.

I spent many days alone in the house, reordering my outer world to come into alignment with the order I had found in my inner world. This was hard emotional, mental, and physical labour. After a day of spending energy connecting joy to hundreds of items from my over-stuffed closet and dresser, I was exhausted. But it did grow neural pathways that recognized which items elicited present-moment joy and which ones to thank for the memories. The house felt lighter as stuff went to the donations pile or out to the garbage. Tidying the physical world decluttered my mental world. Marie Kondo was right: This work is magical.

LEAVING FULL-TIME WORK FOR CONTRACTING

Shortly after the disability claim was approved, I was offered a six-month contract from the one interview I'd had in March. They needed me to start in three weeks, and although it was during my disability pay period, I wanted to leave JumboTek as soon as possible. I hadn't expected my job search to be successful this fast, but I was happy to get out of the hustle of the interview process.

Like tidying my clothes, I was able to let go of JumboTek with gratitude for the good memories and friends while recognizing this company no longer served me well. I was sad to no longer be part of the school, and I would miss working with Rosie and engaging with the mindfulness and coaching communities. Yet, I knew to go back would disconnect me from my values and risk my mental and physical health. Work was not worth dying for. It was with mixed emotions that I sent in my letter of resignation.

Maeve asked if I was sure I wanted to leave while I had disability pay.

"I'm no longer sick," I said.

I knew I had made the right decision when I read through my contract for my new job. It laid out the rate I would be paid per hour and the maximum number of hours in a week unless otherwise agreed to. As a full-time employee in IT, I had had no protection to assure I would be paid extra if I worked extra hours, yet as a contractor, I had that assurance. But the best part of the contract was what wasn't written. Time away from work was unlimited, plus there wasn't a performance review to determine my worth or compensation. There would be no carrot-and-stick dynamic. I probably would never again bond with people at work like a family, as I had done at JumboTek, but that was okay now. The impermanence of the role was ironically comforting to me because it meant I could be a temporary visitor and deal with whatever toxic culture might exist, knowing I had an end date to leave.

Another positive thing about my contract was that the responsibilities were much less than I had at JumboTek, which assured me I could deliver more than expected and still work fewer hours. Doing great work was important to me, and I could achieve these objectives easily without burning myself out. I needed to avoid a high-pressure situation as I made this big transition.

And lastly, the pay was about 50 percent more, but most of that would go towards costs I would pay for now, such as insurance (medical, dental, life, disability), retirement savings, and time off without pay. I was disappointed when I was told I was too much of a liability to qualify for disability due to illness because I'd had a recent claim for depression. All I could qualify for was disability due to a physical injury. It was a risk to work without full coverage, but I felt contracting was the right decision.

CITIZENS OF BREATH

I went one last time to JumboTek to say goodbye to the people who had loved me through my illness. Rosie and I hugged and said we were sisters forever. I now knew it was not my job to be her protector — that this had to come from within her. She told me I had inspired her to be more sure of herself at work. We made plans to meet up, and she excitedly suggested that Jessica, Sophia, and I visit soon for dinner.

The group of friends from the prayer group surprised me with presents and cookies. I opened the gift bag to find a framed print of *Inhale, Exhale* written on a big white background. It was a meaningful gift because the wordless white space was where we had bonded in meditation sessions when we first met each other. It reminded me that although we came from all walks of life, we were citizens of breath. I told them how much I felt their love during the darker days of the depression and how their prayer, posted on my fridge, gave me support.

They also signed a copy of *Oh, the Places You'll Go!* by Dr. Seuss. Their inscriptions on the title page said I positively impacted them, but I could say the very things about them that they wrote for me.

"I'm a much better person because of you."

"You have been a rarity and a breath of fresh air…"

"Thank you for your inspiring light and positivity."

"Thank you for being such a great leader in Mindfulness!"

"Thank you for your positive reinforcement."

"Thank you for teaching me to take the time to inhale and exhale. Thank you for making a profound difference in my life."

I was embarrassed and overwhelmed by their gratitude and feedback, but I knew how special it was to have this kind of love at work. I had had so many dark, sad feelings at work in the last few months. How could they see any light and positivity in me? Maybe even with a mental illness, love can shine through. Their words remind me that no matter what is happening, it's possible to generate tremendous love and positivity with a group of compassionate people. They were a Sangha community, just like True Peace.

I set the *Inhale, Exhale* print next to the framed print of *go as a river, go as a sangha,* both now in front of my meditation cushion. I reread the inscriptions they wrote in the Dr. Seuss book. I felt great love and wrote to my inner child, who also wrote back.

May 3, 2018, Journal Entry: *I am truly blessed for how these people came into my life.*

To my inner child, Little Sunita,

Do you see the joy? How much we are loved? How safe from harm, how we are held in loving-kindness and live in joy?

We are strong and free, my dear one. I am connected to you now and won't lose you. Remind me if I do. I'll come back at playtime and naptime, and mealtime.

Inhale, exhale. Beginner's mind for us, dear one.

Love, Big Sunita

May 3, 2018, Journal Entry: *Dear Big Sunita,*

I am playing. I am safe. Slow down. Don't do so much. Have more fun and ease in your life. Put us first.

Love, Little Sunita

I think the wisdom of my inner child, a subconscious part of me, knew that I was prone to doing too much, getting consumed by my work and personal projects. I would be stressed out starting a new job and be driven to make sure people were happy with my work. These life-long tendencies could sink me if I didn't stay mindful and connected to the part of me that wanted to slow down and have fun.

I felt like weights were lifted off me after Dr. Joshi confirmed I was healthy again and after the claim decision came in as favourable. I closed the chapter at JumboTek with good wishes from my colleagues and my own inner child consciousness for the next part of my career.

CHAPTER 29

Finding the Dharma in the Real World

It was a warm, sunny day when we drove to the farm in Lindsay to bring Harvey the Doodle home. He was quiet on the ride home, emanating a calm presence. Once free in our house, he roamed everywhere, exploring his new toys and crate. He had big green eyes, and his stubby baby tail was adorable. Sophia swaddled him like a baby in old towels that he didn't seem to mind. He was so easygoing and willing to please, and I loved him. But a puppy is a lot of work, and much of it fell to me since I was home all day. I found that being frustrated with a puppy was a dharma door. After only two days of having Harvey at home, I felt unbalanced with the demands on me.

May 7, 2018, Journal Entry: *I'm angry about:*
　　—*People wanting my energy.*
　　—*Harvey not doing it right.* (house-training)
　　—*My time going back to a work schedule instead of stillness and do-nothing.*
　　—*Being too serious.*
　　—*Housework.*
　　—*People needing me.*
　　—*People using me.*

Simply noticing and acknowledging my anger was the first step I had learned about in the retreat. I was labelling these thoughts and seeing that they were mental formations, which reduced their emotional charge. I recalled the advice in one of the retreat dharma talks that breathing is like taking the air away from the fire of anger, helping cool it. Mindful walking and breathing together helped me defuse the anger and remember how joyful it was to just be alive. It helped me remember to be grateful for my family and the privilege of having a sweet puppy. Mindfulness also helped me remember I needed to take it slow as I transitioned from one career to another and cut myself a break because I was only freshly recovered from illness. But without the clarity of Noble Silence and the collective energy of the True Peace Sangha, I had to have the presence of mind to not get carried away by these everyday stressors.

I had so many great tools (listed in Appendix B), but the challenge was to apply them when my mind was in turmoil. Fortunately, project management has a process for working through turmoil which I adapted to help me respond with the dharma of compassion when I felt hijacked out of a peaceful state of mind.

PROJECT DHARMA

A core part of engineering and project management is bringing people together into a team with a singular mission. Psychologist Bruce Tuckman recognized that a small group doesn't bond instantly. Its members go through predictable stages to overcome their individual differences before they can "gel" and become a high-performing unit. Having a step-wise process helps the team trust that even if its members start with their own ingrained ways of working, they will eventually grow and adapt to what works best as a collective to achieve the goal.

The stages are 1.) forming, 2.) storming, 3.) norming, 4.) performing, and 5.) adjourning.

Figure 2: Stages of a Team

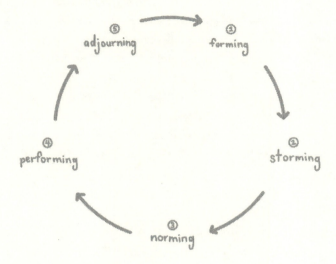

Forming Stage: First, the team forms and is given information for what it will do.

Storming Stage: Initially, the team members have good intentions but feel the emotions and unease of adapting their personality to the group.

Norming Stage: Through real-time experience, they eventually start to know one another's strengths and weaknesses.

Performing Stage: When the team members can divide the work, communicate well, and feel the flow of their togetherness, they become high-performing towards their mutual goal.

Adjourning Stage: Eventually, when the work ends, they disband to start the process all over again on a new mission with new team members.

I have adapted this model to support my mission statement of bringing peace to my life, which I call Project Dharma. The forming and storming stages still apply to what happens as part of daily living. However, the last three stages adapt to how mindfulness meditation can help me respond using what I learned in the retreat: discerning, transforming, and returning.

Figure 3: Project Dharma

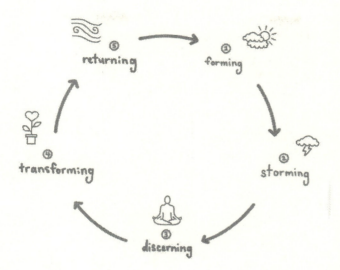

Dharma Forming Stage: The present moment forms in my mind with awareness, and my brain does a first pass on the information it discerns. My brain will form some thoughts. These are mental formations. Often this will be a habitual or negative response because they carry more weight in my survival-focused brain.

Dharma Storming Stage: My mind becomes unsettled if I don't like the present moment or feel dissatisfaction. Even though I feel love and gratitude, sometimes I feel fear creep in because one day I could lose what I love. Even when I have privilege in my life, I can still feel sad. I can be quick to anger and long to recover from feeling hurt. I'm easily carried away by tumultuous thoughts and feelings, but if I can just see the storm within and catch the moment, I can begin to normalize my breathing and raging emotions to find the message in the storm. These moments are the dharma doors that are really learnable moments. The key is to not run away but to open the door and feel the storm.

Dharma Discerning Stage: This is where I pivot to real-time information rather than the story my mind is spinning to understand things better. I try to break through the deception my mind can project from fixed, habitual patterns. To get an accurate view beyond habit thinking, I ground myself in one of my toolbox's present-moment-finding techniques (Appendix B). Of all the tools, I have five that are my go-to methods: 1.) breathing meditation, 2.) loving-kindness or metta meditation, 3.) the self-compassion break, 4.) body scan, and 5.) thought inquiry. This stage is like being a data scientist who needs to find out what is really happening versus what my mind-talk is saying. It is seeing reality as it is in the eye of the storm.

Dharma Transforming Stage: After becoming present via the breath, the natural world, my body, or the feeling of love, it's like I shift into the high-performance mode of my consciousness. I uplink to the consciousness of the collective intelligence in the universe. In teaming up with my Observer, inner child or body wisdom, I have insights that cut through unconscious bias, judgment, false thinking, negative thought formations, or other neural patterns my brain likes to employ to fit its narrative. I can drop the need for certainty, which is really a need for control and safety. I can drop beliefs that keep me separated from others and disrupt my peace. I also tend to lose the sense of a separate self as I cultivate interbeing. When I see a cloud in my tea, a rose in the garbage, or my grandmother in the shape of my fingers, I see that the nature of reality is complex, nuanced, and completely interdependent. When I see that it's all a dance of interbeing, then there is no more storm.

In this stage, I can go beyond my mental boundaries to spiritual experiences that knit me into a whole person, like the visualizations of meeting my ancestors or conversing with my inner child. I see deeper into the present in the transforming mode and find more peace and joy, no matter what formed initially in my mind. My nervous system calms down and recognizes at a creature level that this moment is not the painful past nor the scary future. I can calm the story's emotions and come to wiser conclusions.

It's a significant yield for the mental effort invested and transforms my previous understanding of reality to one that is more peaceful, loving and kind.

Dharma Returning Stage: My connection to the Observer and inner child comes and goes. Every time I've been on a team, I've emerged stronger for having been with those particular people, working together on that specific challenge. I feel fulfilled by both the collaboration and the achievements. Similarly, after joining the Observer or inner child consciousness, I feel whole and fulfilled, like I grew into my best and highest self a little more. This mode completes the stress cycle and returns me to a more balanced state. It celebrates the insights or peace achieved, which is spiritually healthy, and returns me to the world with an invitation to bring that new understanding forward in my life.

Project Dharma describes how I have shifted my relationship with life since the retreat. Many think slowing down and meditating is unproductive and not worth the effort. Yet what I've found is that mindfulness meditation is wildly productive. I've often said that we have to slow down to go fast in project work. It's counterintuitive, but I believe we will finish on time or even early if we pause at the beginning of the project to properly analyze and plan and avoid the temptation to jump into haphazard action.

With meditation, I believe going slow is going fast. That pause to become mindful provides much better information to take action. For me, that means I get less stressed, speak with more kindness, listen with more attention, and act with more care. If I fail, I can become aware of it and try again. I gain clarity to see solutions and not take things personally. I put less negativity into the world and my body by finding a more peaceful and loving way. Now that's productivity.

CHAPTER 30

Dharma Doors

It takes concentration and intention to keep watching thoughts, experiencing the flow of emotion and breath, and staying grounded in everyday life. When someone doesn't stop at a four-way stop and takes my turn, I get angry and yell, "Asshole!" Sometimes, I'll notice this harsh, angry response within myself and follow my breathing until I can get into the discerning stage. Then my compassion rises, and I wonder if they had a hard day. I send them loving kindness as their car disappears down the road. I've poured love rather than anger into the world.

The five stages of Project Dharma help summarize many complex teachings from Buddhism into something I can use practically in a stress-filled life to not get swept away into negative mental states. Going through this process repeatedly, I've come to see that each moment of life is a chance of a lifetime to move to a higher level of love, peace, and joy. The more I apply this process, the more efficient I've become at recognizing the forming and storming stages. Instead of getting stuck there, I can intentionally enter the discerning stage and see my way through to the transforming stage, where inevitably I'm called on to respond with love.

One morning, a year after we got him, Harvey illuminated the power of the Project Dharma transforming stage by bringing compassion to the world. Although Harvey came into our life by chance after I went to a silent retreat, he was indeed the perfect dog for us. His canine personality was so centred and soothing that he became a kind of therapy dog to us. His sweet, gentle soul was always uplifting, and I enjoyed our 6 a.m. routine of walking together outside.

A few minutes into one of our walks, I heard a strange sound. I thought it was some birds, but I realized it was crying as we approached the intersection near our house. I looked around and then saw a person sitting on the grass by the curb across the street. Looking closer, I saw the person was a young woman.

I crossed the street, unsure of what was going on, and wondered if this could be a domestic fight. I half-expected an angry man to pop out from behind the nearest bush. But there was no one else at this early hour. It was just her and me and Harvey.

She looked to be late teens or early twenties and had mascara running down her cheek. She wasn't dressed warmly enough for the chill of the spring morning or the wet dew on the grass. I asked if she was okay and if there was anything I could do to help. She shook her head, seemingly too emotional or maybe embarrassed to speak. I got still, dropping into the present moment. I gazed at her, trying not to let any judgments or mental formations take over the moment. I felt the cool air, smelled the grass, heard the birds, and as fully as I could, I felt her pain too.

Just discerning into the present moment gave me an intuition that Harvey could help her. I asked her if she wanted to hold my dog and warned her that while he was gentle, he was still a puppy and liked to jump on people. I didn't want her to be frightened if he got over-excited. The young woman said she would like that very much, so I let Harvey go to her. She took him in her lap while still crying, and Harvey did not jump around. He laid his head on her leg, forming an intimate, loving embrace. I stood by, not wanting to influence this scene. Harvey was the perfect soul to remind this girl's soul that there is goodness and love in the world. Finally, she stopped crying, and I could tell her energy was calmer. Thanking me, she separated from Harvey and let him go. I asked again if she needed help — if I could call someone, take her somewhere, or get her a cup of tea. She refused firmly but politely, and I could tell she didn't want to talk. I knew it was time to go. What needed to happen at that time had taken place, the Project Dharma transforming stage. It was the returning stage now.

This was a beautiful example of the power of the present moment and intentionally not letting any energy but love fill it, not even worry, fear or speculation. I needed this superpower in my contract work as well when I was faced with difficult situations. Even though being a freelancer gave me more autonomy and balance in my work life, I still encountered people who threatened my psychological safety. Sometimes I felt sad just like the young woman I found crying on the grass. Project Dharma helped me respond appropriately when I got tangled up with people at work who embodied the power-over dysfunction that I so dislike in corporate culture. I suffered through periods where these people disrupted my sense of peace no matter how much I tried to douse the anger with meditation techniques. When my family was fed up hearing me complain, it was a sign I was wallowing in wishing my life was different. I knew the villains in my work life were dharma doors pointing me to some unmet need I had to fulfill, or they were a call-to-action from the universe to pour loving thoughts instead of anger.

THE QUEEN BEE GETS A PASS

I entered the sphere of a senior woman, Beth, who was territorial and easily threatened by women at her skill level or above. I learned from my female peers that Beth had campaigned with senior leaders to discredit women she didn't like, to the point that women quit the organization or were fired. I knew I was on the outs with her when she interrupted me in meetings and asked me sweetly, but without giving me a choice, to take my point offline. She never interrupted the men this way. My intuition was that Beth didn't want female competition and wanted others to think that I had little to offer. I vividly remember when another senior leader, Jean-Francois, asked her to include me in a series of meetings, and she didn't respond with an agreement. Instead, Beth suggested they discuss it offline. I was stunned to see her openly resist this direct request to be an inclusive leader. Later I learned that there is a term for women like this in business: Queen Bee syndrome.

The next day, Jean-Francois followed up with me. "Sunita, I'm sorry," he said. "I tried to reason with her, but she doesn't like you. I feel terrible about it."

What the fuck, I thought. *How does this woman get away with bullshit like this in a professional setting? Is this work or high school?*

I was outraged and could feel how tight my body was when I sat down for meditation. Because I was so agitated, I meditated using the Four Establishments of Mindfulness. This is the power tool I bring out when I'm really bothered. It's a direct teaching of the Buddha that Thich Nhat Hanh translated, and it works for me. I went through all of the breathing exercises:

> *Breathing in, I am aware of my whole body.*
> *Breathing out, I am aware of my whole body.*
> *Breathing in, I calm my body.*
> *Breathing out, I calm my body.*

Ironically, saying these phrases helped me see how un-calm I was. I watched the emotions ebb and flow and realized it was *hurt* that I was experiencing. I was … hurt. Once I could see that, I thought to do another meditation that helped with the hurtful parts of life: the Mindful Self-Compassion break. This meditation has three parts — first, to acknowledge suffering or pain, second, to realize we're not alone, and third, to bring warmth.

I first learned this tool from Chris Germer, a leading clinical psychologist, meditation practitioner, author, and teacher of mindfulness and compassion in everyday life. He taught it to a classroom full of adults during a one-day workshop. Chris explained that showing warmth and kindness can improve well-being and help overcome obstacles like anxiety. Afterward, I wanted to learn more, and took an eight-week course in Mindful Self-Compassion (MSC). In that training, I learned hard emotions, like anger, cover softer feelings of hurt and feeling unworthy. The MSC course profoundly changed the way I treated myself. During the course, I journaled *self-compassion is adding kindness to struggle, compassion to hurt, love to hate, and warmth to coldness.* I came to see that self-compassion is like duct tape in my toolbox of mindfulness tools. It makes many broken things function better.

The MSC break is part of the Project Dharma discerning stage, where I cool off the hot emotions to see what softer feelings lie underneath. I did the steps of this meditation, first becoming mindful, second understanding I was not alone in this experience, and third feeling the energy of kindness. In the second step, I realized that other people at work worldwide feel marginalized when kept from having a voice at the table. Great compassion flowed out of me for women, people of colour, and people of different sexual orientations who have felt discriminated against at work. In the third step, I placed my hand on my heart to feel its warmth and acknowledged this was a painful part of my work life. I felt compassion flow inwards. I admitted that it hurt to not be liked by someone. I connected that this present-day situation was bringing up approval needs in me.

This short five-minute meditation gave me insights into what was really happening. I recognized that I would be upset seeing anyone in a position of power mistreat another because my inner child consciousness was sensitive to that dynamic from the past. Being shut out and minimized were the same toxic tactics Rosie experienced at JumboTek, and it felt like that was happening to me now.

After giving myself this compassionate understanding, I could offer compassion to Beth. I realized that she could feel threatened by me, and that this was her response mechanism. I communicated to my inner-child consciousness that we were safe and it was okay if someone didn't like us. My fear centre settled enough to see the truth that she really couldn't harm me with her behaviour. I could feel myself relax. At that point, feelings of gratitude came up when I looked at the situation differently and realized that Beth had given me a gift of time.

She marginalized me so much that I had little work to do. I was bored at work for weeks because of her shutting me out. But during that time, I practiced compassion and appreciated the lighter workload, which gave me a chance to get caught up on other things. Then one day, during meditation, an idea downloaded into my mind nearly formed. I saw a management report based on charts and spreadsheets that I could create. I used my free time to go deep into the data and play around with Excel spreadsheets until I found meaning and insights. This work had a flow quality about it, and I enjoyed it. When I showed people my findings, they were both thankful and impressed. I couldn't have found that inspired idea or unlocked that achievement if Beth hadn't cut me out of many meetings and made me upset enough to turn to meditation.

I could not change the fact that she did mistreat me, and it was even more egregious that she had a history of bullying behaviour and was allowed to get away with it. Working with her could have been biologically toxic if stress hormones flooded my body because I was angry and hurt. However, mindful self-compassion helped me switch to the parasympathetic nervous system, supporting mental well-being and creative thinking. This situation actually gave me a more fulsome view of how abuse of power triggers me and how to unwire that trigger point just a little bit more. This woman wanted to put me down, but instead, she was a dharma door that strengthened me spiritually.

THE MACHO MAN GETS A PASS

"Luigi is old-school Italian, Sunita," a colleague said when I told them that someone on our team was difficult to interact with.

"He's an alpha male who doesn't like to work with women. But, he's really good at what he does," my colleague explained. "Even the men he works with need to treat him like the alpha male."

The words *he doesn't like to work with women* should never be uttered at work. Yet they were, without shame or pause.

What the fuck, I thought. *Are we in the 1950s or part of some wolfpack?*

I woke up the following day at 4:30 a.m. thinking about Luigi. I did not want Luigi in my bedroom again, so I knew I had to work this out in meditation. This time, metta meditation helped me with the simple phrase, "May I be safe," spoken while holding my hand over my heart.

My inner Voice whispered, *Luigi is Me. You are Me. You can't love Me, or yourself, without loving Luigi.*

Damn, I remembered thinking right on the meditation cushion. *Luigi is a person who, just like me, wants to feel safe. If I really believe in interbeing, I need to send him love, not condemnation.*

I realized that my inner children were the ones Luigi made feel unsafe. Even after all the inner work, if any person threatens my peace, the inner child in me needs reassurance that all is well. Like Beth, Luigi doesn't like me, and it hurts. I sat with that yucky feeling for a bit, and the pain grew less significant as I watched. The resistance to Luigi lessened until I had a sense of interbeing to see we were all one, just like my inner Voice said.

After the Project Dharma forming, storming, discerning, and transforming stages of working through my initial aversive reaction to Luigi, I went to the returning phase. This is where I saw that I could use Luigi as an opportunity to deepen my skills of interbeing. It was a hard pill to swallow seeing a man get a pass and have his ego stroked by the corporation. Yet I saw these things were beyond my control to change. Instead, I focused on working with Luigi and changing my reactions to ones of compassion and interbeing. Luigi did not interrupt my sleep any longer.

Beth and Luigi did make my working life awful for a while. There were times I wished I was wealthy enough to stop working and get away from them. When co-workers like Beth and Luigi make me feel marginalized or outraged that the world is not fair, it can bring unhealthy mental states. I worry about the depression coming back because work is getting more stressful with each passing year. It seems that since financial markets have been on a roller coaster due to the pandemic, work is squeezing people harder, forcing them to do more in less time. The workplace is full of people who are burning themselves out trying to meet the unhealthy demands of work culture, and I must be careful not to get sucked into that mode. Leaders at the top can be adept at being two-faced to look like they care while operating ruthlessly. Such people are slippery, don't walk their talk, and I hate being in the culture they create, even with the psychological protection that I gain from being a contractor.

***

Jessica and Sophia play a video game together, and they have so much fun. I hear bursts of laughter and excited voices when I walk by the room on the night a game update happens. Their joy is contagious; the update means new characters drop, and there will be new challenges to overcome. Seeing dharma doors in the workplace as opportunities to uplevel my skills transforms the work world for me. However, work is not a game, and the real challenge is not to compromise health, values, or integrity. The consequences are real if the time spent at work results in toxic hormones and chemicals being injected into my body, disrupting sleep, digestion, immune function, heart function, and mental function. Just like in the video game, characters do "drop" into the work world, and difficulties arise out of my control. The difference now is that instead of wanting it to be different, I see it as a dharma door and try to see which stage of Project Dharma I'm in and respond accordingly with my superpowers of awareness, concentration, and insight. I am guarding the gate against things that would harm my world, and I am building myself a refuge where I can fill my cup with the love I need to bring to the world.

And like a video game, I've leveled up with each work situation. I couldn't have found peace in an increasingly crazy world if I wasn't skilled at being in the present moment. Then one morning in the second year of the pandemic, 2021, I was unexpectedly given a gift during meditation. It was a gift that took living in a loving way to an entirely new level for me.

CHAPTER 31

The Heart as CEO

Thanks to the pandemic work-from-home lifestyle, I made morning meditation a regular part of my day. I managed to sit for twenty minutes daily and often added walking or mindfulness moments throughout the day. I had set up a meditation corner tucked under a window where I could see the sunrise. On this morning, the dark night sky had a hem of fiery orange light where the sun was rising. I paused before sitting on my cushion to appreciate the miracle of daylight that comes without fail. Nothing was bothering me, and I felt relatively peaceful, just breathing. After a few minutes, a vision sprang into my mind of a group of children who had been cast out of a warm home with a fire on the hearth. They were dirty, hungry, cold, and dressed in rags. This vision was like a vivid, waking dream.

Spontaneously I saw that these children were parts of me that I had cast out of my heart a long time ago. I resisted opening the door and letting them into my clean, perfect home. I could feel that in their heart they wanted to reunite with me. Still with hesitation, I opened the door and let one child in while the others waited outside. There was a warm bath in the room, and as the child was bathed, dressed in clean clothes, brought to the fire, and given food, I could see that this child represented failure. In the safety of the hearth, I felt like failure was something I no longer feared. By accepting this child into my hearth and heart, I welcomed failure as a part of life. I felt more complete.

I went to the door and let the next child go through the same routine. I welcomed this child and saw she was about my fear of not getting approval. She had split away from me at a young age when I needed approval from others. Now it felt like my survival wasn't contingent on others' approval.

The next child represented love. I had lost her when I lost my ability to feel worthy just by being me. When she came to the hearth, it was like a golden light bathed the room.

May 1, 2021, Journal Entry: *Love was the dirtiest and coldest. But once cleaned up, shone radiantly and cleaned the others with light rather than water.*

The following two children were cleaned up in Love's light and joyfully joined the others. They represented humour and playfulness, two parts of me that I had cast out for the seriousness of studying and working.

Two more children needed to come in, but I was much more afraid to let them in. I had pushed these two very far away and knew that I would be most vulnerable to the world if I let them in. The second last child represented courage. I had taken the safe way in life many times, and this part of me wanted to live life daringly. She didn't want to be out in the cold anymore.

Finally, the last one, the hardest one to reunite with, was the child who was the truth. This child felt dangerous to let back into my heart because, with this reunification, I was committing to living an awakened life. I didn't want her to cross the threshold because she would disrupt habitual thinking that I had used like armour to protect myself from hurt or blame. This child was going to cut through the bullshit I told myself to make myself feel righteous and a victim of others. I was scared of her. I thought about closing the door for several moments. But the child who represented love pressed me, and I let the child that was the truth cross the threshold. She would make me vulnerable, but I had to accept that to become whole.

I left this meditation with wonderment because I felt at home with myself in a way I never knew was possible. The image of me as a young child dancing on the pile of hay in Guyana and fist-pumping the air with joy came to my mind. This was the same image that came to me when I reunited with Little Sunita during the silent retreat.

That little girl seemed to be saying, *Let's run this show differently now. It's time to live the biggest, boldest, and most joyful life. It's time to stop being never-not-afraid.*

I could imagine her saying, *Finally, I got you to hear me.*

It was like I had a village of unseen children who wanted to feel safe and loved and experience the fun of life through my thoughts and feelings. These children were demanding too, like most children, when their needs were not met. Although they were parts of my subconscious, I genuinely sensed their message was here to help me stay in peace and integrity. They wanted me to see that when fear of failure or fear of not getting approval arose, I must apply mindfulness practices instead of being carried away by the protection strategies I had adopted way back. They wanted me to bring laughter, play, courage, and truth to my life.

***

Noble Silence during the silent retreat was about getting to know the true nature of reality. As I spend more time in Noble Silence, it's clear that I am consciousness without boundaries. The lost children vision was a specific instruction sent from my subconscious about what was separating me from a joyful life. Like the journaling with Little Sunita, this vision brought me instant inner power. But I wouldn't have "gotten it" as much if it hadn't come through the plane of mindfulness meditation. Outside of this plane, the messages land on my rational mind. The industrial psychologist who assessed me during my 1999 interview with SciTech North gave me insights on how low self-worth and being overly nice at work were things to work on. But that report's information didn't sink into my bones and soul because it was received at my head level, not my heart level. The messages in this vision came from within and dropped like a soul makeover, taking the peace, meaning, and connection I felt to a higher level.

Only when I'm in states of deep awareness do the messages I need land in my soul, infused with meaning and momentum for change. The inspiration comes from inside the spirit, and the most consistent ways I've seen to connect to my spirit are through the compassion, joy, and kindness meditations in my toolbox.

Merriam-Webster's definitions of the word *inspiration* include —

> 3: the act of drawing in, specifically: the drawing of air into the lungs.

> 4a: a divine influence or action on a person believed to qualify him or her to receive and communicate sacred revelation, b: the action or power of moving the intellect or emotions, c: the act of influencing or suggesting opinions.

What I've come to know is that following the drawing in and out of breath, the *inspiration* of breath leads me to spiritual communication that moves my thinking more than any other activity can. Living a more awakened life is not necessarily pleasant because I see more of my tendency to overwork to compensate for low self-worth, need for approval, and fear of failure. By overworking, I laugh and play less and miss out on life. It takes the spiritual effort of compassion to unwind these habits and keep my work hours and stress levels in good balance. I know that Jessica, Sophia, Tom, and even Harvey love it when I'm laughing and happy rather than bearing the world's weight on my shoulders. The seeds of approval-seeking, perfectionism, and the need for control are easily sprouted and can run my life like a maniacal Chief Executive Officer. It's time for this old-school CEO to step down and let the original CEO, these lost children who don't fear vulnerability, run the show.

Awareness helps me avoid thinking like a dysfunctional CEO who is stuck in a command-and-control mindset, driven by fear, including fear of failure, and obsessed with self-preservation. Awareness helps me see when I am being a ruthless boss of my life who doesn't allow time for self-care or downtime because I'm holding myself to such a demanding to-do list in a day.

In a moment of mindfulness, I realized I don't give myself breaks during meetings to get a glass of water or go to the bathroom. There was a moment of awakening during a self-compassion meditation when I realized how harsh I was to cut it so close to catching the train home. I would not leave meetings when they ran overtime or politely cut off a conversation, and that had me running down the sidewalk and racing up the platform stairs. Sometimes I missed the train, and other times I launched my sweaty self into the train car, fighting to catch my breath. In the light of self-compassion, I realized just how unkind I was to myself. And each meditation gave me enough awareness to change my patterns and let people know I needed to leave to go home or be late for a meeting so I could take a break.

As the skills of awareness have taken root with repeated meditation practice, I've seen just how dark my thinking, emotions, and moods can be. I've come to accept that I'm prone to depressive, dramatic, spiraling thinking that I must guard against. When I'm short-tempered or miserable, I know I am likely putting too much pressure on myself or setting the bar too high with my standards for doing a good job. Even writing this book has taken me off the path of peace as I repeatedly set unrealistic goals. The stress of wanting to "get it right" and the fear of "doing a bad job" made me grouchy and absent from a family that needed me and wanted me to be happy. In her direct way, Sophia asked me to never write another book while she was still in high school and living at home. While this hurt to hear, my heart saw the truth that I did have to find a balance between writing and working full-time. I listened to my heart's intelligence when it was time to stop writing and be with my family.

An unhealthy workplace was the trailhead for my journey to see what needed to be healed and reconciled in my mental world. Just as I rebel at work if I sense unethical practices or a lack of integrity, my inner child consciousness creates a storm of protest if my self-talk creates a culture of harshness and unkindness.

CHAPTER 32

The Real Work

It's not lost on me that these inner truths are coming at the end stage of my career and certainly in the last half of my life. As Oliver Burkeman starkly points out in his book *Four Thousand Weeks: Time Management for Mortals,* someone who lives to be eighty years old will have about four thousand weeks on Earth. I quickly calculated that I have about eighteen hundred weeks left until eighty, and three hundred of those still need to be high-income years to make it to retirement. That leaves only fifteen hundred non-working weeks, and a good part of those could be spent living with reduced health or suddenly single if a spouse dies.

Fifteen hundred weeks seems quite short, but it makes me more determined to enjoy the present moment. Life is a miracle, but even so, it takes daily effort to see that, because life has moments that suck the joy right out of things. The depression and dark times at JumboTek showed me that love has to be there when things are going right and *also when they are not.* I think this is what the career counsellor wanted me to see during my sick leave when he recommended that I read *Man's Search for Meaning* by Viktor Frankl. In line with Buddhist thought, this book teaches that having an attitude of love, even in suffering, transforms the experience.

The meaning of life is to bring up love and compassion as a first response, especially for the crappy parts. My purpose was to find love where I was.

And this purpose was not one I just got out of the blue. I learned about kindness and love from my parents and grandmother early in life. It was like I went on a journey to find answers that were in me all along. I realized I still had access to the person who embodies love, despite having suffered physical and emotional hardship. She has lived well over four thousand weeks in her eighty-five years. I was curious what Nani's message would be from her life experience.

GRANDMOTHER WISDOM

I drove Nani home after taking her for her second COVID-19 vaccine at a clinic near my house. She lives about forty kilometers away. I took the opportunity of having alone time with her to ask her about my childhood memories that had surfaced in the silent retreat with the True Peace meditation group.

I didn't want to bring up something that might prove to be too traumatic for her. I was scared to initiate the topic of domestic abuse, which I had never heard spoken about directly in my family. Over half the drive had passed without the words coming. I knew this time alone with my grandmother was a gift, and I didn't want to let it slip by.

Finally, I said, "Nani, I don't remember much of childhood. But I remember being scared. Was Nana bad to you?"

She got a faraway look in her eyes, but her voice was solid as she replied. "Your Nana was very bad to me," she said. "One time, my whole head bus' open."

She meant that she was struck so hard it caused her head to burst open and bleed. Her words were terrifyingly direct, but her energy was pure love.

I know Nani has a photograph of my grandfather, who I called Nana, on her altar in her home. Even though he passed many years ago, Nani prays daily loving thoughts to her husband and visualizes him in heaven. So I know her words about being struck violently have no bitterness to them. She was just stating a fact, but there was no emotional pain attached. Her absence of hurt let a dharma teaching into my life about the power of love:

Nani could clearly recall the past but held no ill will toward it. She didn't deny what she went through, yet she held no bitter story about it. She had no victim mindset, shame, denial or weakness that I could sense. Nani has endured being married as a child, by our standards today, and serving her husband and his family as someone lower in the social system. She is also an abuse survivor. Yet, her heart is big enough to see past the harshness of life and be at peace. She has no high school diploma. She never had a career. Yet she does the highest work of all — being a loving person.

I took one hand off the steering wheel and held hers. We continued to chat, and Nani told me that prayer helps her the most. I marveled at how she channels her energy to see goodness and generate love. I pulled into the driveway of her apartment building, where she was still living on her own. I released her seatbelt buckle for her and went around to help her out of the car.

She held my hand to step out and thanked me for helping get her the vaccine appointment and driving her door to door.

"Bless, bless, bless you, meh pickney," Nani said as she hugged me tight.

When Nani brings her being into your sphere, and you feel her vibration of love, and when she goes one step further to give her blessing directly to you, it's divine. Hugging her is like connecting to the live wire of love. I tried memorizing the feel of the love pouring out of her. Through her as a role model, I knew that pain from the past doesn't need to live in the present. I didn't have to live my life as if I was a hurt or powerless child. All I had to do was go forward and bring love, just as Nani is doing.

GREAT-GREAT-GRANDMOTHER WISDOM

I wondered how our paths to peace were related. Religion has never given me the sense of meaning and connection that meditation does, yet prayer is what Nani is all about. A few months later, we had alone time once more as we chatted in my living room, waiting for her COVID-19 booster appointment. Harvey the Doodle, who excitedly still jumped on visitors even though he was three years old, came to lie at her feet as if guarding her. It was like he sensed her calm energy.

"How did you come to have two religions?" I asked.

"From little, we go through a lot," Nani said. I thought she was talking about her marriage, but she was referring to her mother. "My mother died when she was only forty, and my father didn't care for us."

I couldn't imagine seven children losing their mom. Nani would have been twenty-two years old with two children of her own, grieving the loss of her mother. My mother was only five years old at the time.

"My grandmother, my Nani, taught us to pray. When I was crying for my mother, my Nani said my mother was gone, and my father wasn't going to help us. She told us that Lord Krishna was our mother and father now. She teach us to pray, and we prayin' all the time."

Nani's Nani was her maternal grandmother. I tried to picture this great-great-grandmother of mine, and it felt like I was meeting a new family member. I imagined her teaching a young mother how to grieve such a loss even while she was grieving a daughter. Nani said her grandmother's parents had been born in India. I imagined my great-great-great-grandparents leaving their country to seek a better life. I had read that these indentured workers were deeply religious, and that's what got them through the trauma of the ocean crossing and the slave-like working conditions in their new homes, like Guyana.

"But, how did you come to pray to Jesus too?" I asked.

"I always have a picture of Lord Jesus, even in Guyana," Nani said. "People dis come to deh house and talk to us about Jesus." I thought she must mean missionaries.

"Then, when I come to Canada, there was only church here. And I wanted to go pray, so I had to go to church. It was hard to leave Guyana. Your Nana wanted to go back, but we had to stay here. Jesus helped me."

"Sometimes when you deh in a problem, you say, 'God, I don't know how to do dis thing.' And because you pray, God send the right person to you. Prayer is good. You don't know which is a bad day for your children. You don't know what is a bad day for you. I pray every day, and if I miss a day, it don't feel right."

Nani's hazel eyes sparkled behind her glasses with deep feeling as she spoke. It was clear to me that Nani truly believes in prayer, that it supports her through finding solutions to her problems, and that she trusts there will be help if something bad happens. This felt very much like my meditation practice. I feel out of sorts if I miss a day without time in contemplation and present-moment awareness. And I've seen so many times that starting my morning off in meditation helps me drop anxieties, feel light-hearted, and yield insights that help me with my problems. The Observer or my inner Voice, as I call my non-self, helps me see that I have answers within me that I can access. If unwholesome reactions of hurt, fear, and anger storm through, then the next step is to bring up seeds of non-judgment, compassion, and kindness to water them.

Nani also believes God sends people to help when you pray. The depression was a dark time for me, and many people helped me. There was the prayer group where JTekkers prayed together in a conference room at lunch. In the Mindful@Work Pod, we meditated together. In the Coaching Pod, we came together as a worldwide group of caring people to provide coaching services. These were workplace expressions of love, and looking back, I believe they saved my mental health from being more damaged. I think they saved my life, to be honest. Before the depression, my friends Julia, Patrick, Liam, and Ben were there, and I found Greta, a caring and compassionate manager. I also met genuinely caring people at the U of T Mindfulness program and True Peace Sangha. My inner Voice and the Observer also help me channel my inner wisdom. I can't imagine this ocean of help wasn't called to me.

"Nani, I don't pray," I said. I felt odd confessing this to my religious grandmother.

Nani shook her head swiftly and spoke firmly. "Don't worry. Don't make da bother you. It doesn't matter to God. Be truthful, be kind and be loving. You know what is right from wrong. You know fire. If you put your hand in it, it will burn. So why put your hand in? That's how right and wrong work. That's how we grow up from back home."

Nani, sitting in my living room with Harvey at her feet, shared her grandmother's wisdom about how doing good is what life is about.

"Doing good is like a bank account. When you put in money, the interest will grow. The same will be when you put in good. You will receive it back."

"You do a lot of kindness to people," Nani said to me. "You help people with their problem. Like today you bring me, and you do good to help me get the vaccine. You do a blessing. That is putting in kindness. My Nani taught us we have to keep on doing the right thing all the time."

She had conviction in her voice as she said, "You don't have to pray."

My great-great-grandmother helped my grandmother ease her suffering by teaching her to do good. In my ancestors' world, doing good was through prayer. But my grandmother had the wisdom to tell me that doing good didn't have to follow that one path. Nani was telling me to do the work of distinguishing right from wrong, which meant, in her teaching to me, to be loving and kind. I wondered if the love that found me at work, from my inner consciousness, and in my local communities was because of the loving-kindness I tried to give to people who cross my path. It seemed very likely.

INDISCRIMINATE LOVE

Buddhism, like Nani, doesn't believe there is one path. Dharma is not exclusive. I think it lives in all teachings that are based on love that is indiscriminate and in all hearts that embody that practice. I can see dharma in Hinduism, which I was born into, in Christianity, which I married into and practiced for my children, and in Buddhism, which seemed to be a path I was led to by the universe when I asked for help during my depression. I can see dharma in the Indigenous beliefs I learned of — the Seven Grandfather Teachings and the Haudenosaunee Thanksgiving Address. I can see it in the Zulu greeting of Sawubona, "I see you." I can see dharma in the Western-based research on self-compassion I learned from Kristin Neff, and Chris Germer's Mindful Self-Compassion course. My meditation practice asks me to see all of life and respond with love equally.

Because that's what everyone is asking for.

To be seen.

To be known.

To be responded to with love.

CHAPTER 33

Healing a Toxic Work World

I believe bringing indiscriminate love to the workplace is the way to make many people's lives better. My line of work exposes me to dysfunctional people and organizations, as many lines of work do. People promoted in technology can be wonderful leaders, but some can be cutthroat, smiling assassins. It only takes one of these people to take away psychological safety and well-being from many who work beside and below them. It's a reality that a counter-culture is generated by a few people who leave their kindness at the door to gain power, wealth, and market share. Their behaviour gets a pass because organizations are too blind or too determined to succeed.

This might sound like an ungenerous statement, but the reality is there are a lot of people suffering in the work world. Statistics and cost-impact analyses exist to prove that with very reliable data. There are also the un-documented, non-quantitative feelings of people who are contemplating suicide right now. There is the undocumented, non-quantitative worry that supporting family members have for the health of their loved ones. Sometimes in meditation, I feel this collective pain and send loving-kindness to each soul that is suffering. I recognize that even the people who create or tolerate the psychologically harmful workplace also need my energy of loving-kindness. I visualize a warm golden light and send it out of my heart indiscriminately to everyone.

Off the meditation cushion, when I'm in the bustle of the workday, the stages of Project Dharma help me know what the kindest thing to do is. I can bring love to work by planning a project well and saving people from wasted meetings and anxiety. I can listen to the person who no one else thinks is important to listen to. I can recognize someone who is overlooked. I can stand up to bullying. I can acknowledge burnout and push for a more human pace of work. I can do the right thing in the clarity of present-moment awareness.

"MAKE EVERYTHING AS SIMPLE AS POSSIBLE, BUT NOT SIMPLER." —ALBERT EINSTEIN

The mental health problem our world faces is complex, but I believe the solution is simple. We can make things better by acting with kindness, compassion, or love in any given situation. The influential people at the top of organizations are trying to improve the workplace without going through an inner change to cultivate kindness and compassion. Without embodying these states, I don't think they will fix much because they cannot see the issues from the point of view of the people suffering them. Work will become less toxic when ordinary people stand up for the rights of ordinary people, when they call out disrespectful behaviour and when they choose to not tolerate fakeness and abuse of power.

WHAT I KNOW FOR SURE

My mindfulness meditation practice is well beyond the workplace mindfulness I first learned, which focused on stress reduction, increased happiness, and productivity for the workforce. The mindfulness I learned at the silent retreat is more spiritual. Like the field Rumi speaks of, I communicate with a loving presence when I go there. I can hear the frightened and wise parts of me and attend to them. They want to be seen by me and enjoy it when I drop into stillness and meet up with them. There is a distinct language of wordless communication that happens in this space, and it has the definite purpose of furthering the completion of the expression of life. The stillness wants to remove fear, or maybe the illusion of fear. I just have to allow that space to open. When I pay this attention on the inside, my cup is filled, and I have the true form of love inside of me to pour back onto the world. This aspect is not really discussed in workplace mindfulness programs because it cannot be scientifically measured or proven. Yet this felt spiritual connection and connection to the inner wisdom enables me to keep my integrity, peace, and health in a toxic work environment, and even bring light to it.

The supernatural experiences I had in my life seem to show me that the universe sees me too and wants to awaken me to a truer reality. The dream where my inner Voice asked me to pour love onto souls leaving the Earth felt like I had a universe of love coursing through me. After my first yoga class, I was deeply in the present moment, then had this experience of spontaneously melting into oneness. When I started to run at Cades Cove, it felt like the Earth wanted to join up with me, and I had a high-powered experience of connection with Mother Nature herself. My subconscious gave me a rich visualization in my brother's hospital room that flooded my body with ancestor love so that I didn't bring fear energy into the room. These experiences tell me that life, *including me*, is full of love in ways and quantities I cannot imagine.

When I was a young girl, I picked up notions of women being "less than" in society. I thought I had to be an overachiever to be worthy. I sought educational achievement and then work achievement. At the start of my career, an empowerment seminar and a life partner showed up to help me find my sense of self-worth. An industrial psychologist told me I was prone to overwork, yet I still proceeded to burn out and had a major accident. In my mid-career I fought to find a way to work and be in integrity with my values.

Since I became a mother and have juggled work with my home life, I've sought balance. However, the balance I needed was not in the time realm but in the spiritual realm. A heart-wrenching drawing from my daughter shifted me to understand my energy impacted people around me and started a learning journey through coaching and mindfulness training. My heart became depressed with work and the unjust treatment of vulnerable people I cared about. The depression said, *Pay attention to what is buried and unhealed.* My heart also became hypertensive when fear at work triggered a childhood fear in my subconscious. My blood pressure said, *Don't tense up and hold things inside.* The illnesses were alarm bells to wake me up to heal the past and become more complete.

The loss of mental health was a blessing because I learned how to meditate, accept my spiritual connection, find a channel to my inner wisdom and love myself. In the letter to Little Sunita, I understood why I tended to play small because drawing attention to myself was dangerous. To fully grow into my best self, I need to stand in my truth without reservation, and I've learned to put old fear into perspective and channel courage through the work of self-compassion. My inner child showed me if I unconditionally loved others but not myself, that was an equation that could never balance.

As I set my purpose to be in an awake state, I'm finding that there is a dance between the outside world and the inside world. The difficulties outside of me point to difficulties inside of me. The dysfunctions outside of me point to dysfunctions within me. The toxic workplace practices point to toxic thinking practices I have adopted. My quest to find approval in my job was a quest to be the one who liked me for who I was, even if I fell short of the mark. I wasn't striving for workplace psychological safety, I was striving for psychological safety in my mental world. The lack of justice, integrity, and trust I rebel at in the workplace point to where my self-talk is unjust and out of integrity, and breaks my trust to be a kind and loving person. As I untangle one, I untangle the other.

If my purpose is to truly know myself and live my best life, then the hard parts of life are the parts that I need to integrate to make me more whole. And so will washing dishes and taking out the garbage if I allow those activities to illuminate interbeing. It's good that these simple daily activities can be a lighter path to joy amid the heavier path of dharma doors. The key is to be present no matter what and go with the flow and be unknowing. To be awake to what is.

THE CALL TO ACTION

Each day requires effort and practice to stay mindful and remember the teachings of the silent retreat, to do the right thing and not fall into illusions of intolerance, judgment, and polarization.

Across time, knowledge keepers and enlightened beings seem to have one message: *We are one interconnected being, none independent of the other. The source that created this miraculous planet and the life She sustains is the energy of love. BE love.*

I know for sure that everyone wants to feel seen, known, and loved the way grandmothers can do. Grandmother-love is the love I'm seeking to receive and give to others and to myself. I believe animals and plants and all life forms feel love when I send it to them, including ancestors and planet Earth. Doing the inner work of self-compassion flows out and pours love on every expression of creation, heals suffering across generations, and brings collective spiritual growth.

Yet, I know how easy it is to *not* be kind and *not* be loving. I have harsh thoughts about my weight gain and hair loss as I enter menopause. I constantly need to "guard the gate" against social constructs of beauty. I fear change and loss, as listed in the Five Remembrances. I'm scared as I see how my kids are growing up and moving away, and register how vulnerable everyone's lives are. Many of us will get less than four thousand weeks, and it is scary to never know when our time is up. I enter modes of feeling petty, wallowing in negative thinking, and judging others — especially when villains like the Queen Bee and the Macho Man make it so easy for me to be judgmental and offended. I work hard to undo the ingrained habit energies of judgment and never-not-be-afraid thinking. I catch myself going through a day of a privileged life and missing the opportunity to shore up my "island of refuge" when I don't take deep pleasure in, or feel gratitude for, a cup of tea, a hot shower, or the freedom to walk outside.

It takes mental energy to be intentional, grateful, and present in life's simple moments, like washing hands or taking out the trash. It takes concentration to see past surface differences to the truth that we are all citizens of breath connected through interbeing. It takes insight to see we exist in an energy field of love so great that it is always there, even in the darkest and heaviest of times.

Whenever I can catch my negative moments and take them through Project Dharma, using the tools from my mindfulness toolbox, I produce love like a power generating station and transform the experience. Mindfulness meditation also fills my cup with goodness, and I have that energy on tap to pour onto whatever disrupts my peace.

I have a village of inner children in my heart who keep me accountable and throw tantrums to get my attention if I fall short of the mission statement to be kind and enjoy life. In meditation, I'm giving my presence back to the Observer and the Creator of all things. It is a sacred relationship I've come to accept as my spiritual side, an essential component of myself I can no longer disregard.

We are each a light, and somewhere along the way, that light has diminished, been cast out, or gotten split apart from its source. I think this is why we have fallen so far off our goal to build a better world, one where we have spiritual balance and treat all people, animals, and the Earth indiscriminately with kindness. We won't get to that inclusive, balanced world without each of us listening to our inner Voice, healing our hurts, and bringing our awakened selves to the table to work better together.

My life's work now is to restore that wholeness and light one act of love at a time, which lights not just my soul, but every soul in every dimension of space and time. The path I've walked since the depression has shown me that if I can be in the present moment without an agenda, that's where all the good happens.

Begin Again

I've done something I've never done in a twenty-seven-year career. I quit without having another job on the horizon.

I started this contract with high hopes of being part of a high-performing team with a challenging project. Then a person I couldn't avoid working closely with said I was "calling [them] out and attacking [their] work" by asking too many questions. Unbelievably, they asked me to limit questions to private discussions. But it was a clear threat when they said I had been given free passes, which would end now. I did not know what that meant, even after asking directly about it, and it was disturbing.

I knew this situation threw me into the Project Dharma storming stage. As I practiced mindfulness in that bizarre meeting, I realized my inner child saw this as a threat, my breathing was no longer relaxed, and my mind was warning me that I could not let my voice be silenced in such a heavy-handed way. But I also felt fierceness arise. My inner child did not want to be shushed. I was not the same person I had been during my previous toxic work situation. My voice was stronger now. Having gone through the Project Dharma discerning stage, I knew how I needed to respond. I spoke back with as much authority as they were using. I explained that I had every right to ask questions because they were intended to foster understanding, which was critical to the success of the project we were working on. I said that this way of doing things by limiting questions would create a culture where people are afraid to speak up. I sensed my words were not making an impact, and that just perhaps this person wasn't expecting a woman, especially a South Asian one, to talk back.

I reported this incident, but the response from management was disappointing. As a result, I doubted my inner Voice and sought feedback from the people I worked with. But their perspective was so different and they told me my questions were insightful and helpful. It felt surreal when my colleagues told me how much they appreciated my style. So now it was a gaslighting scenario which I know is highly toxic and dangerous to work within.

My body and emotions also confirmed that things were not right. I woke up at 3 a.m. stressed out, and with stomach issues. I was not myself with my family. I knew I could not ignore these physical signs from the previous loss of health due to workplace stressors. I did not want my body to get my attention with wake-up calls involving accidents or illnesses. Yet, I didn't want to be a quitter so soon into my contract. I wanted to finish this project and work with the other team members, who were professional, kind, and smart. But I hated turning on my computer each day and being in the work environment. My body again told me, *Let's get the hell out of here,* and my brain said, *Let's just see if things get better.*

Even with meditation, I felt stuck. It felt like I needed a silent retreat and the power of a Sangha for this. This inner call for help opened a path for me, just like last time. I found a retreat website I'd bookmarked on my iPhone home screen months before. They had a two-day silent retreat starting in a week, just a short drive away. It was a Vipassana retreat at Harmony Dawn, a retreat centre that included Qigong and Tai Chi Chuan. I had not done either of these things before, but something had to help my nervous system calm down. Impulsively I sent an email to register and got a reply within a couple of hours that two spots had opened up due to cancellations. The date was four years less a week from my silent retreat at Sugar Ridge. I felt the zap of synchronicity and didn't question that I was being guided to this retreat.

It was again a grey spring morning. As I set out on my drive, I had a déjà vu feeling that I would return a different person. But this time, I didn't have the lost, numbed-out feeling I'd had before. I felt life was friendly and warm. I was fatigued by the emotional stress at work but was strong in spirit. At the end of my journey was a dirt road to a winding gravel driveway that led to an architecturally unique house on a hill. The roof was full of solar panels, and large windows filled the lower level.

The woman who had registered me opened the door. She seemed to vibrate with joyful energy and had the biggest smile. "Welcome," she said in a cheerful voice. "You must be Sunita."

She showed me to my cot on the third floor, one of about ten in the airy communal sleeping area. I made my bed with the bedding I had brought from home. I was grateful to have the CPAP machine I'd acquired after being diagnosed with a sleep disorder because I didn't want to disturb people like I had last time. I went downstairs, where I again met strangers I would intimately spend Noble Silence with — a new Sangha community.

I checked out the agenda posted outside the meditation room and saw the retreat didn't have nearly the structure of the True Peace retreat. There wasn't the same group dharma sharing or chanting. I felt a bit bereft. As the meditation practices started, I noticed my resistance to the different ways of this retreat and used that as a dharma door to become more accepting. I struggled with the forty and even sixty minutes of sitting meditation because twenty minutes was my max. My knees and lower back hurt during practice on Friday evening and the multiple sessions on Saturday. But I kept following the instructions of the meditation teacher when I lost my concentration. He told us, if we struggled, to repeat the words, "Acknowledge, let go, begin again."

I did not have much success because my work problem kept invading my attempts to be in the moment. Then on the last day, Sunday, I felt such a peace. Sunday felt like days had passed since Saturday for how settled and peaceful I felt. In the second sitting meditation, I had a vision of walking up a mountain through a pine forest and feeling like there was no separation between me, the sunshine, the trees, or the mountain itself. As I stayed with that vision, my inner Voice came and said, *It's not quitting. It's beginning.*

It was such a moment of clarity when those words came into my consciousness. I knew I could not continue working *and* be true to myself.

I knew I needed time out of work to recover from burnout and toxicity so I could fill my cup again. I would not be afraid of having no income, nor would I be anxious about not having another job lined up. These were flashes of insight transmitted with those five words. I felt such certainty and security, like a column of light had filled me, and doubt and fear could not take hold in that energy. An expansive feeling of freedom settled into me.

I came home Sunday afternoon and resigned on Friday morning. This time I was open about leaving for my mental health and taking a sabbatical. This time, I was strong enough to talk about it. Many people told me I was doing the right thing and supported me. One colleague called me to ask why I was leaving, and when I told him, he shared that he was also burning out. Before I left, he called again and was in high spirits. He said my openness about mental health helped him decide to ask for a department transfer. When we follow our truth, sometimes it lights the way for others.

As my last day approached, people reached out from my team to let me know I had positively impacted them. Then on my last day, I got a call from someone I hadn't worked with directly.

He said, "You know, Sunita, one of the things I most admire about you is your lack of bias." I was not expecting such specific feedback from someone I had only met in a few hours of phone meetings.

He clarified, "So many people come with their own view into a meeting, but you see things from different viewpoints. This is a very rare thing in business." He laughed warmly as he said that last part.

This is the happy part of work when people with similar values connect in a human way. It's like a zap from the universe. We realized we lived near each other and planned to meet up for coffee.

His words about not being biased played in my mind along with the meditation instructions "Acknowledge, let go, begin again." Meditation has given me greater ability to see with clarity, which means more interconnection. I see fewer of the differences that my mind tends to amplify if left unchecked. I told my colleague that I think the world is becoming more polarized, and we have less tolerance for different viewpoints. I shared with him that my meditation practice is the thing that trains my mind to see connections instead of disconnection and similarities instead of differences.

I wish I could have stayed on this project, but my inner Voice helped me find the right decision to leave. I know listening to my inner truth will cause friction with people who think macho bravado and ruthless action are signs of strength. But that friction is okay. With the presence of mind, I see these people as dharma doors to deepen my commitment to respond with love and bring light forward. Being in my truth helps others in ways I can't fathom, like a pebble thrown in a lake of energy and rippling out to all corners of the universe.

My decision was not about quitting. It was standing firm in my truth and letting that begin what it may.

The workplace is fragmented by people in their own camps, not wanting to spend the energy to understand the other viewpoints in the room and those not in the room. It's deteriorating our ability to create a peaceful world. If more of us stand in our values, it will positively impact our organizations.

Whether tech, healthcare, politics, or education, organizations will not change themselves. But individuals can create change when they choose to call out the worst behaviours and not allow them a free pass. My co-worker, the one who couldn't tolerate my questions, is the one who needs to not get a free pass. Despite others feeling like I did, upper management still allowed them to remain because they deliver results, even if they come with a trail of destruction.

I think about the hundreds of thousands of people who must work and live with destructive people. I wish things could be better, and I know the first place to put that wish is in my heart, directed at myself, then my loved ones, and then all people, even the ones causing the pain, because they most of all need compassion.

This last experience with toxic work has strengthened my resolve to practice mindfulness and continue living in the rhythm of interbeing. It's the only state of mind where peace truly exists. And when I forget, or the world disrupts my peace, I will pause to drop into the discerning stage and follow the instructions to find peace again.

Acknowledge. Let go. Begin again.

A Note on Honouring Buddhism

Buddhism is made up of a diverse range of traditions and streams of practice. Buddhism migrated from India to the East over thousands of years, and then spread to the West starting in the late nineteenth century. The tradition I encountered on the five-day silent retreat in 2018 with the True Peace Sangha is Zen Buddhism, originating from the Mahayana branch of Buddhism. This retreat was in the tradition of Thich Nhat Hanh, who promoted engaged Buddhism, a practice that "should help people re-enter society in order to rediscover and accept the good things that are there in their culture and to rebuild those that are not."

On the other hand, the tradition of Buddhism that I encountered on the two-day silent retreat at Harmony Dawn in 2022 was in the Vipassana (insight) meditation tradition, originating from the Theravada branch of Buddhism. This retreat felt like more of a personal quest to me.

Both traditions of Buddhism that crossed my path blessed me with inner truth and peace.

There are many other expressions of Buddhist traditions, each with their own set of practices and emphases. By writing about the streams of Buddhism that have touched my life, I don't mean to exclude other traditions, or comment in any way on the experience other practitioners may have with Buddhism.

There are many paths to becoming awake in the world: secular, Indigenous, formalized religions, nature, art, service to others, and so many more. I honour all of them.

Acknowledgements

My loving thank you to my life partner, Tom, who supported me by being the first reader of my work, encouraging me to take unpaid time off, and running the household so I could spend hundreds of hours writing and revising this book. To Jessica, Sophia and Harvey who grace my life with their presence and allow me to grow as a human being by being in service to their souls. To Mom and Dad and Nani, who cherish and parent me with all their love. I am a continuation of you.

I had no idea what a soul-shaking journey writing a memoir could be or that it takes a village of champions to get to the finish line. I might have given up if poet Jaclyn Desforges had not helped me see the good in my writing. Susan Scott, guest speaker at the Creative Nonfiction Collective Society, generously met me for a chat and challenged me to write about spiritual content in a way that completely discomforted me. This turned out to be exactly what I needed to hear at that time. Thank you to the Humber School for Writers Summer Workshop — Naben Ruthnum for my first editorial review and Ai Jiang, Gabrielle Marceau, Ian Darragh, Jacinthe Paillé, and Maya Nikolovski, you helped me take the craft of writing to the next level. Thank you to the Productivity Mastermind group for holding me accountable when the writing got heavy and taxing. Thank you to my writing buddy, Rose Mina Munjee, who gave me immeasurable confidence to write about Buddhism and my South Asian background. Our check-ins and pep talks filled me with joy and fueled me to write. Thank you to Maya Spector who generously gave me permission to use her delightful poem, "Jailbreak," which resonated with my own jailbreak from fear. Namaste to Vicki L. Flaherty who lit the path for me to travel in mindfulness, generously shared her feedback on this book, and sent me her poem, "Finding Peace," when she knew I was in a dark place.

I am blessed to have had my family doctor (a.k.a. Dr. Joshi), counsellors, and mindfulness teachers who truly listened and made me feel seen. Although work had some definite downsides, it also had a human side that enriched my life — to the real people behind Takashi, Nikoli, Luiz, Yulia, Peter, Liam, Ben, Anders, Greta, Rosie, and Rachel, friends from the mindfulness, coaching and prayer groups, you were angels who travelled with me.

I had no idea what an editor could do to a manuscript until I met Lee Parpart, who somehow read between my lines and saw into my mind to know what I wanted to say and then helped me say it. I am forever grateful to Iguana Books and Greg Ioannou who helped me find you, because you are a kindred soul and your stylistic editing is an artform that turned a manuscript into a book. I thought I had a polished manuscript until it fell into the expert hands of Jennifer Trent. It's truly amazing how you made this story more readable with copy editing. Thank you to Laura Boyle who was a dream to work with on book design. I squealed with delight when I saw your cover designs and you made it hard to pick just one.

To all of these wonderful people and to you, dear reader, the light in me bows and humbly acknowledges the light in you.

Lastly, a deep, abiding thank you to the Observer/Voice/Creator and to beloved Thầy — Thich Nhat Hanh — for guiding me to the true nature of reality, connecting me to the power within Little Sunita, and inspiring me to attempt to put that ineffable experience into words.

Mental Health at Work Log

If you are concerned that your psychological health or safety is at risk, please talk to your doctor or other licensed professionals to seek help. The information below is not medical or legal advice or recommendations.

This log lists the thirteen psychosocial factors identified in the Psychological Health and Safety in the Workplace Standard and includes a place to document when the safety standard is not met. Keeping records can help aid discussions with management and mental health or legal professionals. Supporting evidence — feelings (such as worry, nerves, stress, dissatisfaction, or impressions of unfairness), meeting notes, names, emails, capturing dialog, or hurtful or demeaning behavior are all worthwhile to document. Depending on your social threat/reward motivations, such as in the SCARF model, some factors may impact you more than others.

More information is given at:

https://www.csagroup.org/article/cancsa-z1003-13-bnq-9700-803-2013-r2018/

https://mentalhealthcommission.ca/national-standard/

https://www.guardingmindsatwork.ca/about/about-safety
https://www.ccohs.ca/oshanswers/psychosocial/mentalhealth_risk.html
https://neuroleadership.com/research/tools/nli-scarf-assessment/

Note: The following table is for illustrative purposes and is not exhaustive. Please reference the sources above and consider that research, regulations, and case law may redefine safety standards.

Psychosocial Factor	Example of Psychosocial Hazard /Injury	Notes
1. Balance	Workload (too much/too little), comments made such as, "I never have time to take my breaks," "I always work through lunch," or "I don't have enough work to do."	
2. Civility and Respect	Comments made such as, "That person does not speak to me the same way as they do to others," "I have to be careful what I say," or "I don't feel I can raise that issue with that person."	
3. Clear Leadership and Expectations	Comments regarding uncertainty about the individual's role. Comments about communication or function/ dysfunction of the group.	

Psychosocial Factor	Example of Psychosocial Hazard /Injury	Notes
4. Engagement	Comments regarding not knowing about some-thing, lack of feedback, no response, receiving only negative comments, etc.	
5. Growth and Development	Lack of opportunities for training or professional growth.	
6. Involvement and Influence	Comments that suggest inappropriate and unfair decisions around work policies and rules — for example, approval (or lack of approval) regard-ing leaves or training requests.	
7. Organizational Culture	Feeling a disconnect with values, beliefs, meanings, and expectations that group members hold in common.	

Psychosocial Factor	Example of Psychosocial Hazard /Injury	Notes
8. Protection of Physical Safety	Hazards include ergonomic setup, indoor air quality, noise, etc. Interruption of concentration. Violence.	
9. Psychological Competencies and Demands	Comments made such as, "I don't know which item to work on first" or, "I have so many priority projects, I don't know if I will get them all finished in time." Comments about little or no participation in decision-making.	
10. Psychological Protection	Employees do not feel able to put themselves on the line, ask questions, seek feedback, report mistakes and problems, or propose a new idea without fearing negative consequences to themselves, their job, or their career.	

Psychosocial Factor	Example of Psychosocial Hazard /Injury	Notes
11. Psychological and Social Support	Comments made such as, "I'd be the last person to know" or, "I'm never told that."	
12. Recognition and Reward*	Comments that practices are unfair, biased, or secret. Feeling disrespected by how you are rewarded or recognized.	
13. Workload Management*	Rushing to complete tasks or taking shortcuts. Working extra time (paid or unpaid) to complete work, including working through breaks or lunch, after or before scheduled hours, on days off, etc. Comments about not feeling supported by the supervisor or scheduling conflicts.	

*Factors 12 and 13 are stress mediators, which means they are highly influential towards feeling psychological safety. For example, having a supportive manager can make up for other factors, but a terrible manager will be hard to ignore even if all the other twelve factors are in good shape.

Compassion, Joy and Kindness Toolbox

This is a list of activities that help me find the present moment and deepen peace and joy. They support me in the discerning stage of the Project Dharma process. All of these fill my cup with goodness. An online list with links to source material is available at www.SunitaAlves.com.

THE QUICK AND EASY TOOLS

These lightweight tools yield a lot of positivity for little investment of time.

- Mindful Breathing
- Mindful Self-Compassion Break
- Supportive Touch
- Body Scan
- Gathas
- Gratitude
- Petting or playing with Harvey the Doodle
- Mindful Walking
- Acknowledge. Let go. Begin again.

THE HANDY TOOLS

These take a bit more time and intention but help bring on the transforming stage of Project Dharma.

- Loving Kindness/Metta Meditation phrases often give me an *aha* moment that my inner child's consciousness is sad or fearful, and I have to do inner work before any problem on the outside gets resolved.
- Chanting (Plum Village Playlist, Namo Avalokiteshvara)
- Poetry
- Songs to feel Peace and Joy (such as "I Am" by Kirtana; "Oh My (What a Life)" by MILCK; "Breathing" by Joe Reilly; "I'm on Your Side" by Michael Franti & Spearhead)
- Eating Meditation
- Working Meditation – mindfulness of mopping, vacuuming, laundry, gardening, etc.
- Tidying up as a way to lovingly let go of what I have accumulated that no longer brings me joy.

THE POWER TOOLS

These tools power up compassion and joy, but they take a greater investment of time and concentration. I often communicate with my inner child consciousness and have insights from a part of me beyond my human form, such as my inner Voice or Observer.

- 20 Minutes Silent Meditation with Morning Chant (Plum Village App)
- 40 Minutes Vipassana Meditation
- Breathing Meditation, described in the Four Establishments of Mindfulness
- 16 Exercises of Mindful Breathing
- 32 Parts of the Body Meditation
- Thought Inquiry (thework.com)
- Journaling

- Compassionate Letter Writing
- Touching the Earth Meditation (Plum Village App)
- Deep Relaxation (Plum Village App)
- Dharma Sharing
- Imago Dialog
- Community/Sangha gatherings — retreats, workshops, etc.

APPENDIX C

Glossary

Term	Explanation in my words. Note: These may not be the official or accepted definitions.
Buddha	Enlightened Being.
Creator / universe	Intelligent energy that created all physical and non-physical reality.
dharma	The teaching of Buddhism; the nature of reality.
dharma door	A circumstance in life to deepen understanding and compassion.
equanimity	A balanced way of being and thinking.

Term	Explanation in my words. Note: These may not be the official or accepted definitions.
gatha	Short verse to support being mindful right now in everyday activities, such as washing hands or drinking tea. It reinforces that we are in a state of interbeing. https://thichnhathanhfoundation.org/practice-right-now
guarding the gate	Keeping unwholesome sensory input from entering consciousness, for example, limiting social media or eating healthy foods.
interbeing	Seeing life as continuous across time and space rather than viewing life forms as separate with a discrete birth and death.
island of refuge	Building a store of compassion, joy, and love in myself to fill my cup and have that available to give to others.
Observer	It is a mental mode of meta-awareness where I separate from my thoughts to be with the energy that is aware of my mind's activities.
mental formations	The totality of all wholesome and unwholesome mental formations or "seeds." Fifty-one mental formations are identified in this list. https://plumvillage.org/transcriptions/51-mental-formation/ The idea is to enable spiritual growth by acknowledging an unwholesome thought like anger and then intentionally bringing up a wholesome thought like humility.

Term	Explanation in my words. Note: These may not be the official or accepted definitions.
Mindful Self-Compassion (MSC)	The ability to send kindness and warmth to myself. https://self-compassion.org/the-three-elements-of-self-compassion-2/#definition
Noble Silence	The space that arises when the mind minimizes distractions to know itself.
Sangha	A community joined together for the common purpose of love, compassion, and joy.
Sawubona	Zulu greeting. As it was shared with me, the greeting is, "I see you," and the response is, "I exist."
SCARF	A model to understand social threats and reward motivation. https://neuroleadership.com/research/tools/nli-scarf-assessment/
Thầy	Teacher, which is a loving reference to Thich Nhat Hanh.
the Standard	"The National Standard of Canada for Psychological Health and Safety in the Workplace (the Standard) — the first of its kind in the world, is a set of voluntary guidelines, tools and resources intended to guide organizations in promoting mental health and preventing psychological harm at work." https://mentalhealthcommission.ca/national-standard/

Term	Explanation in my words. Note: These may not be the official or accepted definitions.
the Voice	Words are spoken from an inner Voice that seems to come from another source than my conscious mind.
Truth and Reconciliation Commission (TRC)	A group in Canada commissioned to learn, witness, and publish findings to foster truth-telling and reconciliation of harm done by the Indian Residential School system in Canada. https://nctr.ca/records/reports/
Vipassana	Often called Insight Meditation or seeing the true nature of reality. A definition can be found here: https://www.vridhamma.org/What-is-Vipassana

About the Author

Sunita Devi Alves (she/her) is a professional engineer and project manager working with technical teams across the IT industry. Her experience with toxic work led to illness and learning how meditation can restore well-being, protect mental health, and grow inner peace. She is an immigrant from Guyana and settler who works in T'karonto/Toronto, Ontario, on the traditional territory of many nations, including the Mississaugas of the Credit, the Anishinaabeg, the Chippewa, the Haudenosaunee, and the Huron-Wendat peoples. She loves hiking and RVing with her husband and Harvey the Doodle. You can contact her at: https://sunitaalves.com/

About the Illustrator

Jessica Marta Alves (she/her) is a chemical engineering student at Queens University, situated on the traditional territory of the Anishinaabeg, the Haudenosaunee, and the Huron-Wendat peoples. She clearly overcame her dislike of math mentioned in her Grade 3 booklet but still loves to draw. She loves a well-organized bookshelf and chocolate croissants and is the person Harvey the Doodle targets first for treats. You can connect with her on Instagram: https://www.instagram.com/jessicamalves_/